TRADE
OPPORTUNITIES:
Saskatchewan/Canada–
Shandong/China

TRADE OPPORTUNITIES:
Saskatchewan/Canada– Shandong/China

edited by

EDMUND H. DALE

Western Geographical Series   Volume 28

Department of Geography, University of Victoria
Victoria, British Columbia
Canada

1993   University of Victoria

Western Geographical Series, Volume 28

editorial address

Harold D. Foster, Ph.D.
Department of Geography
University of Victoria
Victoria, British Columbia
Canada

Since publication began in 1970 the Western Geographical Series has been generously supported by the Leon and Thea Koerner Foundation, the Social Science Federation of Canada, the National Centre for Atmospheric Research, the International Geographical Union Congress, the University of Victoria, the Natural Sciences Engineering Research Council of Canada, the Institute of the North American West, the University of Regina, the Potash and Phosphate Institute of Canada, and the Saskatchewan Agriculture and Food Department.

TRADE OPPORTUNITIES
(Western geographical series; ISSN 0315-2022; v. 28)
Includes bibliographical references.
ISBN 0-919838-18-9
1. Canada—Commerce—China. 2. China—Commerce—Canada. 3. Saskatchewan—Commerce—China—Shantung Province. 4. Shantung Province (China)—Commerce—Saskatchewan. I. Dale, Edmund H. II. University of Victoria (B.C.). Dept. of Geography. III. Series.
HF3228.C6T72 1993   382'.0971051   C93-091025-7

ACKNOWLEDGEMENTS

The preparation and publication of this book represent a concerted effort by many people and sheer persistence by the editor. The preparation itself spans four years, largely because of many difficulties, not the least of which were translation, the death of one of the contributors, and finding a publication subsidy in these years of economic recession.

The main financial contributors were the University of Regina, the Potash and Phosphate Institute of Canada, and the Saskatchewan Agriculture and Food Department. Also Mr. Lorne Bryden, Director of Development Services Unit, Saskatchewan Economic Development; Mr. Ray Chan, his able assistant; Mr. Harvey Johnson, Director of Communications Branch, Saskatchewan Agriculture and Food, assisted in making applications for publication funds.

Other persons included in the preparation process were Mr. Paul Osborne of the Executive Branch of the Saskatchewan Government, and Professor Hou Mingjun of the Foreign Languages Department of Shandong Teachers' University, Jinan, Shandong, People's Republic of China. Professor Hou undertook the translation of Chapters 8, 9 and 10 from Chinese to English, and the editorial comments from English to Chinese for the benefit of the authors of those chapters. Dr. Anqing Xing, his wife, Mengchun Zhang, and his brother, Minjing Xing, expedited the mechanical preparation of the manuscript by formatting computer disks and providing computer print-outs of the material. Mr. Stuart Mann, Vice President Emeritus, University of Regina, keenly interested in the trade potentialities between Saskatchewan and Shandong Province, gave moral support throughout the preparation of the book.

Several members of the Department of Geography, University of Victoria also co-operated to ensure the successful publication of this volume of the Western Geographical Series. Special thanks are due to members of the technical services division under the direction of Ian Norie. Diane Macdonald undertook the very demanding task of typesetting, while cartography was in the expert hands of Ken Josephson. Their dedication and hard work are greatly appreciated.

To all these persons and others who gave assistance in various ways, we extend our whole-hearted appreciation.

Edmund H. Dale, Editor   Harold D. Foster, Series Editor
University of Regina   University of Victoria
Regina, Saskatchewan   Victoria, British Columbia
February, 1993

PREFACE

This book discusses, however inadequately, the trade potentialities between two acknowledged groups, the one Chinese, the other Canadian, or more specifically, Shandong/China and Saskatchewan/Canada.

The attempt has been fraught with difficulties, owing partly to language differences and partly to different decision-making processes arising from different systems of government. The first is readily overcome, but the second is obstinate because under centralized planning, characteristic of Shandong and of China in general, information is privileged. Confidentiality and secrecy forbid public access to relevant information for research purposes. In short, the foreign researcher is barred access to a body of reliable information or vital statistics from which he/she may draw deductions and conclusions. To overcome this difficulty, it was decided to divide the subject matter of the book into two parts, the one on Shandong/China written by resident Chinese in Shandong, the other on Saskatchewan/Canada written by Canadians. In this way, the Chinese authors might conceivably have access to information denied a Canadian researcher.

The language difficulty was resolved by finding a Chinese professor Hou Mingjun, who is fluent in English, to translate the work from Chinese to English and vice versa. But, however excellent the translation may be, and Professor Hou Mingjun must be commended for his valiant efforts, certain nuances of the two languages are bound to be lost. In the circumstances, we ask of the reader understanding, if not leniency, in what has been a truly difficult exercise.

The original intent of the book was to focus on Shandong and Jilin, but in the end difficulties made for the omission of the Jilin material. However, the economic policies of both provinces are similar, and the needs of each and the opportunities that each offers are similar. In chapter after chapter these points are made clear. Still, to reinforce the importance of Jilin in the discussion, Chapter 2, an official statement, is added.

The message of the book is that there are indeed considerable opportunities for trade between the two groups. The discussions show that whether we are dealing with agriculture or industry or transportation and tele-communications (in particular, fibre-optics transmission systems), whether computing technology or electronic systems, Saskatchewan has much of what Shandong needs, and the economic sectors of Shandong equally reveal avenues for trade with Saskatchewan/Canada, particularly in joint-venture enterprises and other investments.

The book is specifically addressed to governments at both the provincial and municipal levels and their agents and planners, and to the business sectors. But generally, anyone who is interested in international trade, including geographers, economists, urban and rural planners, indeed the the general public, should find the information presented useful.

Born of realism which recognizes the potentialities for trade in the twin relationships of, and friendly accord between, the two groups, the book recommends as it encourages the exercise of enterprise, resourcefulness and optimism in drawing closer the links that hold in embryo trade benefits for the two groups.

Edmund H. Dale
February, 1993

TABLE OF CONTENTS

6   TECHNOLOGY, EXPERTISE AND TRANSFER: COMPUTING SYSTEMS

LIST OF TABLES

LIST OF FIGURES

LIST OF PLATES

SASKATCHEWAN C A N A D A

Regina

0   1000 kms

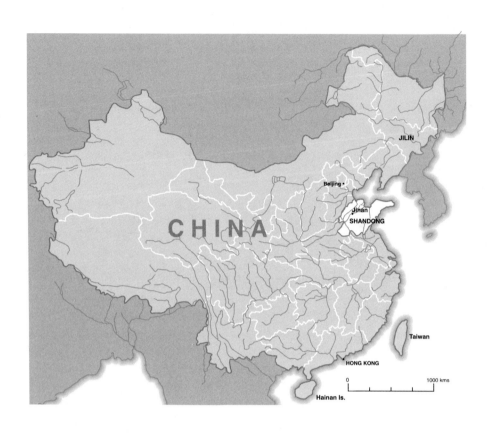

CHINA

JILIN

Beijing •

Jinan
SHANDONG

Taiwan

• HONG KONG

0   1000 kms

Hainan Is.

1 INTRODUCTION

Edmund H. Dale
Department of Geography
University of Regina

Canada's recognition of, and establishment of diplomatic relations with, the People's Republic of China (PRC) on 13 October, 1970 won for Canada potential trade benefits (later declined); again, recent twinnings of Saskatchewan units with Chinese units are likely to foster trade, given political initiative and entrepreneurial boldness.

The twinnings of the Province of Saskatchewan with the Province of Jilin (PRC); the City of Regina, the capital of Saskatchewan, with the City of Jinan, the capital of Shandong Province (PRC); and the University of Regina with Shandong University have fostered cordial relations and exchanges and, besides fostering friendship and cultural understanding, have created a climate conducive to trade. Considered closely, trade between Saskatchewan and these two Chinese provinces, properly and aggressively explored and exploited, seems very promising. It could conceivably transcend narrow provincial bounds and become an integral or significant part of bilateral trade between Canada and China. From the early 1970s, China has regarded Canada as a most-favoured trading partner, and the contacts, agreements, exchanges and twinnings of Canadian and Chinese provinces, cities and universities have greatly heightened the relationship. But even before the 1970s, Norman Bethune, the Canadian medical doctor who attended Mao Zedong's soldiers during the Chinese Revolution and is today regarded virtually a saint in China, had established for Canada abiding friendly relations with China. What seems necessary at present is for the Saskatchewan business-entrepreneurial-investment sector to seize the initiative and progressively and aggressively promote Saskatchewan/Canadian goods, services and expertise in China as, in turn, China should seek to promote in Saskatchewan/Canada more of its own specialized goods, services and labour.

In particular, the trade potentials between Saskatchewan, on the one hand, and Shandong province, on the other, are not being exploited to the full and could be. This is the central theme of this book which is addressed primarily to both Canadian and Chinese readers, particularly to those in the business-trading sectors. It attempts to explore the commodity-resource sectors which can supply each other's needs: the agricultural sector, the manufacturing-technology-expertise sectors, the communications and investment sectors. So also it considers the official agencies responsible for individual aspects (economic and political) of the trade, no less the strong humanitarian desire of Canada, its provinces and people to surmount narrow self-interests and help developing or Third World countries, a status that China assumes. But for this trade to be successful, each side must know what the other needs and can sell, and the respective official departments or private agencies that are involved.

The production-construction units in Shandong province, like those in Jilin and other provinces of China, are beginning to adjust to new circumstances and new opportunities. Shandong seeks guaranteed markets for its goods and services, especially its labour-intensive manufactures like textiles and hand-made woollen carpets. It desires, as well, to replace its aging machinery with modern equipment, much of which can be supplied by Saskatchewan and Canadian firms until the Chinese are able to produce them themselves. Among these are agricultural equipment, like silos and grain dryers; high technology goods, including computer software, telecommunication and transportation equipment; and a wide range of manufactured goods.

Trade between the two sides has yet to be fully explored, as the *Handbook of Selected Statistics on Saskatchewan Trade, 1988*, clearly reveals. Of the total value of trade ($459.1 million) between Saskatchewan and China in 1987, the agricultural sector (grain, seeds, flour) accounted for as much as 85 percent and potash the remaining 15 percent—a slight improvement over the value of the total trade ($421.8 million) in 1982 in which wheat alone contributed 99 percent and potash 1 percent.

It must be admitted that at first sight the ratio of the consumer market appears grossly unbalanced. Whereas the population of Shandong Province is about 88 million (and if we add some 22 million of Jilin Province, the total would exceed 100 million—backed by China's impressive total of some 1.2 billion), Saskatchewan's total is a mere million and Canada's total just over 27 million. Yet, on closer examination, the spending powers of both Saskatchewan and Canada are vastly greater than those of Shandong and Jilin and perhaps of China as well. Also, the availability of modern technology, expertise and investment capital in Saskatchewan and Canada are added factors that may well balance the equation, though the availability and abundant supply of relatively cheap labour are strong factors on the Chinese side.

The prelude to successful trading negotiations is an understanding of the decision-making processes of the two countries. The Saskatchewan/ Canadian business sector needs to know how development policies under centralized planning in China are formulated and effected, and to be aware of the traditional behaviour of the Chinese in conducting business (a slow process, demanding the exercise of patience, the establishing of personal, friendly links, supported by constant, friendly exchanges and hospitality). The Chinese, on the other hand, need to know how Canada and its provinces conduct domestic and international trade, and forge trade links. So a brief survey of the political structures of each country seems apposite.

DECISION-MAKING PROCESS IN CHINA

Public decision-making in the People's Republic of China is mainly a top-down process, that is, all national objectives and goals are set by the Central Government in Beijing, and these are implemented by a descending hierarchical network of administrative bodies, though local ideas may conversely work themselves up the hierarchy and become national policy. China is a unitary State, that is, sovereign power resides in a central government which, like all unitary States, may allocate specified powers of government to its regions and districts. But although a unitary State, the PRC has a socialist system of government "under the people's democratic dictatorship" (Article 1, the Constitution). Also, although the single depository of power is with the Central Government, that power under the post-Mao leaders is decentralized through a National People's Congress (the highest organ of the State) and its Standing Committee (a permanent body), and local people's congresses and their standing committees above the county level. To Canadians this structure may appear somewhat confusing.

Theoretically, there is a three-level administrative structure, with certain variations. The Central Government occupies the highest level of the hierarchy. At the second level, directly under the jurisdiction of the Central Government, are the 23 provinces (including Taiwan and the new province of Hainan), 5 autonomous regions and 3 municipalities.[1]

The provinces, apart from supervising and implementing the laws set by the Constitution, carry out the policies set by the Central Government. Essentially, these policies deal with the national modernization programmes of agriculture, industry, science and technology, and defence, as well as other policies concerning the nation.

The autonomous regions, similar in rank and administrative function to the provinces, are separate in that they were created to consolidate national minority groups and to preserve their traditions and cultures.

The three municipalities are Beijing, Shanghai and Tianjin. Their hierarchical position, constitutionally higher than that of other Chinese cities, results from their special functions. Beijing, with a population of some 10 million, was the ancient, and now the modern, capital of the country. As such, the Central Government saw fit to elevate its prominence. Shanghai received similar treatment because it is the largest city of China and of the world and is of major economic importance both in terms of industry and commerce. It could not be left to be administered by a province. Similarly, Tianjin is a special industrial, commercial centre whose geographical location at the head of China's most important natural harbour also contributed to its second-level hierarchical position. True, there are other cities with even larger populations (e.g. Chongqing) and of equal historic and economic importance (e.g. Wuhan) that might function as municipalities in the constitutional sense, that is, independently of the provinces in which they are located. But they could be regarded as *de facto* instead of *de jure* municipalities.

At the third level of the hierarchy are counties. These are very large areas, chiefly agricultural, and are administered by the provinces. However, the three municipalities under the Central Government also administer counties which are large tracts of land on the peripheries of the municipalities. These lands provide the municipalities with fresh vegetables, chicken, pork, fish and milk. In turn, the municipalities endeavour to speed up the development of their agriculture and industry.

Then there are prefectures. These were created because the three administrative divisions were found to be inadequate. For example, Sichuan Province, with a population exceeding 100 million and about 200 counties, found it difficult to administer so many people and counties. Thus the prefecture was established at key points to help the provincial government to supervise and implement the laws of the Constitution. And in those provinces where there are individual pockets of national minorities, autonomous prefectures and autonomous counties were established to preserve minority culture and tradition.

The structure may appear simple but it is complex. It involves a large number of officials and makes for a "heavy" bureaucracy, nurtured all the more by the Preamble of the Constitution which states in part that:

> . . . all state organs, the armed forces, all political parties and public organizations and all enterprises and undertakings in the country must take the Constitution as the basic norm of conduct, and they have the duty to uphold the dignity of the Constitution and ensure its implementation.

The phrase "all political parties and public organizations" obviously refers to the Communist Party. This added administrative overlay further heightens the complexity of the structure and extends the bureaucracy. However, the Communist Party (or any member of it) may not contravene the Constitution and its laws, though it has a leading role to play in their implementation. The interests of the Party must be those of the people.

By 1982, it was being publicly admitted that the duplication of leadership and economic barriers between town and country, among regions, and among departments had resulted in a wasteful replication of production facilities and public utilities, and that it was difficult to get anything done efficiently (*Beijing Review*, Vol. 27, Nos. 5-6, January 30, 1984).

Thus began a process of simplification—merging the administrative agencies at various levels, dividing their functions and powers, and increasing the role of the more economically developed cities. Today, with the exception of a few national corporations and large key enterprises which are directly administered by central authorities, almost all the other enterprises are now run by local authorities. In addition, the prefectural administrative authority is being revoked and the more developed cities now exercise leadership over the surrounding counties and over construction in the countryside, resulting in the cities becoming the centres of the economic zones (*Beijing Review*, Vol. 26, No. 3, January 17, 1983). Historically famous cities in southern Jiangsu Province (Suzhou and Zhenjiang) have changed their administrative status from prefecture to city. Also, since 1982 the former communes have been changed to townships—rural areas or villages in which peasants develop their own enterprises.

This merging of the city governments with rural administrative areas (prefectural offices and county governments) has made for unified planning and avoidance of problems that formerly militated against developments. In short, it is now the cities that promote their own economies and industrial bases, and exercise leadership over their tributary areas which provide them with goods and services. More especially, the three munic-ipalities of Beijing, Shanghai and Tianjin, and the coastal cities are now empowered to approve projects with investments up to $30 million US each, and the provinces' autonomous regions and ministries under the State Council projects up to $5 million US each. But projects involving more than $30 million US must be examined and approved by the Ministry of Foreign Economic Relations and Trade (*China in Focus*, 1989, p. 17)

The Saskatchewan/Canadian entrepreneurial sector should therefore look to these Chinese cities as the decision-making bodies of local trade. The twinning relationships between Saskatchewan and Shandong Prov-ince (the city of Jinan and Shandong University), and with Jilin (Chang-chun, the capital city) thus make for good trade prospects. Jinan, for instance, has now established industrial zones in parts of the city, each specializing in a certain branch of industry: petro-chemical, metallurgical, light industrial, and heavy industrial. Jinan's industrial policy is geared to supplying the needs of agriculture, and from its industrial zones now come steel, rolled steel, trucks, tractors, an assortment of motors, motor cycles, machine tools, washing machines, boilers, textile machinery (for cotton and silk spinning and weaving), chemicals, electrical equipment, and fabrics (dyed, printed, knitted). Flour milling and food processing are among other industrial activities. And all are controlled to make beneficial the marriage between industry and agriculture.

Jinan's industrial policy also utilizes a number of neighbourhood organizations. It seeks to tap the potential of that part of the neighbour-hood's labour force which would otherwise be ignored. This sector is the seasonal, under-employed, part-time and especially female workers, who can make, and have made, a significant contribution to production and construction. But to make this possible, certain neighbourhood facilities, including schools, daycare centres and social services had to be provided. These are under the direction of residential organizations. In a very real sense, the goal is towards increased production through full employment. Thus Jinan has entered a new era of industrial development. But its industrial machinery is somewhat out-moded, needing modern technolo-gy, technological expertise and investment capital. Indeed, Saskatchewan should be able to make a marked contribution here, apart from supplying grain and potash, for available is a huge reservoir of capital in the form of personal savings for economic development either in the province or elsewhere. This pool of capital is said to be far greater than in the other western provinces (Government of Saskatchewan, 1984, p. 13).

Similarly, in Jilin Province, Changchun and Jilin City (former seat of government) are developing both light and heavy industries, based on a wide range of mineral deposits and other resources, including iron-ore, molybdenum, coal, copper, nickel, zinc, gold, lead, aluminium and petroleum. At present, Changchun boasts a No. 1 Motor Vehicle Plant, which specializes in the production of trucks, and a Railway Passenger Car Works. In like manner, Jilin City has established a Chemical Works complex and a woollen mill which supports a textile industry. Other activities in these cities are the production of hand-made woollen carpets and the processing of ginseng (a root, an aphrodisiac) and deer antlers (both used in the manufacture of Chinese medicine). Other cities of the province are also engaged in the development of heavy and light industries. Common to all these industries is the need for modern technology, equipment and expertise to up-date the plants and render the railway network more efficient in carrying passengers and goods, since this last poses one of the major problems of the country. Again, until the Chinese themselves are able to satisfy this need, Saskatchewan firms could well attempt to supply it.

DECISION-MAKING IN CANADA

We turn next to the decision-making process in Canada, which is quite different from that in the People's Republic. Canada has a federal system of government, based essentially on a division of powers between the national or federal government and the unit or provincial governments. Each level is autonomous within its allocated sphere of control.

The division of powers is such that the federal government has responsibility for matters affecting the State as a whole, such as foreign policy, foreign trade, immigration control and tariff. The provincial governments manage affairs particular to their provinces, for example, direct taxation. Though autonomous within a sphere, the units lack the power of external sovereignty which involves the making of war and peace, and of conducting diplomatic relations with other States.

It was the former British North America (BNA) Act of 1867, (now the Constitutional Act, 1982) which brought the union of Canada into being and divided the legislative powers between the federal government and the provinces. It was done in such a way that the provinces would have exclusive control over a list of enumerated subjects and the federal government would have legislative control over the rest which, according to the Act, "for greater certainty" were listed also. Even so, Section 91 of the

Act authorizes the Canadian Parliament "to make laws for the peace, order and good government of Canada" in all matters other than those reserved to the provincial legislatures. Therefore the powers not expressly conferred on either the federal government or the provinces rest with the federal government; so the provinces were to have certain specified powers and no more.

Among the 29 specific powers assigned exclusively to the federal government are *the regulation of trade and commerce* and the control over matters "declared by the Parliament of Canada to be for the general advantage of two or more of the provinces." Of the 16 subjects that fell within the exclusive powers of the provinces, municipal institutions in the province and education (subject to certain provisions with respect to denominational schools) may be cited. Two powers, immigration and *agriculture*, were given to both the federal and provincial governments. Either or both may exercise jurisdiction in relation to these subjects, but should a conflict arise, the federal law must prevail.

It must be mentioned, also, that Canada's enormous territorial expanse, exceeded only by the former Soviet Union and certainly larger than China's, the third largest in the world, is administratively divided into 10 provinces and 2 territories—Yukon and the Northwest Territories (NWT). The latter occupies one-third of the land mass of Canada but has a small population of some 49,000. It seeks to change its constitutional status. As a result of a referendum held in 1982 in which a majority of the voters approved a division of the NWT into two parts, the federal government agreed in principle to implement the decision, but so far the two new provinces have not been created.

Each of these two territories is administered by a Commissioner, the chief executive officer, who is appointed by the federal government. He is responsible for the administration of the territories under the direction of the Minister of Indian and Northern Affairs Canada. The legislative powers of these territories are similar to those of the provinces in that they have control over all matters of a local nature, but the federal government has control over the renewable and non-renewable resources. And the federal government, if it sees fit, may disallow any act of the territories within a year after it was passed locally.

The Canadian administrative structure is like that of the Chinese in so far as it is three-tiered, but the similarity stops there. Each of the Canadian levels—federal, provincial, municipal—legislates within the sphere allocated to it. Within that sphere each is autonomous. But whereas the federal and provincial governments are each assured constitutional protection under the Constitutional Act of 1982, the municipalities (cities, towns, villages, and rural municipalities, in the case of Saskatchewan) are created by provincial governments which may increase or decrease their powers or even terminate their existence altogether.

The municipal councils, headed by a mayor, are elected by the local residents, except in Quebec where they may be appointed by provincial authorities, to serve for a specific term, usually from two to four years (for Saskatchewan cities three years, towns and rural municipalities two years, and villages three years).

The powers granted to the municipal councils are numerous, including those to enter into agreement or contracts, to conduct its own business, to acquire, hold and dispose of real property. Yet, the councils' exercise of power is subject to control by the provinces and to the consent and approval of a vote of the electors.

It follows that Saskatchewan may conduct trade agreements with Jilin or Shandong or China proper because the federal government has previously established diplomatic relations with China; or Saskatchewan may launch programmes under agreements that the federal government has previously concluded with China, for example, in respect to quotas for textiles. Admittedly, in this matter of quotas, China shows a predilection to deal more with the large cities of central Canada than with smaller cities in western Canada, like Regina, a fact which should invite a more aggressive, competitive approach by western Canadian businessmen.

The federal agencies that may be involved are External Affairs or Regional Industrial Expansion which also administers trade and tourism. But the Province of Saskatchewan also has its own departments that administer aspects of its domestic and foreign trade, including the Potash Corporation of Saskatchewan and PCS Mining and PCS Sales Limited, Saskatchewan Telecommunications, the Department of Trade and Investment, the Department of Science and Technology, and the Department of Economic Development and Tourism. Then, there is the Saskatchewan Wheat Pool, a private agency, that sells wheat produced in Saskatchewan.

DIFFICULTIES, REAL OR IMAGINED

A formidable difficulty to successful trading between Saskatchewan and the two Chinese provinces in question is likely to be ignorance about each other, or each other's way of conducting business. The ignorance is as marked on the Canadian as it is on the Chinese side, a gap that twinning might conceivably fill.

The injustices—political, social, economic—to which the Chinese have been subjected by imperialist powers, especially Europeans in the 19th century, and later the Japanese, had caused the Chinese to regard most foreigners, clearly with justification, as "devils." Today this perception remains, arguably to a much lesser degree than formerly. It is well that the would-be Saskatchewan/Canadian businessman or woman understands this, and, more than this, something of the background of the country and nation, howsoever minimal. A brief summary of this background is not possible here, though a few random, salient points may be noted.

The geography of the People's Republic has had much to do with the country's political and economic history. As Freeberne (1971: 141) has shown, the country is surrounded by natural barriers on all sides. This seclusion explains in part why Chinese civilization has for centuries developed in comparative isolation. The physical geography readily facilitated a 'closed-door' policy of the government. Also, the varied resources of the country, the huge consumer market—the spending power of that market hardly taken into consideration—and the potential as an area for investment have in the past, no less at present, been impressive and attractive. They were attractive enough, it was thought by maritime mercantile powers, to satisfy, in part at least, the export drive resulting from the Industrial Revolution of the mid-nineteenth century. Consequently, it encouraged efforts by these powers to gain a foothold in China in order to penetrate the market. Germany, Russia, France and Britain won leases and concessions of Chinese territories which came under their respective control for varying periods of time. However China did not succumb to a colonial status. Perhaps it was the competition among the powers, or the strong national feelings of the Chinese, or the cultural solidarity of the nation, despite its political weakness then, that defeated the aims of the imperialists—though not altogether, for although the Chinese government had refused to allow the importation of Western manufactured goods, smuggling contributed to Sino-British hostilities and China's defeat in the Opium War of 1839-42. Again, China succumbed to defeat in the Sino-Japanese War of 1894-5. Thus attempted incursions by the imperialist powers weakened the Chinese resolve to isolate itself altogether from the "barbarians" or foreigners. In retrospect, the shameful treatment of the Chinese by these foreign powers served only to advance China to its present position in world politics. Mao Zedong and the Communist victory of 1949 put an end to attempted foreign domination irrevocably.

Whatever it was that ultimately defeated the 'smash and grab' tactics of the imperial powers, China, the Celestial Empire, as it was known, was a powerful magnet that attracted as it repelled and, to repeat, could not be reduced to a colonial status. Apart from the interim period of the foreign powers, the Chinese 'closed-door' policy kept out Western entrepreneurs until 1978 when an 'open-door' policy was introduced. Becoming increasingly aware that the relatively underdeveloped economy cannot provide a high standard of living for the masses, Chinese leaders have resorted to a new policy of allowing, albeit with some concern, foreign capital, technology and technological expertise to enter the country. Without these, China's present modernization programmes are seriously handicapped. But the Chinese leaders are determined to control both their domestic and international trade, mindful of the past injustices of foreigners. Their trade policy is clearly based on the principle "if we buy from you, you must buy from us." And because the West, certainly Saskatchewan/Canada, may have more to sell China than Shandong/Jilin/China may have to sell Saskatchewan/Canada, the potentially unbalanced trade could be a source of irritation between the two trading partners. Already Jilin advocates that Saskatchewan is not buying from Jilin as much as Jilin is buying from Saskatchewan. This charge could also be laid by Shandong. It is paramount, therefore, that Saskatchewan entrepreneurs who wish to trade with Jilin/Shandong grapple with this problem. They must be acutely aware that trade is not a one-way process. To the Chinese such a misconception could be considered blatant arrogance.

Another difficulty of some magnitude is the necessity of each side to promote its goods and services on the other side. Language, of course, may be an inhibiting factor but less a handicap if federal, provincial and city governments have a strong political conviction that twinning of provinces and cities, pursued systematically and wholeheartedly, can be an effective means of bilateral trade. The same conviction is required of representatives and members of the business sector, who should make frequent visits to promote their businesses. To some extent both groups appear somewhat reluctant to exploit fully the economic possibilities to which twinning has given birth. Expecting to have Chinese orders rushing in without active promotion on their part is a pipe dream, hardly the order of the day in business. In the competitive world of today, active promotion is imperative. Visits by Canadians to China readily confirm that Canada has a high profile there. The fact is that throughout China the people have a warm regard for Canadians whom they receive with generosity of spirit. Surely, in such a climate of friendliness business is bound to be made far easier than would otherwise be the case.

Another significant fact about China that Saskatchewan/Canadian entrepreneurs should consider is the entry of China into world power calculations, for it signals that the People's Republic desires to be independent of the United States and the former Soviet Union, that is, non-aligned. China seeks to be a third force in a divided world. Clearly to achieve this status China must continue to import high technology items, including sophisticated transportation-communication systems, computers and oil technology. But the Chinese are a resourceful people and seek to be self-sufficient. As soon as they are able to produce this technology themselves, they will discontinue importing them and end dependency on foreign supplies. This is all the more reason why the Saskatchewan/Canadian business sector should endeavour to establish immediately as many trade links as possible with China.

CONCLUSION

Endowed with fertile soils, a variety of industrial materials and a long tradition of skill, as Tawney (1964, p. 109) has pointed out, China has the potential of becoming a major industrial power and to be able to supply most of its needs. This last was recognized by the Chinese Government as far back as 1793 when it rebuffed the British proposal for closer trade relations with a statement that is often quoted: "Our Celestial Empire possesses all things in prolific abundance, and lacks no product within its own borders; there is therefore no need to import the manufactures of outside barbarians" (Tawney, 1964, p. 109). The statement was certainly true in the 18th century, as East (1971, p. 9) admits. However, times have changed. Today, China needs technology and capital investment from the West. Yet, witness the remarkable speed with which it has established a nuclear capability, developed and launched satellites (even offering to launch them for any country after the temporary U.S. setback with its Challenger space programme), and succeeded in banishing famine which, before 1949, had been a regular occurrence in the country. All this was achieved in spite of U.S. prohibition of trade with China, embargoes by other countries in the 1950s, and the withdrawal of Soviet technical aid to China in and after the 1960s as a result of Sino-Soviet dispute.

Nevertheless, China's industrial potential is inescapably tied to more trading with non-Communist countries, including Canada and its provinces. It is trade that will provide essential equipment to modernize China's underdeveloped and inadequate rail network, the chief means of circulation in a country of considerable proportions and difficult terrain. It is trade that will provide modern technology and power facilities for the country's industrial and agricultural activities. It is trade that will help to raise the living standards of the millions of rural peasants. The post-Mao leaders realize that we live in an interdependent world and that trade is a method by which nations acquire wealth and develop themselves. A sobering fact for the Chinese is that Canada and its provinces, proven friends of the Chinese, have much of what China needs—natural products and specialized manufactures and services—and are willing to trade with the country. Equally, Saskatchewan/Canada should come to the realization that trading with China or any of its provinces begets more than the sale of Canadian products and the importation of Chinese products. Bilateral trading of this kind provides scope for the extension of Canada's humanitarian role in a world diseased with misunderstanding, greed and selfishness. This attitude of the Canadian government and people, which also finds expression in Canada's peace-keeping role, Canada's significant contribution to the developing countries of the world, and Canada's humanitarian treatment of refugees, appears to be its state-idea in embryo. It mirrors the understanding, fraternity, fair play and honesty that are so often missing in State relations. Twinning, ardently and wholeheartedly encouraged, supported by mayors and councillors of city councils, politicians at the provincial and national levels could well vanquish barriers that divide. Certainly trade between Jilin/Shandong/China and Saskatchewan/Canada could point the way.

NOTE

[1]Hong Kong and Macau are soon to become Special Administrative Areas.

REFERENCES

Beijing Review, 26(3).

———, 27(5-6).

China in Focus. (1989). *The ABC of investment in China*. Beijing: Beijing Review Press, No. 34.

East, W.G. (1971). Prologue: The Asian background. In W.G. East, O.H.K. Spate and C.A. Fisher (Eds.), *The changing map of Asia*. London: Methuen and Co. Ltd.

Freeberne, M. (1971), The People's Republic of China. In W.G. East, O.H.K. Spate and C.A. Fisher (Eds.), *The changing map of Asia*. London: Methuen and Co. Ltd.

Government of China. (1983). The Constitution of the People's Republic of China. Beijing: Foreign Languages Press.

Government of Saskatchewan. (1984). *A strategy for the development of rural Saskatchewan*, Report of Special Task Force, Regina, Saskatchewan, p. 13.

Government of Saskatchewan. (1988). *Handbook of selected statistics on Saskatchewan trade*. Regina, Saskatchewan.

Tawney, R.H. (1964). Land and labour in China. London: George Allen and Unwin Ltd.

OVERVIEW OF SASKATCHEWAN-CHINA RELATIONS[1]

Government of Saskatchewan
Intergovernmental Affairs Branch

INTRODUCTION

Apart from what was West Germany, Canada is the most trade-dependent country of all the major western nations grouped under the Organization for Economic Co-operation and Development (OECD). About 30 percent of Canada's total economic production is exported.

Within Canada, Saskatchewan is the most trade dependent of the provinces. Fully 42 percent of Saskatchewan's economic output is exported. This dependency on exports means that the future prosperity of the nation and the province will in large measure depend on the country's and the province's ability to identify, access and develop international markets for the things they produce.

It was recognition of this fact that spurred Canada and Saskatchewan to seek to develop a closer relationship with China, a relationship that is built on a long record of trust and co-operation to the mutual benefit of both countries. China is Canada's fifth largest trading partner and Saskatchewan's fourth after the U.S, the former U.S.S.R. and Japan. With only 4 percent of the country's population, Saskatchewan accounted for about 28 percent of Canada's exports to China between 1980 and 1986. Thus Saskatchewan occupies a disproportionately large place in Canada's economic relations with China.

Saskatchewan has and will continue to have an important role to play in Canada's economic relations with China. The main reasons are obvious. With nearly a quarter of the world's population and less than 7 percent of the world's arable land, China needs to import wheat to feed its people. Despite the fact that China is constantly increasing its wheat yields, periodic droughts and floods make havoc of agricultural production. Further, China requires potash to increase agricultural yields, particularly in those areas with multiple cropping of rice on an annual basis. Not only are supplies of both commodities abundant in Saskatchewan, but they are of high quality and are competitively priced. The mutual benefits of developing trade relations in these areas was recognized by both countries in the 1960s when the excesses of the Cultural Revolution and drought left China short of grain.

On average, wheat exports have consistently accounted for over 50 percent of Canada's total exports to China since the 1960s and, despite China's declining need to import wheat, Canada has managed to increase its share of the shrinking market. This market is expected to continue, ensuring a continuing, strong Saskatchewan presence in Canada's economic relations with China.

The same is true of potash. Saskatchewan is now China's major supplier of potash, contributing between one-half and three-quarters of the total amount imported by China. Projections of future Chinese demand for potash, based on demographic trends, agronomic requirements and agricultural policy indicate that Saskatchewan should continue to have a major role to play in China's agronomic development. In sum, Saskatchewan's traditional export strengths and China's traditional import needs should ensure that Saskatchewan will play a very important role in Canada-China relations well into the future.

Canada's international trade strategy recognizes China as a very important market in Canada's future. A key element of the strategy is the detailed market identification, access, and promotion of exports in China. Similarly, Saskatchewan has developed its own trade development strategy to allow exporters to take maximum advantage of the considerable trade potential of China's developing economy over the medium- and long-term. Saskatchewan's trade strategy is complementary to that of the federal government, but it is not identical to it, given the province's restricted jurisdiction, interests and resources devoted to international affairs.

SASKATCHEWAN'S APPROACH TO CHINA

The province's overall approach to China is based on two general premises. The first is the importance of the Chinese concept of 'guanxi', that is, it is expected that future commercial relations will flow from the initial cultivation of a climate of friendship and trust and the establishment of a record of co-operation, characterized by a spirit of reciprocity.

The second premise is the importance of government-to-government relations; that is, because of China's relatively recent emergence into the international arena with its 'open door' policy, and China's concentration of power and authority in government's hands, there are relatively few government officials with any experience or confidence in dealing with foreigners, especially from the private sector. Consequently, the Chinese tend to put more trust in those initiatives that are explicitly backed by their foreign government counterparts.

The main elements of the existing Saskatchewan 'China Policy' are worth noting. First, like the rest of Canada, Saskatchewan has identified the Asia-Pacific Region (particularly China and Japan) as its second regional priority after the U.S in pursuit of its international interests. These interests are trade, investment, technology transfer, entrepreneurial immigration, tourism, development assistance, cultural exchange and intergovernmental liaison.

Second, Saskatchewan has several policy instruments that it can use in the Asia-Pacific region in pursuit of its international interests. These include the promotion of the interests just mentioned, especially support to exporting businesses, representation abroad through provincial offices, ministerial visits, long-term aid-trade linkages through development assistance, and through 'sister province' or provincial twinning relationships.

Third, Saskatchewan chose to enter a provincial twinning arrangement with Jilin Province in north-east China in order to establish a 'window' on China through the cultivation of friendship and the establishment of cooperation. The idea was not to confine Saskatchewan's activity in China to Jilin alone, but rather to provide a solid and lasting presence and an entry point to the whole country in pursuit of all or most of the province's international interests. It is not overstating the case to say that, while the Government of Saskatchewan's formal bilateral relations with China are focused on Jilin, its approach is flexible enough to accommodate and support commercial and other Saskatchewan initiatives elsewhere in China.

SASKATCHEWAN-JILIN RELATIONS

The Twinning Protocol, signed by both governments of Saskatchewan and Jilin on June 5, 1984, stated clearly that the basic aim was "to deepen their mutual understanding, enhance their friendship and promote trade contacts on the basis of tradition, friendship and existing amicable ties and co-operation between the peoples of Canada and China."

Twinning was motivated by a history of successful ad hoc relations between China and Saskatchewan, as witnessed by Saskatchewan's participation in the Chinese Farmers' Programme, the Chinese Scholars' Programme and the twinning of the Universities of Regina and Shandong, as well as the fact that China's grain imports from Canada and Saskatchewan were apparently destined for large population centres in north-central and north-east China where Jilin is located. Furthermore, Saskatchewan and Jilin share similar geographic, climatic and agronomic conditions—affinities that are as compelling as the complementary import requirements and export capacities in such areas as wheat, potash, the transfer of technology in dryland farming, livestock, and integrated rural development that exist between Saskatchewan and Jilin.

The mutual interests, economic and non-economic, of Saskatchewan and Jilin are expressed through joint Plans of Action which set out exchanges in such areas as trade and development, science and technology, advanced education, culture and recreation. Further still, Saskatchewan has undertaken to assist Chinese trade promotion in Canada, as well as investigate eventually beneficial counter-trade investment opportunities in both provinces and countries.

With respect to technology transfer, Saskatchewan encourages this through such mechanisms as licensing, joint ventures, countertrade, education and training exchanges, and institutional twinnings. The most recent schedule of exchanges is the Fourth Plan of Action agreed to by Saskatchewan and Jilin on February 27, 1991, to cover the next two years. It lists official exchanges; economic and technical exchanges in the agricultural, energy, tourism and manufacturing sectors; educational exchanges in training for academic, vocational or work-study programmes; specialist and vocational exchanges; and exchanges in sports and culture.

The Fourth Plan makes it clear that despite the increasingly economic focus of the Plans of Action, cultural exchanges will continue to be an integral part of the Plans of Action with Jilin. However, for efficiency's sake, cultural exchanges from Saskatchewan may visit other Chinese provinces in which there is substantial public and private sector interest. Thus although bilateral Intergovernmental relations between the Governments of Saskatchewan and China will be focused on Jilin, they are to be broadened on an ad hoc basis to assist commercial and other public-sector (e.g. municipal) interests both in Beijing and in other provinces of China.

Again, the Government of Saskatchewan will continue to expedite access to Jilin and elsewhere in China for other public- and private-sector organizations in pursuit of their own interests (eg. Regina's twinning with

Jinan, Shandong Province; Saskatoon's twinning with Shijiazuang, Hebei Province; university activities in such provinces as Jilin, Shandong and Heilongjiang, and in such Autonomous Regions as Inner Mongolia and Xinjiang.

Finally, the Government of Saskatchewan will continue to be commercially active in Jilin and elsewhere in China through its Crown Corporations (e.g. SaskTel and SaskPower)

CONCLUSION

The current emphasis in both Canada's and Saskatchewan's policies towards China is to improve the coherence and effectiveness of existing China Programmes rather than simply increase the resources devoted to them. But such improvements depend on knowing where China's economy is going and what opportunities may present themselves to exporters as China's economy develops up to the year 2000. It is this information that will help governments, businesses and other interested organizations to orient and co-ordinate their strategies to gain access to the tremendous potential that is China today.

NOTE

[1] This chapter was abridged by the editor of the volume from a larger report, *Saskatchewan in China* (1981), originally prepared by the Inter-governmental Affairs Branch of Executive Council as follow-up to a province-wide conference on the subject in February of that year. The discussion, updated to include references to the current Fourth Plan of Action (1991-1993), represents existing policy directions. These, of course, are subject to change and modification by the government of the day.

3

SASKATCHEWAN'S AGRICULTURAL SECTOR: AGRICULTURAL TECHNOLOGY AND EQUIPMENT

Elaine Carlson

Department of Agriculture, Saskatchewan

INTRODUCTION

Saskatchewan and China share a mutual interest in expanding trade relations. China's current drive to modernize its agricultural sector is accompanied by a need for accelerated mechanization, modern agricultural technology, agricultural processing technology, and infrastructure development. Saskatchewan, Canada's most trade-dependent province, possesses a solid base of agronomic and agricultural technological expertise that can address China's needs.

This chapter examines six areas within Saskatchewan's agricultural sector with the most likely prospects for future trade between China and Saskatchewan: production (commodities), agricultural infrastructure development, agricultural technology, agricultural expertise, barren land development, and opportunities. The purpose is to alert Chinese buyers to the range of goods and services available to them as they seek to modernize their own agricultural sector.[1] The chapter is also directed at Saskatchewan exporters of agricultural expertise, equipment and technology. As the focus of the Saskatchewan-China trade relationship changes from government-led missions to long-term business initiatives, investors and entrepreneurs, agricultural consultants, and producers and suppliers of Saskatchewan agricultural goods and services will play an increasingly important role in pursuing trade with China.

AN OVERVIEW OF AGRICULTURE IN SASKATCHEWAN

Historical Development

Most Saskatchewan farms were settled by families who immigrated to Canada during the late 1890s and early 1900s to acquire homesteads—160-acre (64-hectare) parcels of land offered by the Government of Canada as incentives to settlement on the Canadian prairies. Despite the difficulties experienced by the pioneers—harsh winters, isolation, lack of basic services and comforts—these hardy families were able to clear and break land, grow grain, raise livestock, and establish rural communities. By working together, the early pioneers established schools for their children, churches, hospitals, and a community and agricultural infrastructure. Saskatchewan farm families acted co-operatively to better their economic prospects. They established a co-operative grain-handling and marketing system, a network of credit unions across the province, and co-operative retail businesses. The co-operative movement in the province remains strong to this day. Many farms continue to be operated by descendants of the original pioneers, and the family farm continues to be the main economic unit in rural Saskatchewan.

The Resource Base

Saskatchewan is the fifth largest province in Canada, covering 651,900 square kilometres or 65.2 million hectares of area. Approximately 1,000,000 people, or four percent of Canada's total population, live in the province (Government of Saskatchewan, Agriculture & Food, 1986).

A farm population of 168,500 cultivate nearly 20 million hectares of Saskatchewan's 26.6 million hectare farmland base—half of all cropland in production in Canada. The remaining acreage is used predominantly for livestock production. Average farm size is 420 hectares, with 315 hectares in cultivation. There are approximately 60,000 farms in the province.

Economic Importance

Agriculture is the single most important contributor to Saskatchewan's economy, normally accounting for about 12 percent of GDP and 58 percent of all primary industry (Ibid.). This places the contribution of agriculture to the provincial economy above any province in Canada. As a primary industry, agriculture directly provides jobs for one-fifth of Saskatchewan's labour force. Outside Saskatchewan's two major urban centres, on-farm production accounts for 42 percent of all jobs (Ibid.).

The province's agricultural sector accounts for 20 percent of all public and private investment and provides an economic base for most of the province's towns and villages. The local farmers purchase goods and services worth approximately $4 billion a year. Thirty-eight percent of all service-sector activity is farm-related. Agriculture also is a source of raw materials for many of the province's manufacturing industries; 31 percent of all manufacturing in the province is farm-related. Saskatchewan must export in order to prosper. Only 25 percent of all agricultural production is consumed within the province; the remainder must be exported (Government of Saskatchewan, Agriculture & Food).

COMMODITIES (PRODUCTION)

Crop Production

Saskatchewan is the leading producer of grain crops in Canada, with over 12 million hectares sown to grain crops each year. Wheat is the most important crop, approximating 55 percent of all the wheat produced in Canada (Ibid.). Bread and durum wheat are exported to about 100 countries, including China, the USSR, Japan, and the European Common Market nations. They are used primarily in baking and pasta products.

The second largest crop is barley which is used mainly as a livestock feed, but is also used by the brewing and malting industries. Prairie Malt Limited—Saskatchewan's only malt processor—and malt processors outside the province purchase a large quantity of Saskatchewan malting barley. Export markets include the former USSR, Japan, Saudi Arabia, East Germany, Italy, and other European Common Market nations.

Historically, Saskatchewan has been Canada's leading producer of oilseeds, mainly Canola and flax. Oil from Saskatchewan's canola crop makes up over 40 percent of domestic cooking oil and margarine production. The remainder is exported. Japan has been a significant export market, although canola is also exported to Mexico, the Netherlands, and other countries. Oil from flaxseed is used to manufacture paint. The meal from Canola and flax is used for livestock feed.

Oats and rye are grain crops of lower importance to Saskatchewan. Oats are processed into oatmeal for cooking and baking or used for livestock feed. Rye is used in speciality baking flours, for distilling and for livestock feed. Tame hay and forage are also important crops in the province, ranking high in both acreage and production. Speciality crops such as mustard, lentils, field peas, canary seed and sunflowers are recent additions to the list of Saskatchewan farm products.

The relative importance and production of the various grain crops are outlined in Table 1,3.

Table 1,3   Area and Production of Saskatchewan's Crops (10-Year Average, 1981-90)

Crop	Area (000 ha)	Production (000 tonnes)
Winter wheat	129.5	105.7
Spring wheat	6,544.0	11,558.6
Durum	1,513.6	2,363.5
Oats	362.2	685.5
Barley	1,386.1	3,233.2
Fall rye	170.4	267.0
Spring rye	22.5	32.9
Flax	236.7	255.2
Canola	1,053.0	1,305.1
Mixed grain	26.7	52.0
Mustard	106.2	101.1
Sunflower seed	6.4	5.7
Lentils	87.3	94.8
Field peas	63.3	93.6
Canary seed	63.9	67.0
Tame hay	763.3	2,376.9

An additional 40,000 hectares is used for the production of such crops as buckwheat, corn, fababeans, millet, triticale, safflower, forage seed and fruits and vegetables.

Source: Government of Saskatchewan, Agriculture & Food, 1990

Livestock Production

Livestock production is an important source of farm income in Saskatchewan. About two-thirds of all hogs produced annually are shipped out as either live hogs or pork. Twenty percent of Saskatchewan's beef production is used domestically. The relative importance of Saskatchewan's livestock industries is presented in Table 2,3.

Table 2,3   Livestock Production and Receipts, 1990

Livestock	Marketing and Production (000)	Farm Receipts ($ million)
Cattle and Calves (head)	1,214	575.9
Hogs (head)	1,002	129.0
Sheep and Lambs (head)	20	1.5
Milk and Cream (kg.)	218,000	93.8
Chicken and Fowl (No.)	11,155	26.5
Turkeys (No.)	786	9.7
Eggs (Dozen)	19,631	18.5
Honey (kg.)	7,257	8.7
Other Livestock		20.1

Source: Government of Saskatchewan Agriculture & Food, 1991

AGRICULTURAL INFRASTRUCTURE DEVELOPMENT

Marketing and Transportation

Saskatchewan is a land-locked province and must transport agricultural products long distances to Canadian and world markets. Orderly marketing and transportation of agricultural grain commodities are achieved through the Canadian Wheat Board—a grain-handling system comprising both farmer-owned and private grain companies, and a national railway system with frequent delivery points across the province.

The Canadian Wheat Board, established by the federal government, serves as the farmer's agent for marketing wheat and barley for export or domestic markets. It allocates how much grain a farmer can market through a system of delivery quotas based on farm size and available markets. Grain is hauled off the farm by truck and delivered to country elevators located on either the Canadian National Railway line, or the Canadian Pacific Railway line. The grain is loaded on to hopper cars and hauled to terminal elevators at Churchill, Prince Rupert, Vancouver or Thunder Bay. There, it is cleaned, dried, graded, certified by the Canadian Grain Commission, and loaded into ocean freighters for export, or into lake vessels for further movement to markets via the St. Lawrence Seaway.

Marketing of rye, flax, canola, oats and feed grains for the Canadian market is handled by private and co-operative grain companies trading on the Winnipeg Commodity Exchange. Farmers also sell feed grains directly to feed mills or livestock producers.

Livestock is sold by auction at live cattle markets or on a carcass basis directly to packing plants. Live and slaughtered animals are then delivered by truck to markets across Canada and the United States.

Marketing agencies have been established to facilitate the sale of livestock and crop production. These agencies govern sales in a broad range of agricultural production, including sheep and wool, chickens, eggs, turkeys, hogs, vegetables and milk.

Research

Agricultural research is a high priority in Saskatchewan. Most of the research has concentrated on the development of crops, livestock, agronomic practices, machinery and implements adapted to prairie conditions. Recently, emphasis has been placed on research into food processing, value-added agri-food production, agri-food diversification and development, and marketing.

Agriculture Canada, the Universities of Saskatchewan and Regina and the Saskatchewan Research Council are the major public research institutions in the province that concentrate on agriculture. The major sources of funding for agricultural research have been the federal and provincial governments.

Private industry and producer groups also support an increasing number of research projects through sponsorship by grain companies, machinery companies and chemical and fertilizer suppliers, or through producer "check-offs"—funds accumulated through a collection of fees when producers sell their products.

Private-sector research is also expanding through the establishment of research facilities and firms in conducting research under contract. It offers consultant services to the industry, or establishing turn-key operations at home and abroad.

Technology Transfer

The transfer of technology has traditionally been the responsibility of the Saskatchewan Department of Agriculture and Food, in co-operation with the University of Saskatchewan College of Agriculture and Agriculture Canada. In recent years, the government extension function has been transferred to the Saskatchewan Department of Rural Development. Another government agency, the Saskatchewan Agriculture Development Fund, concentrates its efforts on industry development and diversification. Producer associations, private industry and financial institutions have also become increasingly involved in extension activities to serve the needs of their clients.

Supporting Industries

Saskatchewan's agricultural sector provides markets and raw materials for many of the province's manufacturing industries. Related agri-food industries comprise almost 200 implement manufacturers, over 300 food processors (including bakeries and meat processing plants), and hundreds of farm equipment distributors and farm input suppliers (Government of Saskatchewan, *Saskatchewan Food Processors Directory*, 1990).

Current Trends

Farm income, and the number of farms in Saskatchewan, have steadily declined in the last decade as a result of climatic and economic adversity. This, in turn, has placed considerable pressure on the agricultural infrastructure. Grain elevator and railway companies have started to rationalize services in order to control costs. Suppliers of farm inputs and services have reduced the number of outlets. Farmers must now travel a greater distance in order to take their products to market, obtain services or purchase farm supplies.

The provincial government is committed to strengthen the agricultural sector, lessen its vulnerability to external forces, and create greater self-reliance for the sector. It is placing more emphasis on programmes and policies that will broaden the base of the agricultural sector. The provincial government also has expanded its agricultural focus to include all aspects of agri-food production and processing. Greater emphasis is now placed on value-added processing, economic and sectoral diversification, increased market responsiveness, environmental sustainability, and market and trade development. Saskatchewan's current formal position on international trade calls for a lessening of trade restrictions and distortions, an open marketplace, and fair access to markets.

SHAPING THE SASKATCHEWAN-CHINA
TRADING RELATIONSHIP

The Saskatchewan-China trading relationship is changing. While Saskatchewan's long-term trading relationship with China has been based primarily on wheat sales, these are projected to level off or decline as China modernizes its agricultural sector and steps up its own production.

Saskatchewan has an economic interest in maintaining its trade volume with China and capitalizing on its status as a preferred trading partner by substituting agricultural technology and equipment for agricultural commodities as the Chinese need for these commodities diminishes. This change will also mean a change in the nature of the trading relationship. As non-commodity exports replace commodity exports, the majority of trade initiatives will be undertaken by private-sector interests. Any future China-Saskatchewan trading relationship, therefore, will be one that is business-driven.

As China moves to strengthen its base for the production of exportable commodities, Saskatchewan's private sector looks forward to playing a key role by providing western technology and equipment and becoming investment partners to this end. As investment partners, the private sector will expect to have increased involvement and input in setting priorities and making decisions.

Impediments or perceived irritants to trade will also need to be lessened or resolved. For example, Saskatchewan investors and companies are unlikely to demonstrate a great deal of patience in negotiating a trade or joint-venture opportunities if, after a considerable investment of time and energy, they still have not realized any commercial rewards.

Some perceived irritants to trade may indeed be merely cultural differences, and it will be in the best interests of China and Saskatchewan to continue to create goodwill and understanding through cultural and social exchanges, such as education and training exchanges, cultural twinnings, and other non-commercial exchanges. Governments should continue to support these efforts. However, if the trade relationship of the future is to be business-driven, the trading climate could be improved in a number of ways, not the least of which are:

• simplification of the negotiating process;

• better identification of government policy changes, new projects, and joint venture opportunities;

- better identification of real decision-makers and specific contacts, including a directory of knowledgeable and experienced Chinese lawyers, accountants, bankers and other specialists who would be able to advise interested Saskatchewan business interests;

- increased effort to enhance communications between potential buyers and sellers. A forum where Saskatchewan investors could meet with prospective joint-venture partners in China, and a better distribution of papers and publications on joint-venture opportunities in China would facilitate development;

- more co-ordination among government departments in China, or greater separation of the trade sector from the government sector, would also eliminate impediments to trade and investment.

Another development bottleneck that will require attention is the different currencies; access to credit, foreign exchange and concessional financing; trade balances and debt; and counter-trade issues. Equally China's adoption of international commercial standards would resolve some of the difficulties Western consumers have had in accepting Chinese consumer products.

Western consumers are very demanding and discriminating buyers who simply will not choose goods that do not meet colour, style and size specifications, or that fail to meet minimum standards of performance, consistency, quality and workmanship, endurance and durability, and access to service, repair or replacement parts. Price must also reflect quality.

Again, cultural differences may account for the different expectations of Western and Chinese consumers. In the commercially-oriented economies of Western society, the consumer drives the marketplace and enjoys a considerable amount of choice in the goods or services he purchases, unlike consumers in centrally-planned economies. Consumer goods in Western society are seldom in short supply. On the contrary, there are numerous suppliers of similar goods and services who rely on advertising, packaging, and high workmanship standards to attract and please buyers. As a result of the enormous choice and variety that Western consumers enjoy, a predominant philosophy in the marketplace is that the buyer is always right. In order for Chinese products to be accepted in the Western marketplace, Western consumer standards will need to be adopted.

The Saskatchewan government will continue to expedite access to Chinese markets, to encourage the private sector to establish business relationships with China, and to support Saskatchewan private-sector involvement and investment in China as it modernizes its agricultural sector. However, Saskatchewan also anticipates that trade and invest-ment between China and Saskatchewan will be a two-way street, and that the province can expect to see Chinese investment or joint-venturing in Saskatchewan as part of any future, mutually-beneficial and reciprocal trading relationship.

FUTURE TRADE PROSPECTS

Agricultural Commodities

Wheat

Saskatchewan will continue to be an important source of wheat for bread, baking and pasta products for China's population. However, giv-en China's expected growth in population and agricultural productivity, Chinese wheat imports are expected to stabilize or decline. (Saskatch-ewan wheat is marketed through the Canadian Wheat Board).

Barley

Saskatchewan is the second largest barley-producing province in Canada. Saskatchewan farmers produce six-row varieties (for feed and milling) and two-row varieties (now preferred by the malting and brewing industry). Saskatchewan-grown barley is high-yielding, high quality, shows good tolerance to disease, and meets or exceeds world quality standards. (Commercial barley is marketed through the Canadian Wheat Board).

Feed grains

Barley, oats, rye and some pulse crops (fababean) constitute Saskatch-ewan's feed grains production. Although most of Saskatchewan's pro-duction of these crops is used domestically as a feed source for livestock and poultry feeding, export markets may also access feed-wheat and feed-grade barley through the Canadian Wheat Board.

Canola

Saskatchewan's crop scientists have modified original rapeseed so that new varieties of the crop contain only trace amounts of erucic acid and glucosinolates. In order to distinguish the new varieties from older varieties which contain these compounds, the name of the crop was changed to canola. Saskatchewan's canola production is now recognized worldwide as possessing superior nutritional qualities. The varieties grown in the province are very adaptable to growing conditions around the world. They demonstrate excellent genetic qualities, and yield good quality canola oil (less than two percent erucic acid) and low glucosinolate meal. Canola oil has the lowest saturated fats of all vegetable oils. It also has an ideal balance of fatty acids to make it nutritionally superior to other vegetable oils on the market. (Saskatchewan-grown Canola is marketed to foreign buyers by the major grain companies operating in Canada—Cargill, United Grain Growers, Saskatchewan Wheat Pool.

Seed

Crop seed is also an important commodity. The prominence of cereal grains and oilseed production in Saskatchewan has encouraged extensive research and technology development for its seed industry. Important research is conducted at the Crop Development Centre, Department of Crop Science and Plant Ecology, University of Saskatchewan. For example, in the past 13 years, the Crop Development Centre has developed 14 different varieties of barley in its Barley Breeding Programme (Government of Saskatchewan, *ADF News*, July 1989). Many varieties are now commercially available. Crop scientists also continue to develop new strains of wheat, including spring wheat varieties, winter wheat, durum and triticale; producers can select a large selection of varieties based on environmental, growing season and management-practice requirements of each variety. Grain companies operating in Saskatchewan are also very aggressive in plant breeding and have very active seed departments.

Saskatchewan has a large number of seed growers, most of whom belong to the Saskatchewan Seed Growers Association. They also comply with rigorous, national seed pedigreeing standards to ensure that export and local markets receive pedigree-quality seed-stock.

The pedigreed seed grown in the province may be obtained directly from individual seed growers (Newfield Seeds of Nipawin, Saskatchewan, is already engaged in seed trials in Jilin Province, China); the Saskatchewan Seed Growers Association; SeCan; the Canadian Seed Growers Association, which maintains a comprehensive directory of growers and seed variety and type; or the Canadian Seed Trade Association, a national body of seed trade members and companies organized to facilitate international seed trade).

Saskatchewan's seed growers are prepared to multiply seed from other countries or undertake seed breeding work, especially forage seeds, canola and mustard. (The Crop Development Centre, Department of Crop Science and Plant Ecology, University of Saskatchewan, and the

Saskatchewan Department of Agriculture and Food supply information on Saskatchewan pedigreed seed stocks and growers, new varieties of cereal grains and oilseeds developed in Saskatchewan, and seed multiplication schemes).

Forage and forage seeds

Saskatchewan and some agricultural-producing areas of China share similar climates, raise similar livestock, and use similar feedstuffs. In Saskatchewan, high quality forage seed is produced by pedigreed forage seed producers for use in forage, hay production, and pasture or rangeland production. Alfalfa is the main forage seed, and Saskatchewan leads the country in alfalfa seeded acreage. Other forage seeds produced in the province include bromegrass, crested wheatgrass, and Russian wild ryegrass. Growers can also offer turf grass seed, lawn and industrial-groundcover seed, and amenity or native grasses used in Saskatchewan in wildlife programmes and long-term ground cover programmes. (The Saskatchewan Forage Council, the 250-member Saskatchewan Alfalfa Seed Producers Association, or Saskatchewan Agriculture and Food give information on forage seed).

Because of Saskatchewan's extensive production of alfalfa, the province also has the capability of supplying Leaf Cutter Bees, a domesticated bee used throughout Canada and the Pacific North west of the United States for alfalfa seed pollination. Saskatchewan currently exports bees into the United States, and has the potential to supply large quantities of Leaf Cutter Bees, expertise, and bee-nesting materials and related equipment to other countries.

Dehydrated alfalfa pellets and cubes are important agricultural commodities produced in Saskatchewan to supply both domestic and export markets. A similar product emerging from the alfalfa industry is the dehydrated long-fibre hay bale. Several Saskatchewan firms have developed the capacity to double-compress hay into a compact, easily-handled bale that is ideal for export markets, and that offers superior nutritional qualities.

Livestock breeding stock, semen and genetic materials

In respect of livestock, Saskatchewan offers one of the most diverse genetic pools found anywhere in the world. It includes over 20 breeds of beef cattle, five breeds of dairy cattle, 10 breeds of swine, 20 breeds of horses, 10 breeds of sheep and 6 breeds of goats. Every year, over 15,000 pure-bred animals are registered in the province (SaskCan Livestock Export Inc.)

Pure-bred beef and swine have been bred, emphasis being placed on efficient growth, maternal characteristics, hardiness, and superior carcass quality. Emphasis is also placed on the breeding of dairy animals for high milk-protein content, high conformation and high production. Performance-evaluation programmes offered by government and breed associations have assisted breeders to identify and select livestock that are superior in these economically important traits.

Because of Saskatchewan's geographical and climatic diversity, its livestock can readily adapt to any kind of environment or management practice. Saskatchewan also has one of the highest animal health standards in the world, and is free from all major animal diseases. Animals are easily exported.

Saskatchewan will also export animal genetic materials. Its export of embryos is handled through Transtec Genetics Limited, an accredited embryo export agency. This agency meets all the technical competency standards and credential requirements of Agriculture Canada and the Canadian Embryo Transfer Association, as well as the requirements of the international community.

A new livestock and genetics clearing house in Saskatchewan will facilitate the export of Saskatchewan breeding stock, semen and embryos. SaskCan Livestock Export Inc. represents all sectors of the Saskatchewan livestock industry, including breed associations, performance testing associations, livestock-producer associations, individual breeders, livestock marketing agencies and breeding service agencies. Its mandate is to promote and market superior Saskatchewan livestock genetics, whether as live animals, embryos or semen, nationally and internationally.

Records of performance programmes, cattle breed registries, embryo accreditation and certification programmes, parentage typing facilities, and breed-improvement programmes operated by governments and breed associations are important means of assuring prospective buyers that Saskatchewan breeding stock and genetics materials are of high quality.

Agricultural Inputs: Implements and Machinery

Saskatchewan is home to an extensive manufacturing sector that specializes in a broad range of agricultural implements, equipment and electronics, many adaptable to farming conditions in other agricultural regions of the world.

Although the provincial government assists and encourages agricultural research and development, the size and successes of Saskatchewan's agricultural manufacturing sector is largely the result of private-sector initiatives. A large number of agricultural manufacturing and supply industries that now market their product across North America grew from on-farm activities and innovations; Saskatchewan farmers are known for their inventiveness, ingenuity, and ability to build or modify equipment used in farming operations.

In 1990, there were almost 200 Saskatchewan-based implement manufacturers. Indeed, the range of implements manufactured in the province is extensive. Soil preparation and tillage equipment includes rock pickers, rock rakes, rock management equipment, rod weeders, cultivators, dozers, equipment for land levelling, and scraping equipment for levelling and drainage trenching. Crop and fertilizer application equipment are air seeders, fertilizer and chemical applicators and sprayers, and sprayer tanks. The harvesting equipment comprises swathers, swather belts, double swath attachments, combine pick-up belts, and pickup teeth. Grain handling equipment made in Saskatchewan includes a variety of utility and grain augers and grain elevating equipment, grain dryers, grain vacuums, hopper bottom bins, hopper cones, and steel bins.

Haying, forage and feed-milling equipment are also manufactured: mowers, balers, bail wagons, round bail carriers, roller mills and other milling equipment. Equally significant is cattle handling equipment: stock trailers and flat decks, ventilation systems for stock barns, heat exchangers, computer controlled ventilators, electronic cattle feeding equipment, and corral sections, such as gates, chutes and headgates.

Other equipment manufactured in the province include snow blowers, post drivers, fibreglass and plastic tanks, and a lengthy list of monitoring equipment, and computerized controls for a variety of applications.

(Information on all these activities is available from the Saskatchewan Department of Economic Diversification and Trade which publishes a Saskatchewan Manufacturers' Guide that includes a listing of agricultural-related manufacturers. Similarly, the Saskatchewan Department of Trade and Investment produces an annual Saskatchewan Implement Buyers' Guide; and the Prairie Implement Manufacturers Association publishes an annual Prairie Implement Manufacturers' Guide). These and other directories will provide more detailed information about the range of agricultural implements, machinery and equipment available from Saskatchewan manufacturers).

Farm chemicals

Although Saskatchewan farmers apply large quantities of farm chemicals, including herbicides, pesticides and fertilizers, a Saskatchewan-based farm-chemical industry is still in the developmental stage. Two formulating plants now operate in Saskatchewan. Hoechst Canada, Inc. formulates the wild oat or grassy weed herbicide Diclofop Methyl and other broad-leaf and grassy weed herbicides. Shamrock Agri-Tech Inc. formulates trifluralin products. By the fall of 1992, Saskferco Products Inc. and Cargill Limited will begin producing anhydrous ammonia and granular urea at a plant now under construction at Belle Plaine, Saskatchewan.

Major grain elevator companies operating in Saskatchewan are the primary retailers of farm chemicals in the province. Because of their expertise in farm chemical sourcing and farm chemical formulation, these companies have the capability to fill foreign orders for farm chemicals.

Animal feed ingredients and supplements are also manufactured and distributed in Saskatchewan. Prairie Micro-Tech Inc. manufacturers micro-level feed ingredients and vitamin, and trace mineral premixes formulated for all types of livestock with different nutritional needs, a synthetic milk substitute for mother's milk so that the milk can be used for human consumption, and feed flavour agents to maximize feed intake.

Livestock barns and ventilation systems

Because of Saskatchewan's cold winters and climatic extremes, swine, dairy, and poultry must be housed in totally confined, heated buildings. Many Saskatchewan firms have developed and manufactured modular air-to-air heat exchangers, ventilation systems, exhaust fans, air inlets and heating systems for livestock applications, and computerized systems for barn ventilation, including control systems for multi-operation facilities operating several rooms. Del-Air Systems Ltd., Bantle Engineering Research Limited, and Sheltek Systems Inc. have developed considerable expertise in this area.

Other Saskatchewan manufacturers, such as Dyna-Fab Industries Ltd., manufacture pre-fabricated barn and hog pen structures, heavy-duty feeding equipment, animal waste management systems, farrowing crates, floor systems, weanling decks, liquid feed tanks, penning, gestation stalls, slurry pumps, dairy stalls and penning and plastic feeders.

High-tech equipment

A rapidly increasing number of Saskatchewan manufacturers and innovators are incorporating high technology into farm and agriculture-related equipment and specializing in agricultural and industrial electronics. High-tech products and systems include seed-management equipment, such as computerized or robotic seed-cleaning systems that use camera monitors to identify visually substandard seed, and grain-colour sorters.

Among the high-tech seeding equipment and systems are air seeders; monitors and automatic depth controllers for air seeders; seeder-shaft alarm systems; ultrasonic equipment for non-contact tillage depth and header height control; and minimum till seeding machines capable of addressing trash clearance, fertilizer placement, seed clearance and seed depth.

Also, there are the various high-tech harvest and grain handling equipment, such as grain-loss monitors which monitor the amount of grain lost during combining; moisture testers; high-performance, grain-drying equipment; ultrasonic, bin-level sensors; bin-temperature monitors; bin aerators; and a chaff collection and ammoniation system that improves the feeding value and protein levels of chaff and straw.

Other high tech equipment includes solar fences, solar water pumps, shaft and sprayer monitors, weighing equipment, and computerized agricultural equipment and electronic control monitoring equipment.

AGRICULTURAL TECHNOLOGY

Agricultural Bio-technology

Saskatchewan-based research into agricultural bio-technology is motivated by a number of factors. As a major agricultural producing province, it has always been in the best interests of producers and the sector to stay on the leading edge of any research that would promote agronomic excellence, increased production, and responsible use of agricultural resources. When these demands are matched by increasing demands for environmental protection and a country-wide push for sustainable agriculture, the move into agricultural bio-technology is a logical progression.

The primary vehicle for facilitating bio-technology research and development is Ag-West Bio-tech Inc. which is a non-profit company, developed in partnership with the Government. Its purpose is to co-ordinate and facilitate the production of agricultural bio-technology products in Saskatchewan, to open the channels to national and international markets for these products, and to promote information exchange on every aspect of agricultural bio-technology development.

The University of Saskatchewan is involved in undertaking contractual and basic research specific to agricultural bio-technology in the disciplines of crop science, animal science, soil science, micro-biology, bio-chemistry, engineering and veterinary medicine. Current projects include studies into bio-mass and crop waste uses, environmental detoxification studies, and studies into the production and use of free and immobilized enzymes for the food and feed industries.

The University of Regina is also involved in stimulating and facilitating opportunities for mutually beneficial research between industry and the university. The university's contractual and research programme involves research into genetically-engineered bio-pesticide controls, phytotoxicity of herbicides, computer plant growth modelling, and geographic information systems and their application to both game and land-use management.

The Saskatchewan Research Council (SRC) is another agency which offers considerable support to Saskatchewan scientists and firms. The SRC will undertake research and development functions on behalf of a client on a contractual basis.

The National Research Council (NRC) plays a role in Saskatchewan-based, agricultural bio-technology. NRC's Plant Bio-technology Institute, located in Saskatoon at the University of Saskatchewan, concentrates on utilizing crop wastes for the feed industries, new crop varieties, and on developing plant cell and gene technology. It produces novel transgenic plants and has a nation-wide programme of research training and industrial partnerships.

Similarly, Agriculture Canada operates four Agriculture Research Stations and two experimental farms in Saskatchewan.[2] Their major role is to transfer and implement new technologies, as well as to offer extensive consultations and to conduct co-operative research with producer organizations, universities and industry. Scientists and researchers in the province have access to and support from these research and development centres to facilitate the transition of their technology from the abstract to the concrete. Current projects include research and development of canola and mustard with built-in resistance to disease and insect infestation, the development of a bloat-free alfalfa, origination of better-performing grasses, the breeding of root-rot resistance into wheat and barley, and biological pest control.

Research into bio-technology, natural herbicides and biological control of plant and animal diseases and pests has advanced so far that several companies are now commercializing the results of bio-technological research. Philom Bios Ltd., a new company, is involved in development of non-chemical control agents for plant diseases and insects. Its products include microbial inoculants, bio-herbicides and bio-fungicides. The company will soon be producing and marketing Bio-Mal, a biological herbicide for control of round-leafed mallow, a serious prairie weed problem.

BIOSTAR Inc. is the commercial arm of the Veterinary Infectious Disease Organization (VIDO) at the University of Saskatchewan. Its goal is to develop and market bio-technological products, such as vaccines, immune regulators, disease predictors and disease diagnostics for the prediction, diagnosis and prevention of infectious disease in livestock.

MicroBio RhizoGen Corporation develops products to enhance crop production, placing particular emphasis on products for dryland farming. The company specializes in work with rhizobial strains of bacteria, and is a major producer of legume inoculants in Western Canada.

(The Ag-West Biotech Inc. makes available information on Saskatchewan-based bio-technological research, products and manufacturers).

Livestock Genetics Technology

Saskatchewan enjoys an excellent reputation for its work in animal genetics. The Western College of Veterinary Medicine, University of Saskatchewan, is the foremost centre of research in herd medicine and reproductive physiologies. The College has a reputation for world leadership in all aspects of genetic embryo transplant technology, including surgical and non-surgical embryo transplantation technology, embryo preparation for export, semen storage and freezing, sexing, blood testing for disease resistance and parentage, and DNA and molecular genetics.

Saskatchewan's body of knowledge and expertise in embryo transplant technology is supported by the Saskatchewan Research Council (SRC). The SRC maintains a parentage bovine blood-typing laboratory at the University of Saskatchewan. Current research attempts to identify pedigree lines, parentage and disease resistance through blood typing. The SRC also undertakes DNA technology research and development for better identification of animals with preferred genetic traits, and the genetic identification of disease-resistant animals through blood testing procedures. This new technology shows potential for incorporation with embryo transplant technology. The SRC also maintains a registry of beef and dairy cattle breeds in Saskatchewan on a fee-for-service basis. Several programmes established by breed associations, industry and government also enable producers to identify better superior genetics in their livestock and improve the country's livestock genetic base.

(Most breed associations, the Agriculture Development Branch of Agriculture Canada, the Saskatchewan Department of Agriculture and Food, and the Western College of Veterinary Medicine will provide information on Saskatchewan livestock, genetics materials and technologies, and export procedures).

Livestock Disease Control Technology

Saskatchewan is a North American leader in many areas of animal health management, and most significant livestock diseases have been eliminated from the province. There are many reasons for this. First, there is a high level of animal health expertise, research and technology available in Saskatchewan to support the livestock industry. Second, livestock producers themselves have developed a considerable body of production and management expertise. Third, livestock producers have access to excellent, readily-available Saskatchewan-grown forage and grain feedstocks. Fourth, there is considerable animal nutrition and ration formulation expertise in the province. Fifth, breed associations and government agencies offer excellent animal health management programmes that contribute to livestock health.

Agriculture Canada has overall responsibility to respond to and provide services related to exotic and reportable livestock diseases, such as tuberculosis, brucellosis, foot and mouth disease, and African swine fever, among others. Agriculture Canada also controls the import and export testing of livestock, and provides federal inspection services at two sites in Saskatchewan.

The Veterinary Branch, Saskatchewan Agriculture and Food, provides diagnostic pathology services for Saskatchewan livestock producers on a fee-for-service basis. The Veterinary Branch is also responsible for the provincial meat inspection programme, with inspection services provided at ten abattoirs across the province. The Western College of Veterinary Medicine, University of Saskatchewan, provides a similar service to producers and practising veterinarians on a fee-for-service basis. The Department of Agriculture and Food also administers a number of other animal health and health management programmes.

Most research into animal health and livestock diseases is conducted at the University of Saskatchewan, largely through the Western College of Veterinary Medicine (The Departments of Herd Medicine and Theriogenology, and Veterinary Pathology). The University's Department of Animal and Poultry Science also operates many livestock programmes

(Prairie Swine Centre, Dairy Herd, Beef Research Station, and others) that embrace animal health and disease control components.

The Veterinary Infectious Diseases Organization (VIDO) is also located at the University of Saskatchewan. VIDO serves the livestock and poultry industries by researching and developing non-residue forming animal-health and production-enhancement products, preventative medicine programmes and improved management techniques. VIDO's activities are organized into three scientific disciplines: bacteriology, virology, immunology, and animal care and research-support services. The organization has expertise in the areas of molecular and cell biology, gene cloning and expression, microbiology, immunobiology, virology, epidemiology and veterinary science.

Livestock Production Technology

Animal health is closely linked to animal management. Saskatchewan is a leader in animal management technology, animal nutrition and ration balancing, and pasture and rangeland management. Access to large quantities of excellent cereal and forage feedstocks also contributes to animal health and productivity. The application of advanced technology in livestock shelter and habitat, rangeland management, animal nutrition and ration formulation, feeding, and best-cost production techniques also enhances the productivity and quality of livestock produced in Saskatchewan.

Saskatchewan now raises high performance hogs and operates some of the best-managed swine production units in North America. Although the dairy industry in the province is small relative to the rest of the country, milk production per cow and per herd keeps pace with the national average. Saskatchewan is also recognized world wide for its productivity in beef. Livestock-production technology has been advanced by producers, livestock and breed associations, governments, research organizations, the feed industry and other organizations.

The University of Saskatchewan plays a major role in developing livestock production technology. Research activities specific to livestock-production technology involve the university's Department of Herd Medicine and Theriogenology, the Prairie Swine Research Centre, the Animal and Poultry Sciences Department, and the College of Agricultural Engineering.

The University operates a dairy herd that is consistently among the top five producing herds in the province. The University's work in dairy nutrition, ration balancing and food testing is known worldwide. It also operates a Beef Research Station for research on feedlot feeding, feeding of the cow-calf unit, supplementation and feed evaluation. Other research includes the use of enzyme technology to eliminate anti-nutritional factors or to increase the use of poultry feedstuffs that were thought to be inferior. The University's College of Agricultural Engineering has developed considerable expertise in intensive livestock-housing technology (barn design, construction and setups, ventilation systems) and in the design and development of computer-assisted livestock management technology.

The University of Saskatchewan offers the Master of Science and Ph.D. degrees in a range of subjects related to the livestock industry. The University's research capabilities and expertise in livestock management and production may also be accessed via contractual arrangements.

The Saskatchewan feed industry is a source of information on feed processing, feed formulation, feed evaluation, and other feed-related technology and information. Many feed companies operate their own animal nutrition research departments, incorporating research findings into new feed products, or extending feed management information and programmes to their clients as part of an overall package. The Saskatchewan Chapter of the Canadian Feed Industry Association includes most Saskatchewan-based feed or feed-component manufacturers and processors.

Because the feedlot industry is one of the most competitive in North America, Saskatchewan's feedlot industry has developed a considerable body of expertise in feedlot management and production efficiency. Many different computer programmes have been developed specifically to enable the feedlot operator to achieve the best production at least cost. They address such matters as initial cost of animals, interest costs, capital costs, overhead costs, feeding costs, projected rate of gain, and projected market value. Computer software programmes have also been developed in the area of ration formulation for feedlot cattle to enhance the feedlot's ability to do a least-cost ration formulation that will provide a balanced ration that meets the nutrient requirements on a minimized cost basis.

The Saskatchewan Cattle Feeders Association is a reliable source of information about feedlot technology. Various livestock and breed associations and livestock marketing boards have a vested interest in the development, demonstration and adoption of improved livestock production and livestock management technology.[3]

Other sources of livestock production technology and livestock management information include the Saskatchewan Livestock Association (Beef Herd Management System, Record of Performance Programme), the Agriculture Development Branch of Agriculture Canada, the Livestock Branch of Saskatchewan Agriculture and Food, and the Agriculture Development Fund (ADF).

Pasture and Grasslands Management Technology

Saskatchewan is developing knowledge and gaining expertise in pasture and grasslands management, and related technology. At present, the Government of Saskatchewan and the Government of Canada are co-operatively encouraging increased research, development and demonstration of these technologies in a number of areas. These include rangeland resource inventory and analysis, economic analysis, proper distribution of grazing pressures, stocking rates and grazing distribution, range-cattle breed compatibility, rangeland conditioning and monitoring, pro-active range management and grazing systems planning, stock watering, appropriate vegetation or cropping, chemical or biological management procedures, pasture renovation, fertilization, introduced forages, experimental cropping, related seed production and storage, rotational grazing systems, fencing, ecological and eco-physiological considerations, conservation tillage and soil conservation technologies, and wildlife grazing.

Rangeland management technologies enable livestock producers to maximize their benefits, maintain the productive potential of rangeland, reduce their financial risk, and ensure more stable production throughout a period of potentially variable or adverse climatic conditions.

(Information about emerging pasture and range management technology that have been researched, developed and demonstrated in Saskatchewan may be obtained from the Department of Crop Science and Plant Ecology, the University of Saskatchewan; Agriculture Canada—Prairie Farm Rehabilitation Administration, or Agriculture Canada Research Stations at Swift Current, Melfort, Saskatoon and Regina—Saskatchewan Agriculture and Food; Saskatchewan Rural Development; and the Agriculture Development Fund.)

Other agencies and organizations have also developed expertise in pasture and rangeland management, such as the Saskatchewan Research Council, the Saskatchewan Soil Conservation Association and Ducks Unlimited Canada. Many of these agencies will work through CIDA to extend rangeland management expertise to other countries.

Plant Breeding, Plant Genetics, Crop Disease, Crop Production, Seed Production and Related Technology

The Crop Development Centre and the Department of Crop Science and Plant Ecology, University of Saskatchewan, are important centres for scientific expertise in plant breeding, plant genetics and crop diseases in the province. Research by crop and plant scientists at this institution has resulted in the commercialization of many new varieties of cereals and oilseeds suitable for Saskatchewan's agronomic conditions, climate and growing season.

The Crop Development Centre also conducts plant breeding work on a contractual basis, and will facilitate the training of people in plant breeding technology, supervise seed multiplication schemes, and source seed and facilitate germ plasm exchange.

Agriculture Canada is also involved in plant and crop research and development at four Agriculture Research Stations in Saskatchewan. Its activities include development of canola and mustard with built-in resistance to disease and insect infestation, the development of a bloat-free alfalfa and better performing grasses, the breeding of root rot resistance into wheat and barley, and the development of new varieties of medium quality spring wheat and rye.

Scientific expertise in crop disease is concentrated at the University of Saskatchewan's Biology Department, the Crop Pathology Section of Agriculture Canada, and the Agriculture Research Station, Saskatoon. Saskatchewan has special expertise in canola and lentil diseases as a result of research conducted in the province.

All the institutions discussed in this section transfer and implement new technologies, offer extensive consultations with Saskatchewan producers, and conduct co-operative research with producer organizations and industry. There is significant producer-based expertise in seed production and seed cleaning technologies in Saskatchewan. (This information may be obtained from individual seed producers or through the Saskatchewan Seed Growers' Association).

Irrigation and Water Use Technology

Saskatchewan currently has the two largest pressurized pipeline irrigation systems in Canada. They are multiple-use water supply systems, providing municipal water supplies, wildlife enhancement projects, and domestic water to farms, as well as providing a supply of water for agricultural irrigation purposes. Another notable feature is that the systems are designed to accommodate the disposal of livestock effluent by means of the irrigation distribution system.

Responsibility for management of the province's water resources rests with the Saskatchewan Water Corporation (Sask Water), a provincial crown corporation. Sask Water has developed considerable expertise in irrigation technologies and methodologies, including development of a method for evaluating irrigation potential that considers soil issues along with their geological and hydro geological background.

Sask Water works closely with two Saskatchewan-based irrigation and water-use engineering consultants, SNC Inc., and Cochrane Lavalin Inc. Both firms also have expertise in irrigation projects outside Canada and have the capability to establish BOOT (Build, Own, Operate, Transfer) operations in foreign countries. In this capacity, they are able to design and build an irrigation project, using equity provided by Canadian investors, to operate the project for a pre-specified period of time, and to transfer ownership of the project back to the country at the end of the specified period. This format enables the cost of the project to be spread over a period of time, serves as a proving technique, allows the developer to receive revenue from the project to re-coup costs, and ultimately results in a no-cost transfer of ownership of the project.

Irrigation technological expertise is also developed at the Saskatchewan Irrigation Development Centre at Outlook, a joint Saskatchewan-Canada project. Using the latest technology and information, researchers, farmers, and governments work together to research all aspects of irrigation and water management, including soil reclamation, soil irrigation, tile drainage, and research into crop varieties suitable for irrigated fields.

Advanced Technology Applicable to Agriculture

There are several sources of information on advanced agricultural technology, including the Saskatchewan Research Council, Ag West Biotech Inc., the University of Saskatchewan, the Agriculture Development Fund, private sector consultants and agrologists, and the Prairie Agricultural Machinery Institute (PAMI).

The Agriculture Development Fund maintains a data base of all ADF research, development and demonstration projects undertaken in the province, as well as data from agriculture-related projects from other agencies, such as Saskatchewan Water Corporation, and Saskatchewan Economic Diversification and Trade. This data base ties in with the ICAR (Inventory of Canadian Agricultural Research) data base developed by Agriculture Canada.

Ag West Biotech Inc., established to spearhead agricultural bio-technological initiatives in Saskatchewan, maintains communications channels between industry, scientists, governments, financiers and specialists on a global basis. The organization has the capability to facilitate and coordinate research, and development and commercial opportunities between Saskatchewan interests and those in other countries. It is also interested in new technologies outside Canada that might have applications in Western Canada.

PAMI operates testing and evaluation centres at Humboldt, Saskatchewan, and Portage La Prairie, Manitoba. It is jointly subsidized by the governments of Manitoba and Saskatchewan. One of its functions is to test and evaluate key components or equipment used by prairie farmers in prairie farm conditions. A second function is to conduct research and development work on a fee-for-service basis for designers and manufacturers of agricultural systems, equipment and implements. This could include concept and pre-prototype evaluation, engineering evaluation of components or complete machines, evaluation of systems such as harvesting or ventilation systems, development of guidelines for system application, and other assistance that would enable manufacturers to develop machines designed to address specific problems related to prairie farming conditions.

PAMI's work with individuals or companies is done in a confidential manner. However, should a manufacturer agree to market a machine as tested, using PAMI recommendations or modifications, this information is incorporated in an evaluation report. Reports published by PAMI are then made available to the public. As an agency involved in the forefront of agricultural implement engineering, design and production innovation, PAMI also serves as a referral agency and can direct inquiries to appropriate agencies and manufacturers.

The Saskatchewan Chapter of the Canadian Consulting Agrologists' Association (CCAA) also provides referral and consultant services that put clients in contact with sources of advanced agricultural technology. All members within CCAA are professional consulting agrologists. The major focus of CCAA members is to enhance the productivity of clients involved in the agricultural sector. The diversity of expertise within the organization ensures the capabilities to meet the needs for agricultural development in the fields of project management, farm production and management systems, soil and land-use systems, livestock management and production, recommended agricultural practices under intensive, large-scale farming regions, machinery design and selection, and agriculture and environmental issues.

Agricultural Technology Consultants with Turn-key Project Capabilities

Many of the Saskatchewan-based consultants and firms have experience and capability in establishing in developing countries turn-key operations that include all aspects of agricultural project development relevant to a specific area. The WECAN Project Development Inc., for instance, offers integrated livestock project development expertise that includes all relevant operations from nucleus breeding stock to product marketing. WECAN can:

- examine economic and social feasibility of livestock development projects;
- prepare detailed plans of production complexes for swine, dairy, poultry or beef for any size or purpose;
- prepare feasibility and detailed design for feed-production complexes such as complete feed mills, concentrate and premix units, and supply micro nutrients, storage complexes, transport systems and testing laboratories;
- conduct feasibility and detailed design for slaughter and processing plants;
- develop complete training programmes for livestock management, health management, animal husbandry, nutritional design and testing, using facilities in the client's area or Canadian training facilities;
- contract health management and testing;
- procure equipment, genetics and expertise;
- offer turn-key or contract-project management.

WECAN draws on the expertise of a wide variety of Western Canadian professionals in engineering, transport, economics, food processing, design, project evaluation, finance, expediting, and genetics. WECAN is also registered with the Canadian International Development Agency (CIDA) as an eligible delivery agent for programmes.

Similarly, O & T Agdevco offers similar agricultural expertise in horticulture, totally integrated poultry farms (hatching, growing, feed processing and nutrition, disease prevention and control and sales), dry-land farming, water resource identification and management (well drilling, irrigation, large- scale drainage). It establishes schools, practical and theoretical farm-management expertise delivery and training, technology evaluation, equipment and technology accessing on behalf of clients, and agricultural expertise in many other areas.

Agdevco is registered with CIDA and has been involved in projects in China, Nigeria, Zambia, Sudan, Tanzania, Lesotho, the former Soviet Union and other nations. Agdevco is also prepared to establish joint ventures on projects or to sell expertise directly. Both Agdevco and WECAN are members of the Saskatchewan Chapter of the Canadian Consulting Agrologists Association.

The Association of Professional Engineers of Saskatchewan will also refer clients to member firms or consultants who have expertise in turn-key establishment or management, or who have developed technology for different organizations associated with agricultural development in countries outside Canada. A number of Saskatchewan-based engineers and engineering firms are actively involved in developmental projects outside Canada.

Marketing/Infrastructure Expertise

Saskatchewan has a significant body of expertise in many areas re-lated to agriculture and the production, management and delivery of food, including co-operative formation, product-quality control and grad-ing, the development of comprehensive extension services, bulk handling, and product distribution. This infrastructure expertise may be adaptable to China's agricultural sector. The larger pools, such as the Saskatchewan Wheat Pool, Dairy Producers Co-operative Ltd., and Federated Co-oper-atives Ltd. have expertise in co-operative formation in areas related to agriculture and food production, processing and marketing.

Product Quality Control/Grading

The federal government has primary responsibility for product safe-ty, quality control and grading. However, the provincial government also has an infrastructure in place to insure that Saskatchewan consumers receive safe, quality foods, free from disease, toxins, or harmful residue.

The laboratories at the Western College of Veterinary Medicine in Saskatoon and the Provincial Laboratory in Regina provide diagnostic information to veterinarians and farmers and serve as a surveillance sys-tem for all diseases in livestock. Reportable diseases are referred directly to Agriculture Canada. Other diseases are treated and managed by the farmer and the veterinarian. The Prairie Swine Research Centre at the University of Saskatchewan also plays a valuable role in the treatment, diagnosis and elimination of swine disease.

Saskatchewan also provides inspection services for the slaughter, grad-ing and control of meat products sold within the province, including beef, hogs and poultry products. Milk quality is controlled by the Saskatch-ewan Milk Control Board. Other products, such as meat intended for export outside Saskatchewan, eggs, dairy products and processed foods, come under the jurisdiction of Agriculture Canada or Health and Welfare Canada.

Extension Services

Extension services are the means by which farm-based producers and farmers learn about the newest, most up-to-date agricultural methodologies and technologies. In Saskatchewan, extension services related to agriculture are administered by the Saskatchewan Department of Rural Development, Extension Branch. Saskatchewan Agriculture and Food also disseminates information to farmers and producers through a variety of publications and newsletters, media releases, and other communications vehicles.

Most grain companies and farm or producer associations also have extension services divisions within their organizations and regularly disseminate important agricultural information to their members or clients. Weather-related information is provided by Environment Canada. The province's media outlets also cooperate in the dissemination of agricultural information, and many rural newspapers, radio stations and television outlets regularly incorporate agricultural columns or broadcasts directed to producers and consumers.

Bulk Handling Expertise

The grain handling industry in Saskatchewan has enormous expertise and capabilities in the agricultural sector. The Saskatchewan Wheat Pool, Canada's largest grain handling company, owned and controlled by 65,000 farmer-members, has taken an active leadership role in the development of the agricultural infrastructure in the province. This includes:

- development of a grain elevator, collection and storage services network for grain (using slip-form technology to build large, sealed, insect-proof concrete elevators);
- a network for the marketing of farm inputs such as farm chemicals, feed grains, shortline equipment items;
- operation of terminal facilities at Thunder Bay and Vancouver, which provide seed cleaning, blending and storage, vessel loading;
- operation of a flour mill, barley mill, bakery mix plant and special crops cleaning plants;
- establishment of a livestock division which operates nine Saskatchewan livestock marketing centres, including auction marketing of livestock, complete order and buying service, trucking services;
- a service department with engineering, construction, project management knowledge and expertise, grain transportation experience;

- expertise in coordination, trading and marketing of Canadian grains and oilseeds world wide through its marketing arm, X-Can Grain Ltd.;
- canola crushing and processing, marketing, researching and technical aid to canola oil customers and refiners and packagers (CSP Foods Ltd.);
- assistance to research and development of alternate energy sources;
- trading experience in speciality-crop trading experience, such as in sunflower and confection processing and fish farming;
- formulation of farm chemicals through Interprovincial Cooperatives.

Marketing Expertise

As shown in Table 3,3, a variety of marketing and promotion agencies have been established within the food industry in Canada to promote sales of many agricultural commodities, including red meats, poultry products and eggs, milk and other dairy products. The list is incomplete, for other livestock breed associations and speciality-crop growers associations also have an interest in promoting the sale and use of these agricultural commodities.[4]

Table 3,3   Marketing and Promotion Agencies

1. The Council of Canada
2. The Dairy Producers Co-operative Ltd.
3. The Saskatchewan Broiler Chicken Hatching Egg Producers Marketing Board
4. The Saskatchewan Chicken Marketing Board
5. The Saskatchewan Commercial Egg Marketing Board
6. The Saskatchewan Dairy Foundation
7. The Saskatchewan Egg and Poultry Processors Association
8. The Saskatchewan Meat Processors
9. The Saskatchewan Natural Products Marketing Council
10. The Saskatchewan Pork Producers Marketing Board
11. The Saskatchewan Turkey Producers Marketing Board
12. The Saskatchewan Vegetable Marketing and Development Board
13. The Saskatchewan Wild Rice Council

Many other livestock breed associations and speciality crop growers associations have an interest in promoting the sale and use of their agricultural commodities.

(The Saskatchewan Agriculture and Food maintains a directory of these and other agencies.)

BARREN LAND DEVELOPMENT

Saskatchewan's expertise in soil conservation technology, soil and grasslands reclamation and management, and water management technology is growing as more emphasis is placed on preserving and managing the productive potential of land in Saskatchewan. The capabilities of Saskatchewan Water Corporation include large scale drainage, multipurpose water pipelines, water control and management, wildlife enhancement, canal and pipeline irrigation and management, and related soil management issues.

Ducks Unlimited Canada, the North American Waterfowl Management, and Saskatchewan Wetland Conservation Corporation have a well-developed level of expertise in the management of land with a multi-use focus, including wildlife resource supports, wildlife management, rangeland use, good soil management and wetland preservation.

The bulk of information about rangeland management, barren land development and soil conservation is available from the Department of Crop Science and Plant Ecology, University of Saskatchewan. Agriculture Canada and the Prairie Farm Rehabilitation Administration (PFRA) also have knowledge in rangeland management. The PFRA operates 56 federal pasture programmes in the province, using state-of-the-art rangeland management techniques. The Soils and Crops Branch of Saskatchewan Agriculture and Food has specialists on staff in the areas of soil conservation, tillage, and management practices for soil conservation technology. The Saskatchewan Department of Rural Development is another source of specific information on rangeland management. It operates community pastures and disseminates information via extension agrologists.

Two other agencies with considerable expertise in soil conservation and rangeland management are the Saskatchewan Soil Conservation Association (SSCA) and the Institute of Pedology at the University of Saskatchewan, a body established for the purpose of developing technology and expertise related to soil and land-use issues. The Institute has representatives from the university, the federal and provincial governments, and the scientific and research community.

The Saskatchewan Soil Conservation Association is a non-profit, producer-based organization dedicated to the promotion of soil conservation in Saskatchewan. It is funded by the Agricultural Development Fund (ADF). Its aim is to encourage soil conservation by promoting agricultural production systems that reduce soil degradation and maintain economic viability. Producers have been joined by many agencies, corporations, and institutions which support the soil conservation effort in the province. The body of knowledge within SSCA embraces extension, research and administration expertise. It has introduced forages (breeding, fertilization, seed production and storage); fossil fuel efficiency; rangeland evaluation (community ecology, ecophysiology, soils); and grazing systems management.

The farm implement sector in Saskatchewan is also a source of technological expertise in land reclamation systems, dryland farming, and soil erosion management. A growing number of manufacturers design, develop and manufacture implements and technologies appropriate to Saskatchewan farming conditions. Developments include a cultivation system to preserve surface residue and lessen damage by wind; barrier strip seeders; sprigging technology for planting rhizomes as a land reclamation technique; wide blade tillage equipment which is ideal for soil conservation and dryland farming activities.

The Prairie Implement Manufacturers' Association (PIMA) and the Prairie Agricultural Machinery Institute (PAMI) are good sources of information on land reclamation or conservation-related equipment and technologies available in Saskatchewan.

AGRICULTURAL PROCESSING TECHNOLOGY

Food Processing

Although Saskatchewan's agricultural reputation has been based largely on the production and export of primary agricultural commodities, value-added agri-food production is increasing. Food products produced and processed in Saskatchewan comprise canola oil, flour, bread, noodles, dairy products such as cheese and yogurt, processed meats, alfalfa sprouts, sauerkraut, chocolates, fresh and preserved wild berries, perogies, lentil soups, honey, beef jerky, wheatnuts and other confections, bottled water, beer, dried herbs, and condiments.

Agriculture Canada and Saskatchewan Agriculture and Food have compiled a Saskatchewan Food Processors' Directory that lists hundreds of processors. Many food processors also belong to the Saskatchewan Food Processors' Association, and many agencies are involved in the development of food processing technology.

The Agriculture Development Fund also supports food product and market development by providing assistance to determine market potential, market testing, the analysis of food products, and to develop, improve or import technology. In exchange, research and development findings are incorporated into the ADF data base.

The University of Saskatchewan's Department of Food Sciences and Department of Microbiology are also involved in research into new food products and new food processing methods and technology.

Dairy Processing Technology

The Dairy Producers Co-operative Ltd. is a major dairy processor in Saskatchewan, and a western Canadian leader in dairy milk processing. It uses state-of-the-art technology and computerized equipment in the manufacture of fluid milk, ice cream, cultured and dried products, and a high-protein milk whey and pea protein product with potential uses as a milk replacement or baking mix. The Dairy Producers Ltd. has also provided consulting services in the design and establishment of dairy processing plants in developing countries.

Oilseed Processing Technology

CSP Foods Ltd., jointly owned by the Saskatchewan Wheat Pool and Manitoba Pool Elevators, is the largest oilseed processor in Saskatchewan. Its Saskatchewan operation crushed over half a million tonnes of canola in 1989-90 (Saskatchewan Wheat Pool, Annual Report, 1990). The company has also established a presence in flour-milling and rapeseed processing. With refineries, hydrogenation and packaging facilities, CSP manufactures and markets a complete range of shortening, margarine and salad oil. As a result of its activities, CSP Foods has developed a reservoir of experience in the oilseed processing industry. CSP Foods was instrumental in the adoption of many improvements that led to canola, and co-operates with the research community to create a world-recognized edible oil. CSP also maintains its own research department and provides technical support to oil customers, and can help refiners and packagers produce a high-quality finished product.

Oilseed research is also supported by the POS Pilot Plant Corporation in Saskatoon. The corporation conducts research on a contractual basis for the purpose of designing agricultural-products-processing operations, including engineering, training, quality control, technical assistance and other assistance that may be required for establishing a food processing plant. POS has recently positioned a contact person in China.

Livestock Feed Processing Technology

Many Saskatchewan-based livestock feed producers market technology as well as product, or extend consulting services to foreign customers. The Saskatchewan Chapter of the Canadian Feed Industry Association has feed and feed-component processors, such as Prairie Microtech and White Fox Forages which have developed high levels of expertise in feed formulation, feed processing, and animal nutrition.

Recent technological advances in livestock feed processing include the use and incorporation of enzymes and enzyme bio-technology to improve utilization of feedstuffs or eliminate anti-nutritional factors. One firm, Redekopp Chaff Systems, developed a unique chaff collection machine that can pick up chaff piles and transport them to an area where they can be ammoniated to increase feed value and fed to livestock. The Saskatchewan Research Council participated in the development of this new technology.

OPPORTUNITIES FOR CHINESE INVOLVEMENT IN SASKATCHEWAN'S AGRICULTURAL SECTOR

Diversification of Saskatchewan's agricultural sector is fuelled by the desire to broaden the economic base of the province. Greater awareness of consumer trends and consumer consumption patterns around the world has also provided the incentive for agricultural entrepreneurship and diversification. Some of these new activities are in the developmental stage, and may be of interest to people in China.

Antler Velvet Production

The game-farming industry is growing in Saskatchewan, and several elk farm units are now producing antler velvet. The quality of antler velvet produced in the province is considered to be among the best in the world. However, since antler-velvet processing is a relatively recent development, the game-farming industry in Saskatchewan may be receptive to assistance with antler-processing technology, and with market identification, assessment, and expansion.

Mushroom Production

Consumer consumption of cultured mushrooms is on the rise in Canada. There are several reasons for the increase. Processed food products, such as pizza, are growing in popularity. Mushrooms also have been identified as a healthy food for health-conscious consumers. Fresh mushrooms are also readily available; supermarkets now carry good supplies of fresh, Canadian-grown mushrooms.

Although there is one mushroom farm in Saskatchewan, the bulk of Saskatchewan's mushroom market is now being supplied from sources outside the province. Saskatchewan is interested in developing a cultured mushroom industry that addresses not only consumer demand within the province, but can export the product outside the province. Assistance with mushroom production technology and market development would be welcomed.

Wild mushroom harvesting is also on the increase in Saskatchewan, and several entrepreneurs are now exporting a variety of wild mushrooms to exotic markets. Since wild mushrooms are plentiful in northern Saskatchewan, a priority is to locate and supply new markets for this product, or to identify potential medicinal or non-food uses for wild mushrooms.

Short-Season, Fruit-Bearing Trees and Shrubs

As Saskatchewan consumer preference for fresh fruits and vegetables increases, so does the opportunity to provide Saskatchewan-grown produce. However, because of Saskatchewan's climate, traditional varieties of fruit trees grown in other regions of Canada or North America are difficult to grow in Saskatchewan. Given China's thousands of years of horticultural experience, there may well be varieties or production technologies that could be adaptable to Saskatchewan's climate and growing season. With the right marketing approach, Saskatchewan consumers—and consumers in the rest of the country—could be encouraged to try entirely new types of fruits that could be cultivated successfully in Saskatchewan. New fruit varieties suitable for cultivation in Saskatchewan, marketing expertise, and production technologies would be welcomed.

Greenhouse Technology

As consumer demand for fresh fruits and vegetables continues to grow, more entrepreneurs are considering ways of meeting Saskatchewan's demand with produce grown in the province. Greenhouse production of fruits and vegetables is the only practical option that would allow consumer demand to be satisfied on a year-round basis. Rural gasification in the province will reduce significantly the costs of greenhouse vegetable production, and prospects for this fledgling industry are good.

Greenhouse production technologies could also be applied to the growth of nursery stock, bedding plants, cut flowers, and speciality foods for ethnic markets. Consumer demand in each of these areas appears to be on the increase and could be supplied from Saskatchewan.

Saskatchewan is interested in adding to its expertise and knowledge of greenhouse production technology, and in developing and securing markets for greenhouse-grown vegetables, produce for ethnic markets, fresh flowers, bedding plants and nursery stock.

Forages

Livestock production is a significant industry in Saskatchewan, and researchers and producers are always interested in discovering new forages, such as salt-tolerant grasses or alkali-tolerant forage plants that can be successfully cultivated in the province to provide forage for grazing animals.

Although Saskatchewan possesses excellent research, testing and plant breeding capabilities, it is always interested in obtaining new plant genetics with potential applications in Saskatchewan.

Medicinal Herbs

More and more North American consumers are interested in medicinal herbs, holistic medicine and non-surgical intervention of illnesses and ailments. Most North Americans have limited understanding about how herbs such as ginseng can be used in medical and non-medical applications, or what processing technology should be used to preserve the potent compounds of these plants. The Chinese, on the other hand, have a very large body of knowledge on herbs.

Several Saskatchewan producers have recently moved into limited herb and spice cultivation and production, and have proven that herbs can be successfully grown in the province's cold climate, given adequate information and technology. Saskatchewan is very interested in adding to its body of knowledge about herbal and natural products, and is also interested in developing markets for Saskatchewan-grown herbs and spices.

Ornamental Plants

It is predicted that gardening will be a major North American trend in the next decade or two. Consumers are showing an increased interest in purchasing and growing exotic and different plant materials, such as ornamental plants, house plants, or flowering shrubbery. It is possible that plants common to China and adaptable to Saskatchewan's growing conditions could supply this developing demand for plant novelties, and as such, it is an area that is worth exploring. Saskatchewan is interested in learning more about Chinese ornamental plants, production technology, genetics materials and marketing expertise related to ornamental plants. (The Saskatchewan Department of Agriculture and Food entertains inquiries on this subject.)

CONCLUSION

The agricultural sector in Saskatchewan is well developed, and significantly supported by state-of-the-art technology, expertise, experimentation and research. In both commodities and infrastructure, it is quite able to supply major agricultural requirements of Shandong/China as they seek to modernize this sector, among others, of their economies. The potentialities for trade in this sector with Shandong could not be more promising, and conditions could not be more agreeable for the governments of Shandong and China, on the one hand, and public and private decision-makers and investors of Saskatchewan, on the other, to initiate agreements that could lead to profitable trading between the two groups.

NOTES

[1] Addresses of agencies and organizations named in the text of this chapter are listed alphabetically in Appendix 1,3.

[2] The Agriculture Canada Research Station in Swift Current, Saskatchewan, specializes in dry-land farming; wheat, rye and forage breeding programmes; range and pasture management development; and crop management and conservation applications for semi-arid agriculture. The Agriculture Canada Research Station in Melfort, Saskatchewan, specializes in forage, beef and grain crops. The Agriculture Canada Research Station in Saskatoon is the centre for oilseed breeding, specializing in canola, mustard and rapeseed, and alfalfa and grass breeding programmes for crops grown in the northern region of the prairie crop zone. The Saskatoon Research Station also operates an entomology section. The Scott Experimental Farm in Saskatoon focuses on crop management rotations and weed control. The Agriculture Canada Research Station in Regina specializes in weed ecology and physiology (biological controls), as well as more conventional weed control methods), and serves as the main weed control centre for Western Canada. It also conducts work on other crops, including cereals, oilseeds, and speciality crops. The Indian Head Experimental Farm conducts variety testing and is a major seed distribution centre.

[3] Saskatchewan livestock associations and boards involved in promoting animal health, nutrition, production management and breed improvement are listed in Appendix 1,3.

[4] Agencies and boards with an interest in promoting the use and sale of their agricultural commodities are included in Appendix 1,3.

REFERENCES

Government of Saskatchewan Agriculture and Food. 1989. "Agriculture in Saskatchewan".

Government of Saskatchewan, ADF (Agriculture Development Fund) News, July, 1989.

Government of Saskatchewan. 1990. *Saskatchewan Food Processors Directory*.

Saskatchewan Wheat Pool Report, 1991.

ACKNOWLEDGEMENTS

The personnel of government agencies and universities, farmers, contractors, commercial firms, among others, have contributed information for this chapter. Brevity does not permit credit to each source. I thank all contributors.

BIBLIOGRAPHY OF HELPFUL SOURCE MATERIAL

Abouguendia, Z.M. 1990. *A Practical Guide to Planning for Management and Improvement of Saskatchewan Rangeland*. Range Plan Development, First Printing 10M, Canada, with funding from the Canada Saskatchewan New Pasture and Grazing Technology Project through the Saskatchewan Agriculture Development Fund and the Economic Regional Development Agreement (manuscript prepared as Saskatchewan Research Council Report No. E-2520-1-E-90 and published under contract with the New Pasture and Grazing Technologies Project "ERDA").

Ag-West Biotech Inc., Agricultural Biotechnology Saskatchewan, Ag-West Biotech Inc., Saskatoon, Saskatchewan, Ag-West Biotech Inc., with funding assistance from the Saskatchewan Agriculture Development Fund.

Agriculture Canada, Industry Science and Technology Canada; Statistics Section, Economics Branch, Saskatchewan Agriculture and Food; Saskatchewan Economic Diversification and Trade; and Saskatchewan Food-Talk—Department of Applied Microbiology and Food Science, University of Saskatchewan, 1990 Saskatchewan Food Processors Directory, Saskatoon, Saskatchewan, Saskatchewan FoodTalk, University of Saskatchewan.

Government of Saskatchewan (author: Paul Osborne), 1987, Saskatchewan in China, a report on the China Conference hosted by the Government of Saskatchewan in February, 1987, Regina, Saskatchewan.

Jie, Lui Shi, (1988), translated by Yu, Wang, Faculty of Administration, University of Regina, Edited by Weymes, Ed., Faculty of Administration, University of Regina, "Doing Business in China", Regina, Saskatchewan.

Pyle, W., and Johnson, W. (Eds.). 1990. *Managing Saskatchewan Rangeland*, Canada Saskatchewan New Pasture and Grazing Technologies Project, funded by the Economic Regional Development Agreement (ERDA) and the Saskatchewan Agriculture Development Fund (ADF).

Saskatchewan Agricultural Services Co-ordinating Committee (University of Saskatchewan, Saskatchewan Agriculture, Agriculture Canada), revised 1987, *Guide to Farm Practice in Saskatchewan*, Saskatoon, Saskatchewan, publication financed by Saskatchewan Agriculture, published and produced by the University of Saskatchewan, Division of Extension and Community Relations.

Saskatchewan Agriculture, ADF News, Agriculture Development Fund Newsletter, Issues: October, November, December 1987; January, February, March, April, May, July, August, September, October, December 1988; February, March 1989, Regina, Saskatchewan.

Saskatchewan Agriculture, "Agriculture in Saskatchewan" (pamphlet), Saskatchewan Agriculture, Regina, Saskatchewan.

Saskatchewan Agriculture and Food, ADF News, Agriculture Development Fund, Issues: February, March, May, June, August, September, October, 1989, Regina, Saskatchewan.

Saskatchewan Agriculture and Food (Economics Branch, Statistics section), 1990, *Agricultural Statistics 1989*, Regina, Saskatchewan.

Saskatchewan Agriculture and Food (Farm Management Section, Economics Branch), 1990, "Cost of Producing Grain Crops in Saskatchewan 1990," Regina, Saskatchewan.

Saskatchewan Agriculture and Food, "Diversification Takes Agriculture Beyond Farm Gate" (pamphlet), Regina, Saskatchewan.

Saskatchewan Agriculture Development Fund, ADF News, "Agriculture Development Fund, Issues," December 1989; January, February, March, April, May, June, August, September, October, November, December 1990; January 1991, Regina, Saskatchewan.

Saskatchewan Agriculture Development Fund, 1990, "ADF On-Farm Demonstration Project Listing 1990," Regina, Saskatchewan.

Saskatchewan Agriculture Development Fund, 1989, Agriculture Development Fund Progress Report 1987-1988, Regina, Saskatchewan.

Saskatchewan Agriculture Development Fund, 1990, Agriculture Development Fund Progress Report 1988-1989, Regina, Saskatchewan.

Saskatchewan Agriculture Development Fund, 1990, Special Report— Milestone Year for ADF, Regina, Saskatchewan.

Saskatchewan Department of Economic Diversification and Trade, 1990, Saskatchewan Manufacturers' Guide 1990, Regina, Saskatchewan.

Saskatchewan Department of Trade and Investment, 1989, *Saskatchewan Implement Buyer's Guide 1989*, Regina, Saskatchewan.

Saskatchewan Pork Producers Marketing Board, 1988, *Pork Industry Suppliers Directory*, Saskatchewan, sponsored by the Saskatchewan Pork Producers Marketing Board through the Technology Transfer Program.

Saskatchewan Wheat Pool, Communications Division, Head Office, 1990, 1990 Annual Report, Regina, Saskatchewan.

The Interdepartmental Committee for International Agri-Food Trade Development (External Affairs Canada, Agriculture Canada, Regional Industrial Expansion, Canadian International Development Agency), 1986, "The Agri-Food Market in China: How Can We Improve Canada's Export Performance?" (draft document), Canada.

APPENDIX 1,3

Ag-West Biotech Inc.
105-15 Innovation Boulevard
Saskatoon, Saskatchewan, Canada
S7N 2X8
Attention: Dr. Murray McLaughlin, President

Agriculture Canada
Agri-Food Development Branch
Room 270 - 1955 Broad Street
P.O. Box 8035
Regina, Saskatchewan, Canada
S4P 4C7

Agriculture Canada
Food Production and Inspection Branch
Room 210-1955 Broad Street
P.O. Box 8060
Regina, Saskatchewan, Canada
S4P 4E3

Agriculture Canada
Melfort Research Station
P.O. Box 1240
Melfort, Saskatchewan, Canada
S0E 1A0

Agriculture Canada
Regina Research Station/Indian Head Experimental Farm
5000 Wascana Parkway
P.O. Box 440
Regina, Saskatchewan, Canada
S4P 3A2

Agriculture Canada
Saskatoon Research Station/Scott Experimental Farm
107 Science Place
Saskatoon, Saskatchewan, Canada
S7N 0X2

Agriculture Canada
Swift Current Research Station
P.O. Box 1030
Swift Current, Saskatchewan, Canada
S9H 3X2

Agriculture Development and Diversification Secretariat
230-3085 Albert Street
Regina, Saskatchewan, Canada
S4S 0B1

Association of Professional Engineers of Saskatchewan
2255-13th Avenue
Regina, Saskatchewan, Canada
S4P 0V6

Bantle Engineering Research Limited
P.O. Box 7805
Saskatoon, Saskatchewan, Canada
S7K 4R5

BIOSTAR Inc.
P.O. Box 1000, Sub. P.O. #6
Saskatoon, Saskatchewan, Canada
S7N 0W0

Canadian Agri-Marketing Association (Saskatchewan)
Attn: Steve Meister
Hoechst Canada, Inc.
295 Henderson Drive
Regina, Saskatchewan, Canada
S4N 6C2

Canadian Angus Association
P.O. Box 3209
Regina, Saskatchewan, Canada
S4P 3H1

Canadian Consulting Agrologists' Association
Saskatchewan Chapter
c/o O & T Agdevco
14-395A Park Street
Regina, Saskatchewan, Canada
S4N 5B2

Canadian Embryo Transfer Association
R.R. 5
Guelph, Ontario, Canada
N1H 6J2

Canadian Lacombe Breeders' Association
P.O. Box 490
Melfort, Saskatchewan, Canada
S0E 1A0

Canadian International Development Agency
200 Promenade du Portage
Hull, Quebec, Canada
K1A 0G4

Canadian Seed Growers Association
P.O. Box 8455
240 Catherine Street
Ottawa, Ontario, Canada
K1G 3T1

Canadian Seed Trade Association
207-2948 Baseline Road
Ottawa, Ontario, Canada
K2H 8T5

Canadian Sheep Breeders Association
P.O. Box 260
Borden, Saskatchewan, Canada
S0K 0N0
Attn: Secretary-Treasurer

Canola Council of Canada
301-433 Main Street
Winnipeg, Manitoba, Canada
R3C 4C5

Cargill Limited
2210 Idylwyld Drive North
Saskatoon, Saskatchewan, Canada
S7L 1B9

Cochrane Lavalin Inc.
Suite 200 - 1230 Blackfoot Drive
Regina, Saskatchewan, Canada
S4S 7G4

CSP Foods Ltd.
870 - 360 Main Street
Winnipeg, Manitoba, Canada
R3C 3Z3

Dairy Producers Cooperative Ltd.
445 Winnipeg Street
Regina, Saskatchewan, Canada
S4P 3A5

Del-Air Systems Ltd.
P.O. Box 2500
Humboldt, Saskatchewan, Canada
S0K 2A0

Ducks Unlimited Canada
P.O. Box 4465
Regina, Saskatchewan, Canada
S4P 3W7

Dyna-Fab Industries Ltd.
P.O. Box 730
Watson, Saskatchewan, Canada
S0K 4V0

Federated Cooperatives Ltd., Head Office
401-22nd Street East
P.O. Box 1050
Saskatoon, Saskatchewan, Canada
S7K 3M9

Flax Growers of Western Canada
P.O. Box 832
Regina, Saskatchewan, Canada
S4P 3B1
Attn: Morris Chevaldayoff, President

Hoechst Canada, Inc.
295 Henderson Drive
Regina, Saskatchewan, Canada
S4N 6C2

Holstein Canada
P.O. Box 40
Vibank, Saskatchewan, Canada
S0G 4Y0
Attn: Keith Flaman, National Director

MicroBio RhizoGen Corporation
Bay 5, 116-103rd Street East
Saskatoon, Saskatchewan, Canada
S7K 1Y7

National Pig Development, Head Office
633 Park Street
Regina, Saskatchewan, Canada
S4N 4N1

National Research Council
Plant Biotechnology Institute
110 Gymnasium Road
Saskatoon, Saskatchewan, Canada
S7N 0W9

Newfield Seeds Limited
P.O. Box 100
Nipawin, Saskatchewan, Canada
S0E 1E0

O & T Agdevco
14-395A Park Street
Regina, Saskatchewan, Canada
S4N 5B2
Attn: Bruce Hansen

Philom Bios Ltd.
110 Research Drive
Unit 104
Saskatoon, Saskatchewan, Canada
S7N 3R3

Pig Improvement Canada
P.O. Box 266
Acme, Alberta, Canada
T0M 0A0

POS Pilot Plant Corporation
118 Veterinary Road
Saskatoon, Saskatchewan, Canada
S7N 2R4

Prairie Agricultural Machinery Institute
P.O. Box 1150
Humboldt, Saskatchewan, Canada
S0K 2A0

Prairie Farm Rehabilitation Administration
1901 Victoria Avenue
Regina, Saskatchewan, Canada
S4P 0R5

Prairie Implement Manufacturers Association
2135 Albert Street
Regina, Saskatchewan, Canada
S4P 2V1
Attention: Ron Zimmer, General Manager

Prairie Malt Limited
P.O. Box 1150
Biggar, Saskatchewan, Canada
S0K 0M0

Prairie Micro-Tech Inc.
363 Maxwell Crescent
Regina, Saskatchewan, Canada
S4N 5X9

Provincial Veterinary Laboratories
4840 Wascana Parkway
Regina, Saskatchewan, Canada
S4S 0B1

Redekopp Chaff Systems
P.O. Box 178A, R.R. 4
Saskatoon, Saskatchewan, Canada
S7K 3J7

Saskatchewan Aberdeen Angus Association
P.O. Box 132
Dundurn, Saskatchewan, Canada
S0K 1K0
Attn: Jud Willis, President

Saskatchewan Agriculture Development Fund
3085 Albert Street
Regina, Saskatchewan, Canada
S4S 0B1

Saskatchewan Alfalfa Seed Producers Association
P.O. Box 148
Zenon Park, Saskatchewan, Canada
S0E 1W0
Attn: Vince Marchildon, President

Saskatchewan Ayrshire Club
Guernsey, Saskatchewan, Canada
S0K 1N0
Attn: John Bartel, President

Saskatchewan Beef Cattle Performance Centre
P.O. Box 3266
Regina, Saskatchewan, Canada
S4P 3H1

Saskatchewan Beekeepers Association
P.O. Box 306
Nipawin, Saskatchewan, Canada
S0E 1E0
Attn: Len Proctor, President

Saskatchewan Broiler Chicken Hatching Egg Producers Marketing Board
P.O. Box 1837
Assiniboia, Saskatchewan, Canada
S0H 0B0
Attn: Gerald Leduc, Chairman

Saskatchewan Canola Growers Association
P.O. Box 2066
Saskatoon, Saskatchewan, Canada
Attn: Norman Maze, President

Saskatchewan Cattle Feeders Association
P.O. Box 8305
Saskatoon, Saskatchewan, Canada
S7K 6C6
Attn: Brian Perkins, President

Saskatchewan Chapter, Canadian Feed Industry Association
P.O. Box 1050
Saskatoon, Saskatchewan, Canada
S7K 3M9

Saskatchewan Charolais Association
P.O. Box 44
Ponteix, Saskatchewan, Canada
S0N 1Z0
Attn: Richard Carlson, Secretary-Treasurer

Saskatchewan Chianina Association
P.O. Box 110, R.R. #2
Saskatoon, Saskatchewan, Canada
S7K 3J5
Attn: Gary La Frentz, President

Saskatchewan Chicken Marketing Board
P.O. Box 282
Abernethy, Saskatchewan, Canada
S0A 0A0
Attn: Charles Stueck, Chairman

Saskatchewan Commercial Egg Producers Marketing Board
P.O. Box 1812
Regina, Saskatchewan, Canada
S4P 3C6
Attn: Ted Weins, Chairman

Saskatchewan Commercial Egg Marketing Board
P.O. Box 1637
Regina, Saskatchewan, Canada
S4P 3C4
Attn: Dave Mackie, Manager

Saskatchewan Dairy Foundation
P.O. Box 1294
Regina, Saskatchewan, Canada
S4P 3B8
Attn: John Nykolaishen, Executive Director

Saskatchewan Department of Agriculture and Food*
3085 Albert Street
Regina, Saskatchewan, Canada
S4S 0B1

(*Direct inquiries to appropriate branch or agency. These include Agricultural Engineering Branch, Agriculture Development & Diversification Secretariat, Agriculture Development Fund, Economics Branch, Livestock Branch, Natural Products Marketing Council, Soils & Crops Branch.)

Saskatchewan Department of Economic Diversification and Trade
International Division
1919 Saskatchewan Drive
Regina, Saskatchewan, Canada
S4P 3V7

Saskatchewan Department of Rural Development
3085 Albert Street
Regina, Saskatchewan, Canada
S4S 0B1

Saskatchewan Egg and Poultry Processors Association
502-45th Street West
Saskatoon, Saskatchewan, Canada
S7L 6H2
Attn: Brad Priel, Secretary

Saskatchewan Farm Builders Association
R.R. #4, Box 236
Saskatoon, Saskatchewan, Canada
S7K 3J7

Saskatchewan Feedlot Association
P.O. Box 445
Indian Head, Saskatchewan, Canada
S0G 2K0
Attn: President

Saskatchewan Forage Council
P.O. Box 100
Nipawin, Saskatchewan, Canada
S0E 1E0
Attn: Ken Stoner, President

Saskatchewan Greenhouse Growers' Association
P.O. Box 833
Outlook, Saskatchewan, Canada
S0L 2N0
Attn: Bill Day, President

Saskatchewan Hatchery Association
402-21st Street West
Saskatoon, Saskatchewan, Canada
S7M 0W4
Attn: Brad Lawson, Secretary-Treasurer

Saskatchewan Hereford Association
201-4401 Albert Street
Regina, Saskatchewan, Canada
S4S 6B6
Attn: B. Guild, Manager

Saskatchewan Horticultural Association
P.O. Box 670
Carrot River, Saskatchewan, Canada
S0E 0L0
Attn: Doreen Gilmour, President

Saskatchewan Institute of Agrologists
100-2103 Airport Drive
Saskatoon, Saskatchewan, Canada

Saskatchewan Irrigation Development Centre, Outlook
P.O. Box 7
Outlook, Saskatchewan, Canada
S0L 2N0

Saskatchewan Limousin Association
P.O. Box 458
Saltcoats, Saskatchewan, Canada
S0A 3R0
Attn: Herb Rooke, President

Saskatchewan Livestock Association
P.O. Box 3771
Regina, Saskatchewan, Canada
S4P 3N8
Attn: Jack Hay, President

Saskatchewan Maine-Anjou Association
Stonehenge, Saskatchewan
S0H 3Y0
Attn: Clarence Oancia, President

Saskatchewan Meat Processors
2548 Garnet Street
Regina, Saskatchewan, Canada
S4T 3A5
Attn: Larry Brossart, President

Saskatchewan Milk Control Board
620-2045 Broad Street
Regina, Saskatchewan, Canada
S4P 1Y4
Attn: Stan Barber, Chairman

Saskatchewan Milk Producers Association
P.O. Box 220
Pangman, Saskatchewan, Canada
S0C 2C0
Attn: Keith Howse, President

Saskatchewan Natural Products Marketing Council
329-3085 Albert Street
Regina, Saskatchewan, Canada
S4S 0B1
Attn: Blair Backman, Chairman

Saskatchewan Nursery Trades Association
256 Habkirk Drive
Regina, Saskatchewan, Canada
S4S 5XB
Attn: Executive Manager

Saskatchewan Pork Producers Marketing Board
2nd Floor, 502-45th Street West
Saskatoon, Saskatchewan, Canada
S7L 6H2

Saskatchewan Pork Pushers Association
P.O. Box 599
Kipling, Saskatchewan, Canada
S0G 2S0
Attn: Audrey Tennant, Chairman

Saskatchewan Poultry Council
101 Langley Street
Regina, Saskatchewan, Canada
S4S 3V7
Attn: Don Conrad, Secretary-Treasurer

Saskatchewan Pulse Crop Development board
P.O. Box 516
Regina, Saskatchewan, Canada
S4P 3A2
Attn: Don Jacques, Administrator

Saskatchewan Research Council
(also: Bovine Blood Typing Laboratory)
15 Innovation Boulevard
Saskatoon, Saskatchewan, Canada
S7N 2X8

Saskatchewan Seed Growers' Association
P.O. Box 1135
Grenfell, Saskatchewan, Canada
S0G 2B0
Attn: W. Allan Hardy, President

Saskatchewan Sheep Breeders Association
P.O. Box 132
Elbow, Saskatchewan, Canada
S0H 1J0
Attn: Ken Webster, President

Saskatchewan Sheep Development Board
P.O. Box 102
Tompkins, Saskatchewan, Canada
S0N 2S0
Attn: Leslie Flaig, Vice-Chairman

Saskatchewan Shorthorn Association
P.O. Box 580
Weyburn, Saskatchewan, Canada
S4H 2K7
Attn: Grant Alexander, President

Saskatchewan Simmental Association
P.O. Box 760
Balcarres, Saskatchewan, Canada
S0G 0C0
Attn: Lionel Stilborn, President

Saskatchewan Soil Conservation Association
#132-3085 Albert Street
Regina, Saskatchewan, Canada
S4S 0B1

Saskatchewan Stock Growers Association
P.O. Box 175
Val Marie, Saskatchewan, Canada
S0N 2T0
Attn: Lynn S. Grant, President

Saskatchewan Sunflower Committee Inc.
P.O. Box 54
Carievale, Saskatchewan, Canada
S0C 0P0
Attn: Murray Firth, President

Saskatchewan Swine Breeders' Association
c/o Saskatchewan Livestock Association
Box 3771
Regina, Saskatchewan, Canada
S4P 3N8

Saskatchewan Turkey Producers Marketing Board
502-45th Street West
Saskatoon, Saskatchewan, Canada
S7L 6H2
Attn: Dennis Billo, Chairman

Saskatchewan Vegetable Growers' Association
P.O. Box 36
Yorkton, Saskatchewan, Canada
S3N 2V6
Attn: Elwyn Vermette, President

Saskatchewan Vegetable Marketing and Development Board
101-2515 Victoria Avenue
Regina, Saskatchewan, Canada
S4P 0T2
Attn: John Langford, Chairman

Saskatchewan Veterinary Medical Association
Suite 11, 1025 Boychuk Drive
Saskatoon, Saskatchewan, Canada
S7H 5B2
Attn: President

Saskatchewan Water Corporation
2nd Floor, Victoria Place
111 Fairford Street East
Moose Jaw, Saskatchewan, Canada
S6H 7X9

Saskatchewan Wetland Conservation Corporation
110-2151 Scarth Street
Regina, Saskatchewan, Canada
S4P 3Z3

Saskatchewan Wheat Pool
2625 Victoria Avenue
Regina, Saskatchewan, Canada
S4T 7T9
Attn: Garf Stevenson, President

Saskatchewan Wild Rice Council
P.O. Box 9
Sandy Bay, Saskatchewan, Canada
S0P 0G0
Attn: Ronald A. Roy, Chairman

Saskatchewan Wool Growers Association
P.O. Box 82
Tompkins, Saskatchewan, Canada
S0N 2S0

SaskCan Livestock Export Inc.
P.O. Box 3771
Regina, Saskatchewan, Canada
S4P 3N8

Saskferco Products Inc.
1874 Scarth Street
Regina, Saskatchewan, Canada
S4P 4B3

Shamrock Agri-Tech Inc.
607-4th Avenue East
Regina, Saskatchewan, Canada
S4N 4Z8

Sheltek Systems Inc.
P.O. Box 324
Rocanville, Saskatchewan, Canada
S0A 3L0

The SNC Group
1600-2002 Victoria Avenue
Regina, Saskatchewan, Canada
S4P 0R7

Transtec Genetics Limited
P.O. Box 8265
Saskatoon, Saskatchewan, Canada
S7K 6C5
or:
205-2nd Street South
Martinsville, Saskatchewan, Canada
c/o Dr. Paulyschyn, Veterinarian

United Grain Growers Ltd.
P.O. Box 160
Elrose, Saskatchewan, Canada
S0L 0Z0
Attn: Roy Piper, President

University of Regina
Office of University Research
3737 Wascana Parkway
Regina, Saskatchewan, Canada
S4S 0A2

University of Saskatchewan*
Saskatoon, Saskatchewan, Canada
S7N 0W0

*Direct inquiries to appropriate department care of the University of Saskatchewan:

The College of Agriculture has the Crop Development Centre, the Department of Crop Science and Plant Ecology; the Department of Crop Science and Plant Ecology; and the Department of Animal and Poultry Science (Prairie Swine Research Centre, Saskatchewan Feed Testing Laboratory, Sheep Industry Development and Extension Centre, Dairy Herd, Beef Research Station).

The Western College of Veterinary Medicine includes the Department of Herd Medicine and Theriogenology, and the Department of Veterinary Pathology.

The College of Engineering includes the Department of Agricultural Engineering.

Other departments/agencies within the University of Saskatchewan that may be of interest are the Department of Agricultural Economics, Department of Applied Microbiology and Food Science, the Saskatchewan Institute of Pedology, and the Department of Horticulture Science.

Veterinary Infectious Diseases Organization
124 Veterinary Road
Saskatoon, Saskatchewan, Canada
S7N 0W0

WECAN Project Development Inc
P.O. Box 2500
Humboldt, Saskatchewan, Canada
S0K 2A0

Western Barley Growers Association
P.O. Box 237
Viking, Alberta, Canada
T0B 4N0
Attn: Richard Nordstrom, President

Western Canada Cow-Calf Association
P.O. Box 82
Fleming, Saskatchewan, Canada
S0G 1R0
Attn: Miles Fuchs, President

Western Canadian Wheat Growers Association
Suite 201-4401 Albert Street
Regina, Saskatchewan, Canada
S4S 6B6
Attn: Harvey McEwen, President

White Fox Forages Ltd.
P.O. Box 119
White, Fox, Saskatchewan, Canada. Carlson is president of Elaine Carlson Word Works Inc., Regina, Saskatchewan.

4 DEVELOPMENT OF POTASH USE IN CHINA

Kenneth M. Pretty

Potash and Phosphate Institute of Canada

HISTORICAL BACKGROUND

Chinese farmers are recognized as among the best in the world in terms of optimizing agricultural output with a minimum amount of purchased inputs. For centuries, traditional food and fibre production has focused on intensive cultivation of a relatively small land area. Even today, less than 10 percent of the land mass is suitable for agriculture.

Soil productivity was maintained by the extensive recycling of all organic materials to provide essential plant nutrients, maintain soil structure, enhance the efficiency of moisture utilization, and limit soil erosion. The sources of organic materials were crop residues, composted materials, green manure crops, animal and human excrements, river mud, and plant matter transferred from the hills and mountains to the fertile paddy (rice) fields below.

Although crop yields were low, production was sufficient to supply the needs of a modest population while remitting to the feudal landlord an amount sufficient to pay the "tax" imposed. The depletion of soil nutrient status was slow so that complete reliance on the use of organic fertilizers was barely perceptible. It was not obvious to leaders of the day that population growth and soil impoverishment were on a collision course.

Historical data show that average wheat yields in China were almost constant over a period of more than 15 centuries (220 B.C. to 1300 A.D.) (Liu, 1988). The increase from the thirteenth to the twentieth century was about 150 kilograms per hectare. Progress in the unit production of rice was more substantial, but at the beginning of the 1950s yields were still below 3000 kilograms per hectare.

THE NEW CHINA

With the establishment of the People's Republic of China in 1949, and the collectivization of agriculture in the early 1950s, some short-term gains were made. Under this early modernization programme for agriculture, including even more intensive cropping (two or three crops per year in the southern parts of the country), nitrogen (N) fertilization was correctly identified as the most essential nutrient to increase agricultural production. Hundreds of small, inefficient but localized plants for the production of ammonium bicarbonate were established, most of which still exist.

The N output from these facilities substituted for the declining area devoted to green manure crops and dwindling supplies of other organic materials. The use of green manure was only one-quarter as much in 1984 as in 1950-54. The hillsides were progressively denuded of trees to supply fuel, so that peasants increasingly relied on crop residues as an alternative source for heating and cooking.

Growth in the use of chemical fertilizer, mainly N, was rapid throughout the 1949-1967 period, averaging about 35 percent annually. Reliance on organic materials to supply other essential nutrients continued.

Scientific research, so essential to establish the course of developments, was largely thwarted by the intervention of the Cultural Revolution (1966-76). During the author's first visits to China in 1972-73 to lecture on needs for potash, it became apparent that, while a certain enthusiasm existed, scientists were helpless in establishing progressive research programmes. A decade of service by many qualified researchers was lost.

At the end of the Cultural Revolution in 1976, scientists once again undertook experimentation on the use of plant nutrient. They tended to concentrate on N and phosphorus (P), the two most limiting nutrients in crop production. As a result of this research, the use of P fertilizers has increased progressively, although the N : P ratio is still out of balance. China uses more N than any other country in the world.

Throughout the 1950s and 1960s, the use of potash (K) in China was mainly supplied by organic sources. As late as 1980, less than 5 percent of the K provided for plant growth was of chemical origin. The popular belief, which still exists in some areas, was that the soils of China were rich in this nutrient, therefore the addition of K in a chemical form was unnecessary and "a waste of foreign exchange."

Fortunately, a few scientists had developed and maintained an interest in studying the K status of a number of soils in China, and needs for K fertilization. With financial support provided in part by the Potash and

Phosphate Institute of Canada (PPIC), these data were summarized and presented at an international conference in Malaysia (Xie Jian-Chang et al., 1981). It was from this limited base that the China/Canada/Saskatchewan Potash Agronomy Program (CCSPAP) evolved, starting in the south in 1983 with progressive expansions into more northerly provinces.

Scientists at the Soils and Fertilizer Institute (SFI), Chinese Academy of Agricultural Sciences (CAAS), had been quietly monitoring the decline in the efficiency of N fertilizers over a period of years. For example, they noted that in 1958 field trials on each kilogram (kg) of N fertilizer produced 16.5 kg of rice. By 1982, each kg of N gave a yield increase of only 10.1 kg. Obviously, the deterioration in soil fertility through an imbalance in the use of nutrient was leading to a stagnation in agricultural production (Zhonggus, 1989).

Droughts and floods in many regions have had a deleterious effect, but these are counter balanced by the introduction of better farming techniques and improved crop varieties with a higher yield potential. Agricultural production did not increase in the 1984-88 period (Table 1,4) and is estimated to have been about the same in 1989.

Table 1,4   Index of Agricultural Production in China (1979-81 = 100)

Year	Index	Year	Index
1977	96	1984	125
1978	99	1985	124
1981	113	1986	124
1982	113	1987	122
1983	115	1988	124

Source: FAO Agricultural Yearbooks

THE POTASH AGRONOMY PROGRAMME

The scientific staff of PPIC and the Potash and Phosphate Institute, USA (PPI), had observed striking examples of K deficiency on several crops in a number of provinces in south China. Chinese scientists believed that K fertilization was required only for certain soils and crops south of the Yangtze River.

As a result of discussions between PPIC staff and the Ministry of Agriculture (MOA) in Beijing, agreement was reached in 1992 to provide support from Canadian sources for the establishment of a comprehensive programme of research, training and development. PPIC would act as the implementing agency with additional financial support from the Government of Canada (CIDA), the Government of Saskatchewan (GOS), and the Saskatchewan potash producers through their international marketing agency, Canpotex Limited. The Bureau of Science and Technology, MOA, Beijing, would serve as the implementing agency for China.

Essential components of the programme are:

a) an expanded research programme to establish more precisely K fertilizer needs when related to the K status of soils and specific crop requirements;

b) provision of training and postgraduate studies in Canada for young Chinese scientists;

c) exchanges between Canadian and Chinese researchers;

d) compilation and dissemination of research results.

The programme began in two provinces in 1983, was expanded to seven in 1986, and at present about 40 projects are being carried out in 20 provinces. A grant provided to PPIC by the Western Diversification Program (WDP) made resources available for the most recent expansions, especially in northeastern China, including the provinces of Jilin and Shandong. Additional staff to supervise the work in China also became possible, culminating in the establishment of a Beijing office early in 1990. More than 15 young Chinese scientists have received, or are receiving, advanced training at Canadian universities, including the University of Saskatchewan (UOS). Each year, two Canadian scientists have been sponsored for lecture tours in China while several Chinese scientific delegations have visited Saskatchewan and other provinces. Opportunities have been provided to observe potash from its underground exploration, through refining, to its end use at the fertilizer retailer and farm levels.

PROVING POTASH NEEDS

The research component of the programme has been, and continues to be, the key activity. Potash use will grow once its role in improving the quantity and quality of crop output has been proven by carefully-planned and well-conducted investigations. In this respect, the eager and enthusiastic co-operation of agronomists and soil scientists at co-operating institutions in China has been a source of great satisfaction.

Space does not allow a complete presentation of experimental results. Only a few are given (Tables 2,4 and 3,4). The data shown in Table 2,4 reflect an increasing response to K over time as crop-management practices improve, and the application of N depletes soil K reserves. In more recent trials, yield increases of over 100 percent have been recorded at certain locations. The SFI in Henan estimates that over three-quarters of the soils require K for optimum yields.

Table 2,4   Increasing Responses to K Fertilization in Henan Province, China 1952-1980

Period	Number of Trials	Percent with Response to K	Average Percent Yield Increase[1]
1952-63	31	29	6
1964-69	20	80	12
1970-80	734	94	13

[1]Average of all sites

Source: SFI, Henan (Cited by Pretty, 1988)

Evidence that soils in the northeastern region respond favourably to K applications is shown by the data in Table 3,4.

Table 3,4   Responses to Potash Fertilization in Henan Province, China

Crop	Number of Trials Conducted	Kg/Ha K_2O Applied	Percent Yield Increase
Cotton	45	120	17
Peanut	13	112	11
Rapeseed	24	112	17
Rice	41	112	17
Soybeen	38	112	17
Wheat	31	112	13

Source: SFI, Beijing (Cited by Pretty, 1988)

Henan Province, which adjoins Shandong, has traditionally been considered an area where K additions were not necessary.

Research in Jilin and Shandong provinces is of more recent origin (initiated in 1988); consequently the extent of K needs has not yet been fully determined. Excellent responses to K additions for maize (corn) and peanut in the respective provinces have been observed. Scientists at each provincial SFI, while eager to push ahead with the research phase, have expressed a note of caution. Potash allocations from the central authority have either been non-existent or minimal. Their concern is appropriate because the development of demand without parallel supply creates frustration and anger among farmers. It is to be hoped that these shortcomings can be overcome in the future.

Potash is in short supply throughout most of China, and as research continues to define further the needs, this deficit will intensify. At the same time, there are tens of millions of farmers who are not familiar with K or its role in enhancing the quantity and quality of agricultural output. They are not aware that as crop yields and cropping intensity increase, K removal also often increases. When straw or stalks are removed for fuel, K removal frequently equals or exceeds that of nitrogen (N).

For example, in one five-year study of a three-crop system of early rice-late rice-barley, the K contained in the above ground parts (grain and straw) was 49 percent higher than a two-crop system of rice and wheat (Beaton & Keng, 1990). In the two systems the K content exceeded that of N by 16 to 23 percent.

TELLING THE NEED FOR POTASH

Research should first establish requirements for K. These data must then be interpreted and shown to farmers before they will invest scarce financial resources in an additional input.

In 1986, Canpotex Limited, together with PPIC/PPI, the original co-operating sponsors, and the SFIs in selected provinces of China, initiated a programme to disseminate results from the newly-accumulated research to tens of thousands of small farmers. The task was made more arduous because, under the agricultural reforms initiated in 1978, individual farmers are free to make decisions on the kinds and amounts of inputs to use. Previously, these decisions had been made by the collective.

The demonstration programme was initiated in one province in 1986 on a pilot basis, and expanded to an additional four in 1987. It is now operational in a total of 12 provinces.

As on-farm demonstrations are a comparatively new educational tool for Chinese farmers, advance preparation included:

- development of a detailed training manual (in Chinese) outlining precise procedures to follow in designing and establishing the demonstrations.

- two-day orientation meetings for extension technicians who would carry out the work.

- development of an appropriate logo—"scientific farming"—to appear on all information for farmers.

The demonstrations consist of three basic elements:

Demonstration Plots

These side-by side comparisons on a wide variety of crops use "common practice" (NP fertilization) vs. "recommended practice" (NPK). Rates of fertilizer application are determined from PPIC-supported research carried out by SFI agronomists.

Farmer Group Meetings

Extension technicians organize small farmer groups to observe crop growth several times during the growing season. Problems in crop management which restrict yields can be identified.

Harvest Field Days

Several demonstration plots in each province are designated as the site for harvest field days. Farmer attendance at these field days has ranged from 1,500 to 6,000 people.

Farmers are asked to guess the yields from the two plots. Winners are awarded prizes, usually in the form of Canadian potash. Educational displays are also a feature of the harvest field days. Field day results are widely reported by newspaper, radio and television, which provide a strong multiplier effect.

More recently, attention has been focused on other improved production practices and the participation of senior officials at local and provincial levels of government, and the Agriculture Inputs Corporation (AIC) of the Ministry of Commerce (Dawdle, 1987). AIC is responsible for the allocation, distribution and sale of available potash supplies at national, provincial and local levels.

Results from the programme have been remarkable. The data given in Table 4,4 confirm that balanced fertilization can enhance crop yields.

Table 4,4   Percent Increases in Crop Yields Obtained in Demonstrations in Several Provinces of China (1989)

Province	Crop	Number of Sites	Percent Yield Increase with K
Guangxi	corn	4	48
Zhejiang	kenaf	1	55
Henan	barley	2	12
	vetch	3	29
	corn	3	36
Jiangsu	rape	11	91
	wheat	15	28
	potato	1	128
Jiangxi	cotton	1	34
	corn	2	39

Source: Canpotex Limited (unpublished).

The Demonstration programme has been enlarged to the extent permitted by financial and manpower constraints, and the availability of confirmed research results. Canpotex and its member corporations have been a leader and innovator in market development and effective promotion in China based on scientific facts. For this they have won the confidence and respect of end-users.

POTASH USE CONTINUES TO GROW

As shown earlier, potash was virtually unknown in China (other than in organic form) until about 20 years ago. The first sale of Saskatchewan potash to China was made in 1972, with initial deliveries in 1973. Fertilizer consumption data over a 35-year period show a dramatic increase in the use of N, consistent growth in P consumption, and a much more modest increase in potash (K_2O) sales (Figure 1,4), at least in absolute terms.

Figure 1,4 shows a nitrogen-phosphate-potash ($N:P_2O_5+K_2O$) ratio of about 100:27:7. Leading soil scientists and agronomists in China have indicated that, based on their research to date, a ratio of 100:40:25 would result in a nutrient balance most conducive to optimum crop output and sustained productivity of soils.

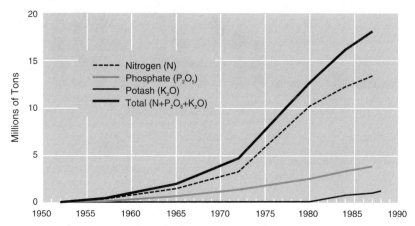

Source: Statistical and China Agricultural yearbooks. Does not include nutrient content of imported complex fertilizers (11.6 percent of total nutrients in 1987).

Figure 1,4 Plant Nutrient Consumption in China for Selected Years (1952-1987)

Canada has consistently supplied half or more of China's potash imports, all on commercial terms. Canpotex Limited has been the largest and most consistent supplier, as shown in Figure 2,4. Data for deliveries do not necessarily coincide with consumption, owing to difference in time frames (calendar vs. fertilizer year) and materials in transit, among others.

Since the mid-1980s Jordan has become a larger supplier of potash to China. Potassium sulphate (SOP), which is required by certain specialty crops, such as tobacco, but which Canada does not produce, is procured from European or US sources.

Chinese farmers have shown a distinct preference for Canadian potash owing to uniformity of particle size, freedom from dust, and other quality characteristics. In fact, retailers report that some peasants decline to purchase potash available from other countries owing to uncertain quality. It is obvious, therefore, that Saskatchewan and Canada have established themselves as a preferred supplier.

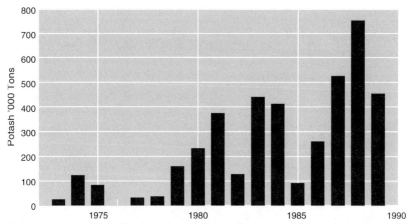

Source: Canpotex Limited. Calendar year basis. Rounded to nearest thousand tons. Does not include smaller shipments by Saskatchewan producers who are not members of Canpotex or by New Brunswick producers.

Figure 2,4   Shipments of Potash by
Canpotex Members to China (1973-1989)

POTASH USE IN JILIN AND SHANDONG PROVINCES

The use of potash in these provinces is still in its infancy, because of (a) a lack of knowledge among farmers, (b) inadequate research and extension programmes, and (c) allocation of the nutrient from scarce national stocks to areas where needs are considered more urgent. It is expected, however, that as research results are confirmed, and farmers are made aware of K needs, the current proportion of use will increase substantially from the current four percent of the national total.

Some knowledgeable agronomists have suggested that growth in K use in north-eastern China may actually increase more rapidly than in the south, even though only one or two crops are produced each year. They attribute this to the higher yields obtained and shorter growing season.

Although this conclusion is debatable, it does illustrate that north-eastern China, including Jilin and Shandong Provinces, do have a considerable potential for growth in K use.

THE FUTURE

Although government policies, shortage of foreign exchange and logistical problems will hamper progress, priorities to strengthen agricultural production will undoubtedly continue. This requires a sustained effort to provide farmers with the essential inputs for production, and massive education programmes to show the financial benefits which can accrue from balanced fertilization practices. China's limited land bases and massive population suggest that any de-emphasis in the agricultural sector could have disastrous results.

It is projected that potash consumption in China could double in the next five years, given enlightened agricultural policies. An increasing proportion likely will be used in the north-eastern provinces, including Jilin and Shandong. PPIC, through its programme to support research, and Canpotex Limited, with its demonstration and education activities, will play key roles. Canada is the only potash producer in the world to make a substantial commitment to market development for potash in China through the co-operative efforts of industry and government.

POTASH VERSUS GRAIN

The argument is often put forth that increased sales of Saskatchewan potash to China result in a decline in grain sales. Such a philosophy is not based on factual information. Inadequate grain sales result from a lack of purchasing power by both countries and consumers. As purchasing power increases, partly as a consequence of improved agricultural production, consumer preferences also change. Consumers eat relatively more wheat and less rice. Japan, Taiwan and Korea are excellent examples of countries where eating habits have changed along with income. It is not entirely coincidental that both fertilizer (potash) and grain imports have likewise increased in these countries.

It can be concluded that in many developing countries, including China, a rise in domestic agricultural production and additional fertilizer use can also increase the need for grain imports.

CONCLUSIONS

The future for expanded potash exports to China in the next five to ten years is bright. Saskatchewan is strategically placed to supply a significant portion of this market. Efforts by PPIC, Canpotex and both the Saskatchewan and Canadian Governments to develop the China market on a scientific basis have been fruitful. This work will not only continue but intensify. The provinces of Jilin and Shandong will form an integral part of this work.

REFERENCES

Beaton, J.D., and Keng, J.C.W. (1990). Potassium: A vital input in sustainable agriculture, *Proceeding of Globe '90 Conference*, Vancouver, March.

China Agricultural Yearbook. (1988). State Statistical Bureau, Beijing.

Dawdle, S.F. (1987). Harvest field day programs show on-farm results in China, *Better Crops International*, Alberta, USA, December.

Liu, G.L. (1988). Grain production and balanced fertilization in China, *Proceedings of the International Symposium on Balanced Fertilization*, Beijing, November.

Pretty, K.M. (1988). The China experience in developing balanced fertilizer use, *Proceedings of the International Symposium on Balanced Fertilization*, Beijing, November.

Zhonggus, R.B. (1989). China's population, land, grain, *Beijing Review*, June.

ACKNOWLEDGEMENTS

The author wishes to acknowledge the information and data provided by the Potash and Phosphate Institute of Canada, and Canpotex Limited.

Information supplied by Chinese scientists, whether verbal or written, is also gratefully acknowledged. Without their enthusiasm, guidance and friendship, accomplishments would be much more limited.

ABBREVIATIONS AND CONVERSIONS

Institutional and Governmental

CAAS	Chinese Academy of Agricultural Sciences
CIDA	Canadian International Development Agency
GOS	Government of Saskatchewan
MOA	Ministry of Agriculture, China
PPI	Potash and Phosphate Institute (U. S. A.)
PPIC	Potash and Phosphate Institute of Canada
SFI	Soils and Fertilizer Institute (s)
UOS	University of Saskatchewan
DP	Western Diversification Program

Technical Terms and Measurements

Ha	Hectares
K	Potassium
K_2O	Expression of K content in potash fertilizer
Kg	Kilograms
MOP	Muriate of potash
N	Nitrogen (elemental basis)
P	Phosphorus
P_2O_5	Expression of P content in phosphate fertilizers
SOP	Sulphate of potash
T	Ton (1000 kg)

THE TELECOMMUNICATIONS MARKET IN CHINA

A.M. Yam

Saskatchewan Telecommunications (SaskTel)

. . . Telecommunications can increase the efficiency of economic, commercial and administrative activities, improve the effectiveness of social and emergency services and distribute the social, cultural and economic benefits of the process of development throughout a community and a nation.

Sir Donald Maitland
Chairman of Independent Commission for World Telecom Development
In *The Missing Link*, January, 1985

CHINA'S COMMUNICATIONS IN THE EIGHTIES

In considering the penetration of the telephone into China, the enormous population, the complexity of government hierarchy, and the fact that manual and semi-automatic long-distance networks were still state-of-the-art in the early 1980s, it is not difficult to understand why upgrading of the communication system was urgently needed. At the end of 1983 only one person in every 200 in China (Billowes, 1986: 5) had a phone in comparison with about 60 per 100 people in Canada and 77 per 100 people in Saskatchewan. In long-distance, inadequate telephone circuits and poor circuit quality contributed adversely to the often congested network. Most long-distance calls were connected with operator-handling, except for a few automatic and semi-automatic long-distance telephone services available among 24 provincial capitals. Similar problems also affected China's international telephone service. Prompted by the need for immediate upgrading, China established a two-decade plan in the early 1980s to increase facilities in the whole public telephone network (China Briefing Book for SaskTel, 1985). It placed emphasis on service to major and coastal cities in the first decade, and on improved public telephone service to private telephones in the following decade.

Progress in the communications sector has accelerated with a series of changes in national economic policy. In 1981, China began implementing its Sixth Five-Year Plan (1981-85). It took a significant step toward China's goal of quadrupling its gross industrial and agricultural output value before the end of this century. By 1984 improvement was just beginning but, as a whole, the plan was being fulfilled. However, state planners found that the economy still lacked solid foundations and adequate infrastructure to support better economic results in production and construction. The strain on energy supplies and transport, the need for convenient communications, and the shortage of materials all hamper higher economic achievements. For instance, international telephone traffic increased by a factor of 15 with an average annual growth of 70 percent in the period 1978-83 (*China Briefing Book for SaskTel,* 1985). To alleviate these problems for the country's 400,000 industrial enterprises, China stressed the need to import advanced technologies. The joint venture signed between the Ministry of Posts and Telecommunications (MPT) and Belgium Bell Telephone to manufacture the 1,240 digital switch was one of 3,000 advanced technologies imported from foreign countries between 1983 and 1985. The approach has been scaled up in the Seventh Five-Year Plan. With the opening up of 14 coastal cities and 5 Special Economic Zones to attract foreign capital and technology, more demand was created in the telephone network. Direct dialling from all these cities became a "must" and modernization of telephone switches and networks was achieved in 1987. This improvement showed the government's determination to provide good infrastructure support for the Special Economic Zones.

Since the state planners announced details of their Seventh Five-Year Plan early in 1986, communications have been a prime target for attracting national and foreign investment. At least 15 percent of the centrally-allocated funds were reserved for capital construction in transport and communications. The government seems to recognize that overall economic reform is unlikely to take shape or reach its potential without modernization of the telecommunications infrastructure to improve quality and accommodate growth (Denny, 1986: 12).

PURCHASE STRATEGY

Though telecommunications in China were not as advanced as those in modern Western countries, a basic telephone network had been established. Improvements to telecommunications under the Seventh Five-

Year Plan depended on more imports of systems and technology. Perhaps more essential is foreign investment.

Short-term Imports and Long-term Exports

Despite the inadequacy of the telecommunications network and inability to produce systems other than analogue equipment, China should not be viewed as a place in which to dump out-dated telecommunications systems. China's future goals are self-sufficiency in domestic consumption and competition in export markets. This means that equipment required for facilities will have to be imported until China's factories attain the technology and manufacturing level to satisfy domestic needs. A large number of factories operate under the direct control of MPT, the Ministry of Electronic Industry (MEI), and the Ministry of Aeronautics. For example, MPT operates 27 plants in medium- and large-sized cities. Each plant has its own specialized line of systems and products. The long-term goal for these factories is to earn foreign income. This strategy means that China will ultimately become a competitor in the world telecommunications market. In the short term, however, the need for more modern telecommunications systems creates opportunities for companies working in the area of digital technology, applied research, manufacturing and management, which are willing to package products with service and technology transfer, and to help China market to other parts of the world. Companies that accept this challenge will likely gain a better market share.

Joint Ventures

Deng Xiaoping, China's recently retired senior leader, realized that only Asia's capitalists and the West could supply the technology, expertise and the hard-currency markets needed to convert China into a "moderately developed" country in the next 50 years. Early in 1979, China indicated that joint ventures were the preferred form of co-operation with foreign firms, as stated in the Law on Joint Ventures Using Chinese and Foreign Investment. On October 11, 1986, the Chinese government promulgated the "Provisions of the State Council of the People's Republic of China for the Encouragement of Foreign Investment" (Arthur Young International Client Memorandum, 1986). The fundamental aim was to improve the investment environment for foreign companies to undertake Equity Joint Ventures and Contractual Joint Ventures. Through these,

China also wants to exploit its manpower potential. According to *The Economist*, China had already approved foreign investment in approximately 18,000 businesses with a contractual investment of over $30 billion US by the first quarter of 1989 (*The Economist*, June 1989: 66).

MPT and MEI have followed this lead very strongly in the telecommunications sector. Large sales of foreign telecommunications systems have been linked to obtaining added items such as technology transfer, manufacturing licences, and system knocked-down assembly in China. Added flexibility on the foreign exporter's part sometimes becomes a crucial element in contract negotiations. Exporters who do not agree to some kind of technology-transfer market will not survive for long. The negotiation of joint ventures can prove difficult for exporters because it is a drawn-out process from initial contact to the signing of the terms of agreement, and involves many levels of the Chinese government where the exporter has little influence or control. There have been many reports of exporters having to resolve tough problems such as language barriers, training, management, finance, new company cultures, quality control, productivity, foreign exchange to maintain new machines, export marketing for the new company, and even executive and partner powers.

Foreign Financial Concessions and Soft Loans

After China regained her seat in the United Nations in 1971, she also became a member of most of the affiliated agencies, including the World Bank and the International Monetary Fund. In 1986, China renewed membership in the General Agreement on Tariffs and Trade (GATT). Willingness to open up to the outside world and accept economic and technical assistance from agencies such as the UN Development Programme was a significant departure from the previous emphasis on self-reliance. China also reversed its opposition to foreign capital and borrowing money from international lending institutions, foreign governments and foreign commercial banks. Unlike many developing countries, the Chinese government maintained an excellent credit rating internationally and did not pile up huge foreign debts. Because of an expansion of exports in the early 1980s, a large foreign reserve surplus was built up. With the decentralization of decision-making, imports of industrial and consumer products surged. In 1984 and 1985, there were huge trade deficits. In order to keep a tighter control on foreign expenditures and focus only on valuable goods for the progress of the nation, China instituted an import- and export-licensing system and devalued the yuan. Though China puts controls on her domestic spending, she continues to invest abroad in different ventures. In 1985, foreign reserves totalled $11.9 billion US (Worden et al., 1988: 347). In 1988 alone, China invested $150 million abroad, and her various foreign joint-venture partners, $120 million, in 168 businesses. In total, China has invested directly in 79 countries. For instance, China International Trust and Investment Corporation (CITIC) has a pulp mill in Canada (*The Economist*, Feb. 18, 1989: 34).

The most successful exporters to China have been obtaining contracts that include a financing package to the buyers in the form of soft loans. These combine a commercial loan at a rate lower than the London Inter Bank Offered Rate (LIBOR), and a grant. The result is that the Chinese buyer often receives a low interest rate with a no-payment grace period and a long-term repayment period. These packages are actually financial programmes set up by the exporter's government to assist the exporter in establishing more sales in this market. Today, this kind of soft loan support from exporting nations plays a decisive role in securing market-share, and China's "poor-man's purchase strategy" has succeeded in attracting over 50 countries to this market. Table 1,5 illustrates in part what has occurred.

Table 1,5   Soft Loans Support

Nation	Loans, Grants and Credit Commitment (billion $)	Effective Interest Rate (percent)	Grace Period (years)	Repayment Terms (years)
Italy	US 1.13	1.50	10	20
Canada*	CA 2.0	3.00	10	13
Japan		3.25	10	30
France		2.50	10	30
U K		5.00	5	15

* Estimated figures. Rates vary in accordance with repayment terms which are not released by the Export Development Corporation (EDC)

Source: Dymond, 1989, Table 6.2, and Intertrade, April 1987.

TARGET CUSTOMERS AND PROCESS

In respect of customers, there are two principal target groups, the end-users and the factories. The end-users are multi-product buyers who see a need for acquiring appropriate systems and specific items for their organizations which have foreign exchange allocated for definite purposes. There is no definite pattern that every end-user adopts in making inquiries about foreign products. Business can start with an agent, a friend of the buyer's organization, a vendor's active marketing, a government source, or as formally as a public request to bid on a project. Obtaining information to determine what exactly the customer wants also varies from case to case. There may be no written specifications or there may be volumes of specifications. The potential vendor must cope with wide variations in customer needs and specifications. However, the approval process in the end-user market tends to be more straightforward because the buyer's primary considerations in the decision-making process are often simply the availability of foreign currency and the local authority's economic endorsement. When the transaction amount runs into millions of dollars, the approval process can get complicated.

Factory-related purchases are more complex. These purchases are often tied to the economic strategy of a region. Transactions normally carry both short- and long-term outlooks. Not only does the factory demand state-of-the-art products to meet the immediate demands of its market in the first place, but the technology is needed to modernize the factory's plant so that similar systems or goods can be manufactured on site for the domestic market. The ultimate goal is to earn foreign currency through exports. Factory purchase is normally a long, drawn-out process dependent on the vendor's willingness to transfer technology and China's willingness to extend favourable conditions. Apart from the 'multi-go-rounds' of business meetings over years, the final approval process is painfully slow for the importer.

Imports are very tightly controlled and monitored by the State before it allows the provincial organization to make procurement decisions. Communication channels for price comparisons among similar products and services are especially well established. The process is set up so that the buying organization can arrive at a better deal; that is, the dice are loaded in favour of the buyer. Figure 1,5 illustrates the process from proposal to the buyer up to the issuing of the Letter of Credit (L/C) by the Bank of China.

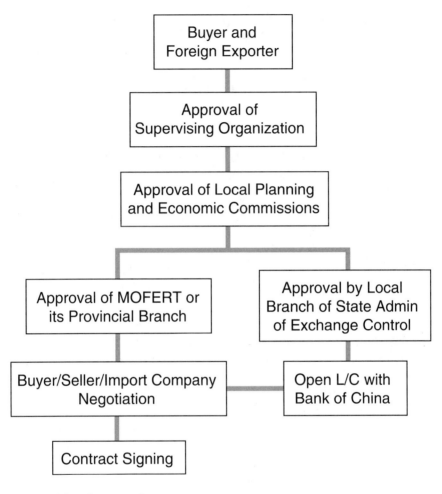

Figure 1,5   Contract Process

STRENGTHS OF CANADIAN EXPORTERS

Political and Historical Advantage

In political terms, Canada has historically been well regarded by the Chinese. In the most tumultuous period of the past 200 years, termed by Chinese historians as "foreign invasion", Canada was never involved in any direct or indirect act of plundering the "Central Kingdom". This is in marked contrast to other countries when one considers that Japan, Russia, the United States, and many European countries all at one time or another took advantage of the corrupt Qing Dynasty in the 1800s and early 1900s. Even if the Chinese Government really wants to be critical, the worst thing Canada has ever done to China was to participate in the Korean War (1950-1953), an action organized by the United Nations first against North Korea and later against China. Following the armistice, Canada's willingness to maintain a low level of commercial relations with China was in marked contrast to the uncompromising stance of the United States. This has created goodwill for Canada in China. Furthermore, Canadians are liked in China particularly because we are countrymen of Dr. Norman Bethune, whom the Chinese always remember and respect as one of the very few national heroes of foreign origin. Canadians, comrades of Dr. Bethune, are treated as sincere friends. This image bodes well for a good relationship between the two peoples.

Canadian Concessional Line of Credit

Though the Canadian federal government developed a national trade strategy in 1985 principally to broaden Canadian access to foreign markets, to strengthen the international marketing of Canadian goods and services, and to improve Canada's competitive position in the world, small exporters received little government support, except for occasional applications under the Canadian International Development Agency's (CIDA) Industrial Co-operation Program. In 1986, the government responded to exporters' desires to compete with other countries by setting up a $350 million concessional tranche in the $2 billion General Financing Protocol (MacDonald, 1986), which the Export Development Corporation signed with the Bank of China in 1984. The Chinese were not interested in the going interest rates on the $2 billion line of credit offered to them. However, by blending the two programmes, the interest rate became much more competitive. This facility supports buyers and Canadian sellers on projects of national interest to China. Canadian suppliers are thus placed on an equal footing with other exporters with access to government financial programmes. So far, two large telecommunications projects have been transacted, using these facilities.

Canadian Expertise

Since the 1970s, the Canadian telecommunications industry has achieved a number of firsts in the application of modern communication technology, in digital microwave, domestic satellite, digital switch family, super high frequency for satellite, direct broadcasting by satellite, packet-switched network, dual band satellite, the Canadarm, a nationwide digital system, longest fibre-optics long-haul network, and national cellular network. Moreover, Canadians efficiently manage two national telecommunications systems with the highest grade of service found anywhere. Canada has technical and managerial expertise as assets, and they are very marketable. In pure technological skill, Canadians have the potential to perform well in both the service and product markets.

WEAKNESSES OF CANADIAN EXPORTERS

Misfit Between Products and Market

Though Canadian telecommunications products are of the highest calibre, they were originally designed for the North American market. Penetration of the Chinese market was not an important item on the suppliers' agenda. In the 1950s, China adopted a switching signalling system close, but not exactly identical, to either International Telephone & Telegraph Consultative Committee (CCITT) R1 or R2 standards to meet the needs of her largely manual telephone system. In transmission systems, China has adhered closely to the standards recommended by the European Conference of Postal & Telecommunication Administration (CEPT), founded in 1959. Only manufacturers who are willing to commit research and development spending to modify their products to meet Chinese standards can compete in this market. However, most manufacturers would not consider such investment after evaluating the short-term product-market, competition and the difficulties of doing business in China.

Almost all Canadian exporters who have compatible products for China have been marketing similar non-switching products to other parts of the world. China just happened to be an opportune area for greater volume sales. For Canadian suppliers, the short-term market does not provide economies of scale. At present only Northern Telecom has the financial resources and ambition to invest in the modification of their DMS switch and in commitment to this market. Switching constitutes the biggest share of the telecom market in China, with about $60 million US yearly purchased from outside (Dymond, 1988: 123).

Weak Urge to Export

One of the most vital factors for success in the China market is commitment. Like customers everywhere, the Chinese want to know that the supplier they deal with is not a "fly-by-night" outfit, nor just coming in for a quick sale with no after-sales support. All new system sales anywhere in the world carry this kind of commitment because there are bound to be problems when the new system is installed. In China, formal contracts place heavy emphasis on guarantees of quality and service integrity. Suppliers often worry about possible difficulties they might encounter in China such as distance, language and ways of conducting business, thus adversely affecting profitability. Unlike the Japanese and Europeans, who rely heavily on exports to boost their Gross National Product (GNP), Canadian industry is weak on exporting expertise. This might be attributed to the complacency of the North American market. We must recognize that countries that do well in the Pacific Rim execute their business plans in the same potentially difficult environment and only those who persevere will secure a strong foothold in the marketplace.

Lack of Counter-Trade

Counter-trade can open doors and lead to more business in China. In counter-trading, Canadian telecommunications companies are not multi-subsidiary conglomerations that can conduct barter or buy-back types of activity. In contrast, Sumitomo (NEC's parent company) and Nokia have the latitude to conduct this kind of trading. These corporations can handle the burden of marketing a wide variety of Chinese products in their domestic markets. The Ministry of Foreign Economic Relations and Trade (MOFERT) favours such activities for obvious reasons based on their eagerness to export in exchange for foreign cash and balance trade deficits. Canada has always enjoyed a trade surplus in trading with China. Figure 2,5 shows exports in 1988 to China to be $2.6 billion, while imports from China were valued at $950 million, and a balance of $1.65 billion in Canada's favour.

Cocom Restrictions

Sales to China are reviewed by the Export Control Section of the External Affairs Department in Ottawa. Each application is normally considered individually. Certain commodities or systems may require approval of the Co-ordinating Committee on Export Controls (COCOM) in Paris, often regarded by China as an unfriendly Western Bloc organization interested in curtailing technology transfer. Certainly, COCOM, as the technology trade watchdog of NATO, wants to maintain this approach to all communist countries. Norwegian police have complained about

Billions of $'s Canadian

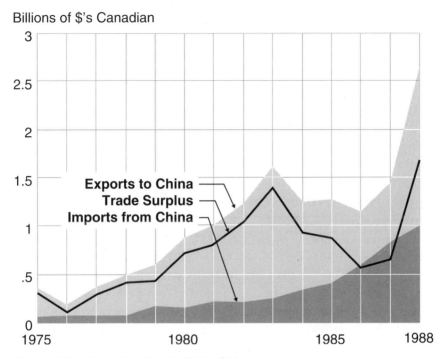

Figure 2,5   Canadian Trade With China

some NATO countries exporting high technology equipment to China in violation of COCOM rules (The Economist Intelligence Unit, China, 1988). If the Norwegian government decides to press the point, the approval process will likely become more bureaucratic. COCOM is particularly concerned about exports that would make a direct and significant contribution to nuclear weapons and their delivery systems, electronic and anti-submarine warfare, intelligence gathering, power projection and air superiority. It is a judgement-call by COCOM when from time to time it approves exports even though they may contribute to Chinese military development.

As this is a newer market for Canadian exporters as well as officials in the Export Control Section, there is much to learn from each individual case. The lead time required from the submission of the application to the issue of the permit is sometimes greater than three months. It is a Catch-22 situation for the high technology exporters who market a product in the first round because they have to make an educated guess as to whether the sales will be approved, as well as promises on delivery dates.

Lack of Logistical Support

Problems of distance, cost, language and culture create inconvenience for the conduct of business in China. Canada is handicapped in competition with exporters like Japan and Hong Kong. In China, business can be built upon local representations because the buyers have limited opportunities to go abroad. Exporters' geographic proximity and ability to place more staff of similar culture who can communicate fluently with the customers are crucial to the building of a strong marketing force.

CHINA'S INVESTMENT SIZE IN COMMUNICATIONS

Though investments in communications were initially estimated at about $4 billion US for the Seventh Five-Year Plan, the yearly investment in this sector has proved to be much higher. According to Dymond (1988: 29), China had already invested about $1.7 billion US in telecommunications by 1987 and, by comparison, Canadian investment in telecommunications amounted to $1.9 billion US, or just over two percent of the world's telecom market of $90 billion (Dymond, 1988: 29). Figures from 1989 (Zita, 1987) show that China has earmarked a minimum of $21 billion US for telecommunications investment up to the year 2000. Thirty percent of this heavy investment in the telecommunications sector will be in imports, which translates into a market of $7.0 billion between 1990 and 2000 (Zita, 1987). Although the total is not as big as international suppliers had hoped, it still represents a strong attraction for exporting countries.

With this amount of investment, the central government has a strong imperative to upgrade and augment the telecommunications network. Its general improvement objectives, according to Lerner (1987: 139), are to:

• improve local telephone service, particularly in large cities;
• develop the toll system and increase trunks;
• install or expand automatic dealing in provincial capitals;
• upgrade major cities to all automatic or semi-automatic service and provide new services; and
• replace open wire with cable and microwave technology.

With limited resources to fulfil these demands, China advocates joint ventures to attract foreign investment to provide technology, machines and management training. In most cases she would provide land, building and personnel. China's new concessions for foreign investors create a more favourable environment. It shows the government's determination to attract high technology ventures to re-tool its factories and increase exports. In brief, there is a clear strategy to buy and absorb technical expertise with limited foreign exchange.

Thus the market represents at least a short-term product market for foreign exporters willing to transfer technology until China masters her own production. There may also be a service market in the long term once China establishes a rudimentary infrastructure for a modern national network.

SERVICE MARKETS AND OPPORTUNITIES

China is a product-oriented market and generally a company must have solid products to sell before any customer interest can be attracted. Up to 1989, most opportunities in the service market have been embedded in business deals that involve system/product sales. When the network grows with assorted equipment and technologies, there will be more problems and they will be more complex. Besides physical transfer of technology and stimulation of foreign investment, high calibre advice on aspects of planning, designing, operating, maintaining and managing an effective public network will be needed.

Consulting Services

One important element that the state planners in China tried to emphasize in the course of modernization is the notion that the West's knowledge is valuable to China. However, either the Chinese do not understand, or do not want to understand, that getting expert opinions costs money. As a general practice in this market, for example, a Request for Proposal by the customer often lures international suppliers/exporters to recommend system design. This means that the buyer will get free consulting on relevant and correlating subjects. This negligence or ignorance of the value of knowledge undoubtedly gives the Chinese short-term advantage in obtaining free information, but in the long run it will cause problems. This free information from suppliers is often incomplete, for the goal is to promote further sales talks. When every deal is structured in this way, network development and deployment of modern technology are implemented in a piece-meal manner. Therefore, China desperately needs, on both national and provincial level:

1. an operational study to assess her network in terms of connectivity, technology compatibility and the need for an effective support system;

2. a planning study to establish an orderly application of new technology on building new network routes for both voice and non-voice service;

3. a feasibility study to develop plans for building network management centres to monitor traffic and maximize plant usage;

4. a pricing study to provide an economical framework for the design of local, toll and international rates—like most developing countries, self-financing of telecommunications development is unlikely until an efficient network is in place and earning a good return on investment. Therefore the study must consider short- and long-term cash flows to address costs of operating and expanding the network. To make things more complicated, it has to harmonize with the socio-economic policies of the socialist government. We must remember that the current transition from a centrally-planned economy to a market-oriented one is difficult. Prices that used to be determined by bureaucratic decision were based on subsidies, the government paying for the real costs. Price reform that reflects costs will invite inflation and suppress demand, at least in the short-term. The study must then lead to an optimal price structure so that the market is sufficiently sustained with solid revenue available for network expansion. And the study must be jointly sponsored by MPT and the National Price Council of the Ministry of Finance;

5. a study to establish a single body to control and supervise the end-to-end performance of China's telecommunications infrastructure—though MPT has jurisdiction over long-distance trunk and international services, the Provincial Telecom Administration Bureau (PTAB) which looks after the local administrations often has closer ties to the local government than to MPT in Beijing. In the absence of an integrated approach to network development, networks lack end-to-end transparency, and the level of service to customers suffers;

6. a study to assess whether future network development should be consolidated into one or two networks instead of continuing with six or seven large ministry networks operating independently of the MPT public networks. It is not the most cost-effective way to run a national telecommunications system, as duplication of facilities to serve a limited number of private customers takes away valuable

resources from fulfilling public needs. This can only be determined by the State Council and the State Planning Commission;

7. apart from political bureaucracies, a study to recommend a single organization fully responsible for the strategy and implementation of the telecommunications modernization plan. The in-fighting between ministries, such as MPT and MEI, on manufacturing, domestic market and joint-ventures with foreign partners is a waste of resources. The ministries do not have to run similar plants. The efforts can be merged and products marketed to the whole telecom market instead of dissecting it into public and private networks;

8. a factory study to eliminate a multiplicity of joint-venture factories using the same technology—there has never been a study on product life-cycles in these joint-venture deals, and a proliferation of redundant factories will not bring efficiency in view of the ever-advancing telecommunications industry. Smaller planned output levels at each of these redundant factories will prevent realization of economies of scale normally associated with manufacturing. Hence low production level, equivalent market prices and different production costs do not go well together. Both MPT and MEI should participate in, and consolidate plans for, an optimal number of foreign joint-venture factories producing different types of products.

With several serious decisions ahead, the Chinese will soon find that, even in an environment of free thinking, it takes expert input to develop healthy solutions. Hardware procurement will make their problems more complex. Free information will not be sufficiently analytical and it may have a negative impact on their modernization programmes. Moreover, they have to operate within limited budgets and under an ideology of Marxism/Maoism, which very often narrows the choice of viable solutions. Canadian companies are very credible to the customers because of Canadian technical experience and historical "blamelessness" in Canada's diplomacy towards China.

HUMAN RESOURCE DEVELOPMENT

Characteristics of Management Infrastructure

The demand associated with economic boom and influx of new technologies has already created much pressure on those who serve in the telecommunications sector. To make the situation worse, the devastating period of the Cultural Revolution in China left industry very ill-prepared for such a sharp transition. It had suppressed progress in almost every industry other than those related to the Military and Space Program. The result was that the education of almost a generation that should be today's middle managers was ignored and the growth of technical managers was completely retarded. The shortage of technical and skilled management personnel is very acute in telecommunications.

While technical training is often negotiated via contracts, there have not been any strong efforts to pursue managerial training. After various dealings with the Chinese, with only a few exceptions, one can identify the following problems in Chinese management:

(a) *The bureaucratic structure is supreme*

The pyramid structure has been so deeply implanted that it affects all levels, from workers to the highest rank. It is highly hierarchical and protocol-oriented. This may help smooth execution of commands but it has two negative effects. First, it creates a management population that is more rank-conscious than oriented to problem-solving. The leader of any group has supreme authority. Second, the bureaucracy becomes so tedious that the lower and middle managers either cannot make decisions because they have limited authority or do not like to make them at all. The unchallenged position of the leader is a replica of the political system which has operated for 40 years; and it creates a slow process of bureaucracy not conducive to carrying on business. Many experienced marketers in China observed that those at a lower level tend to be so indifferent that they merely want to get through the consensus sessions with their equals and leave the decisions to the leader. On other occasions, they even hesitate to consult their leader for the simple reason that they do not want to waste their superior's time. This "don't-rock-the-boat" syndrome does not help to build a strong team and, gradually, creativity is lost.

The problem is serious because both horizontal and vertical communications within an organization are slow and ineffective.

(b) *Leaders are running communities as well as business organizations*

Most presidents of foreign telephone companies who met Chinese directors of provincial PTABs were surprised that their Chinese counterparts were also responsible for the livelihood of their workers. Each bureau actually provides housing for the families of their staff, schooling for the workers' children, and hospitals for the sick. At one time, it even had jurisdiction ranging from food rationing to approval of marriages. In other words, the director is running a community of, say, 80,000 people throughout the whole province. By Canadian standards, the director not only carries a portfolio equivalent to that of Canadian provincial cabinet ministers and president of a telephone company but also looks after the welfare of all PTAB staff. It is not difficult to see that the leader's energy is dissipated in many house-keeping problems related to social issues. This part of the job becomes a number one concern, which he does not want to delegate too much because workers' unrest is unacceptable in China. The next important function becomes the day-to-day operation of the bureau which carries not only telecommunications but postal services as well. It is no wonder that very little business planning goes on. The responsibility in each bureau is also bound to transfer vertically to each manager, making for limited inter-department co-ordinations. This problem exists in all ministries and provincial organization in the nation.

Because people are one of the most important assets in any organization, a balance has to be struck between business management and intra-bureau welfare management.

(c) *Organizations are over-controlled and over-manned but under-managed*

Dealings with MPT in Beijing showed that their officials are more bureaucratic than their provincial counterparts. More significant is a poor perception of important issues by middle and higher management. In a world of high technology, it is easy for engineering managers to fall into the trap of concentrating on technology and to lose sight of objectives and actions required to achieve goals. Their skills in problem-solving are questionable. The supreme authority of leaders exacerbates the problem, as one cannot encourage people to speak up if, in daily routine, the environment is so much controlled. Thus in every session, only one or two voice their opinions, except around tables in the Negotiation Building in Beijing where only the professionals are invited.

MPT operates five educational institutes, which train young engineers in Beijing, Wuhan, Nanjing, Changchun and Xian. Because competition for enrolment in post-secondary institutes is stiff, employees are graduates of very good calibre. However, China is going through a stage where there is an adequate number of line managers with theoretical knowledge but who lack the practical experience and exposure to all disciplines of telecommunications. Though there are some good managers, it may be said, to use a military analogy, that the provincial PTABs have too many soldiers and not enough officers to prepare for the upcoming "digital" war. Important areas that require study and direction from both MPT and PTAB level, but have not been examined, are radio spectrum management, network synchronization, on-going traffic studies, market-demand study, fundamental planning, operator concepts, and records.

Mutual Interests in Training

Given the infrastructure of MPT, most middle and higher managers who want to disentangle their organization from the web of supervision and transform it into a stream-lined operation will face bureaucratic problems for some time. China will not tolerate any external influence for change unless the Standing Committee of the Political Bureau wants to spearhead such change. As a foreign exporter with considerable experience in managing modern networks, Canada's focus must be on helping its organizations in the areas of effective use of manpower, planning and problem-solving techniques. Areas of mutual interest are:

(a) *Training in building effective corporations*

Each manager in the Telecom Bureau must have a well-defined responsibility and should be accountable for that position. This will reduce job redundancy. Systematic development of competence can only be effected if there is a set of precise job-relevant objectives established, a clear programme of training and a plan to measure the effectiveness of training. This will help to employ people in the right positions and define the right person to obtain appropriate training at home or abroad.

(b) *Training in conceptual skills*

Higher managers should be equipped with particular skills to visualize the relationship of the telecommunications business to the social and even political forces as a whole. However, conceptual skills must be provided to distinguish duties as an industrial manager from a welfare administrator. A strategy to delegate responsibilities must be formulated. It must be emphasized that leadership-effectiveness training is important as well. Being appointed a manager does not necessarily make the appointee an efficient one. Effective use of manpower, setting up meaningful incentive systems towards achievement of goals, streamlining the decision-making process, organizing informational and problem-solving meetings are all important skills to enhance productivity of the organization.

(c) *Training in engineering economics*

Though the present method of central allocation of foreign capital funds limits the freedom of PTAB managers to determine capital projects, with the evolution of a pricing strategy and increased international financing activities, there will be a change in their economic thinking. Determination of an optimal solution among viable alternatives based on economics, selecting sources of capital investment and using a project control system from the beginning to the completion of the project are tools which good managers must possess.

(d) *Training in building a financial and management information system*

This type of system must be established. The key to success is to keep it simple so that managers can use it as a tool. It should include modules covering all critical aspects of the telecommunications business.

(e) *Training in computer-aided tools*

Though some MPT departments have used personal computers, their applications are not widespread, particularly in other PTABs. Moreover, there should be a planned approach in using these tools in every PTAB. China has her version of IBM compatible personal computers manufactured and marketed by the Great Wall Industrial Corporation (GWIC). Software tools for outside plant optimization, radio path design, radio interference studies, economic evaluators, and forecasting are marketable.

As the next decade begins, China will find that the effective management of human resources is as important, if not more important than, the choice of an appropriate technology. There are many talented graduates from her Posts & Telecommunications Academies. More and better training has to be emphasized as the higher managers experience the impact of modern network and appreciate the benefits of training. Canadian companies, which often excel in training and development, can do well in this non-hardware domain. The author felt that Canada had made a useful beginning when he visited the CIDA-supported Management Training Centre at Chengdu, a co-operative establishment between the Association of Canadian Community Colleges and China Enterprise Management. Most of the Senior Project Officers and tutors are expatriates from Canada.

PRODUCT-MARKET DEMAND AND OPPORTUNITIES

In terms of network make-up, China has a vast national public switched network operated under the MPT and at least six large private networks dedicated to the operations of the Ministry of Railways, Ministry of Water Resources & Power, Ministry of Petroleum Industry, Ministry of Coal Industry, Military Network and on a smaller scale but concentrating more on satellite communications, the Ministry of Aeronautics. With seven networks all vying to modernize, the demand is enormous in all market segments of telecommunications.

Works such as "Telecommunications in China" (Dymond, 1988), a joint publication of TeleConsult and CIDA, contain many details about the competitive interests in these market segments. There is no need to repeat them here. A brief analysis is sufficient.

Network Switches

After the end of the Cultural Revolution in the mid-1970s, the Chinese switch technology stagnated in the electro-mechanical design, such as step-by-step and cross-bar. There are no analogue stored-programme switches in China. China can leap-frog into the cost-effective, time-space-time, digital-switch technology. One of the objectives of the Seventh Five-Year Plan was to double the number of telephones to 12.5 million by 1990. (see Table 3,5). Since the first digital switch was installed by Fujitsu in Fuzhou in 1982, China has been a fierce battleground for international switch manufacturers. In 1987, the proportion of automatic exchanges rose to 87.4 percent, consisting of 18.7 percent step-by-step, 44.6 percent cross-bar, and 19.3 percent stored-program controlled switches (Zhang, 1989: 13). At present, the Japanese hold 50 percent of the market (Dymond, 1988: 78).

Table 3,5   Telephones: Number and Percentage

	1985	1990	2000
Population (billion)	1.04	1.09	1.23
Telephones (million)	6.20	12.50	33.60
Penetration (%)	0.60	1.15	2.70
Lines (million)	3.40	10.00	25.00

Source: Datapro Reports, 1989

Price per line is cut-throat, starting at about $120 a line. Among Canadian switch suppliers, only Northern Telecom is willing to modify its software so that the DMS family becomes compatible with the China Signalling. China's Integrated Service Digital Network (ISDN) will rely on these new switches to incorporate the CCS7 signalling. The switch market is confined to international telecom giants and allows very little opportunity for entry of small manufacturers.

Switches for Rural Areas

According to Datapro Reports (1989), there are an estimated 1.49 million telephones in rural China, serving a population of 800 million.

China's long-term objective for rural telephone service is to achieve a penetration of one percent and have a basic service to every town and village by the year 2000. This creates opportunities for Canadian products, such as Northern Telecom's DMS-10 and Mitel's GX-5000. General Electric Company (U.K.) has secured a contract to supply its UXD rural exchanges to Guangdong Province. Although the concentrator concept, with direct interface to digital switches, is not well understood in China, it is likely that it will have its own niche in the market of the 1990s.

China has not overlooked the domestic effort to design a switch of this size to satisfy its needs. Continual joint-venture talks with Italy, Canada and even South Korea have been conducted for some time. It is a good investment because the Chinese foresee they can market this product in other Third World countries in the future.

Private Automatic Branch Exchanges (PABX) and Key Systems

The fact that PABXs could be provided by user investment creates an enormous demand, but profit margins in this market drop quickly when training and associated expenses are included. It is a "dog-fight" market, involving many suppliers trying to scoop up as much business as possible before China introduces a digital machine of her own. The target price for a future domestic PABX was speculated to be less than $90 per line, which is incredibly cheap by world standards. Meanwhile, both the MEI and MPT have been talking to suppliers about joint ventures. Today, known PABX deals include Fujitsu with Fujian PTAB, Northern Telecom with Shenzhen to produce SL-1, Nitsuko with Beijing Radio Factory No.3, Mitel with factories of MEI for line cards and hardware production for SX-200, and Philip's agreement to build plants in China. Overall, there will be six PABX factories established with foreign partners.

Transmission Systems—Microwave

Unlike North America, where digital microwave is losing its popularity for long-haul, high-capacity applications in favour of the more cost-effective fibre-optics, China still chooses digital microwave as the technology to fulfil heavy and thin route applications because the microwave spectrum in China is not congested.

In terms of export of transmission systems, the North American telecom industry is creating its own problems because its digital building block of 1.544 MB/S PCM is incompatible with the CEPT standards of 2.048 MB/S PCM which China adopted. In microwave products, Harris

Farinon is the only Canadian supplier with products of 34MB/S in the 2, 7 and 8 GHz bands. To make matters worse, there is absolutely no CEPT digital multiplex supplier in Canada or anywhere in North America.

NEC dominates the Chinese market in the public network. Italian suppliers have had good results in selling to the Ministry of Water Resources & Power. Nokia has been successful in providing systems to Daqing Oilfield in the province of Heilongjiang.

The small number of competitors demonstrates that the market is not very strong, judged by the few projects pursued each year. In 1988, the first large Canadian microwave-system-project contract was signed by Canadian Communications International (CCI), a consortium of SaskTel, B C Tel and Edmonton Tel with the Jilin Electric Power Industry.

Transmission Systems—Fibre Optics

China has put much research emphasis on this stable and interference-free technology, having laboratories in locations such as Shanghai, Xian, Beijing, Tianjin, Wuhan and Chengdu. However, Chinese research teams seem to lack the expertise to commercialize their products. As in the case of digital microwave, Canada falls short as a supplier in CEPT standard electronics. However, there is much market potential for Canadian optical cable because Canada's products are very competitive in price. Sales of optical transmission technology to communist countries are on the Canadian Export Control restriction list. At present, transmission equipment over 140 MB/S is restricted.

Satellite Communications—Earth Segment

The outstanding advantage of satellite systems for a country the size of China is the broadcasting coverage which permits establishment of a nationwide network with one space segment. This is particularly suitable for broadcast and bulk data distribution, neither being affected greatly by the propagation delay of about 250 milliseconds for a round trip. While China has the capability to launch satellites, opportunities for export countries in this area lie in the earth segment of earth station and electronics. Today there are no published plans for satellite communications in China, though broad objectives for civil satellite communications were set out as to:

- interconnect major cities along the coast;
- provide service to remote and rural areas;

- connect offshore oil drilling platforms and islands in the South China Sea;
- provide emergency communication links during disaster and weather early warning; and
- establish dedicated circuits for data services (Dymond, 1988: 86).

Spar Aerospace is the most successful supplier, with 16 earth stations in operation in oilfields from Urumqi to Daqing since 1986 (Canada Department of External Affairs, 1986: 50). Six or seven ministries will likely invest more in satellite communications between their strategic locations. As these ministries expand their data communications for operation, maintenance and processing, the market will become more active. Also the Ministry of Aeronautics is examining products of the Time Domain Multiple Access (TDMA) and Single-Channel Per Carrier (SCPC) technology, and other ministries are planning private networks. Beside Spar Aerospace, manufacturers, like Microtel in B.C., with its "Spacetel", and SED in Saskatchewan, with its "Skyswitch", should have good opportunities if given enough marketing exposure.

Mobile Telephone Systems—Cellular and Others

It is obvious that, without a good basic telephone system in place, modern mobile telephone systems, such as cellular systems will remain a luxury, limited to extremely populous cities. From the systems purchased, it is clear that China had standardized its cellular systems on the Total Access Communications Standard (TACS) Protocol. (Canadian cellular systems are compliant with the IEE-1S3-C Protocol and operating in 800 MHz band).

Beside cellular mobile, there is a smaller-scale market for mobile telephone systems in ministries with localized operating crews, such as oilfields, coal mines and power companies. Canadian companies, such as Glenayre Electronics and Spilsbury, can supply that market.

Data

According to a report presented at Telecom '87 in Geneva (Franco, 1987), the world growth rate for data-terminal equipment is 20 percent annually, compared with four percent for telephone stations. China's growth patterns will be similar or even higher. Meanwhile, a data transmission network is needed for efficiency and economic reasons in China. An X.25 protocol public-packet switching network (CNPAC) has been accepted and will be put into use. The equipment is made in France and Italy, and there will be nodes at Shanghai, Beijing and Guangzhou (Gao, 1989: 34)

As the world's first country to establish a public digital data network on a countrywide customer-to-customer basis as early as 1973, Canada is not short of good suppliers of data communications system equipment. Memotec Data, Northern Telecom, Develcon Electronics, Newbridge Communications, Gandalf Data, Mobile Data International, Intercontinental Data Control are a few among many exporters. The product-line ranges from modems, multiplexers, switching, data transmission systems, LANs, to packet switching. This is a good time to get into the market because most buyers tend to purchase via contacts, and amounts purchased are small enough that local authorities can make decisions. The data market is likely to be developed quickly but, at the present moment, it is informal with little tender activity.

The Changchun Posts & Telecom Institute has a strong association and frequent personnel exchanges with Japan's OKI. It has also had some initial contacts with Develcon in Saskatchewan to the extent that a lightly-loaded data switch was donated to the Institute.

Broadcasting

In China, the broadcasting media is strictly controlled by the Ministry of Radio and Television. The Central People's Broadcasting Station in Beijing controls China's radio network. In 1987, the China Broadcast Satellite Corporation decided to introduce a direct broadcasting service (DBS) by means of two satellites co-located in an orbital position of 92° East, one for use as a spare (Franco, 1987: 66). It is considered the only practical means of providing a national television and radio coverage for the whole country. Operating in the K-band at the spectrum of 11.7 to 12.7 GHz, DBS requires only a one-metre-diameter dish. If this project proceeds, it will create a significant market for cable television (CATV) and television receive only (TVRO) systems and de-scramblers.

Canada, the leader in showing the practicability of using 12 GHz via the HERMES satellite and of using small dishes to demonstrate DBS in 1976, has the opportunity to test China's CATV and TVRO market in the 1990s. Manufacturers like Norsat International, 2001 Satellite Network in B.C., and Lindsay Specialty Products in Ontario should have very competitive products.

Others

Copper Cable: There are no opportunities for Canadian copper cables (telephone paired cables and coaxial cables) in the China market because China has good domestic supplies. Less than 10 percent of its requirements are obtained from imports. Canadian prices are generally higher than those offered by competitors like BICC of the U.K. South Korean copper cables also found their way into this market through the skilful efforts of some Hong Kong agents. There has been, however, interest in Canadian cable manufacturing expertise. In 1986, Phillips Cables of Canada sold a cable plant to China with technology transfer, and helped the Chinese to re-assemble it in the city of Fushan in Guangdong Province.

Tele-Text: Business demand has forced China to place high priority on telex investment. Statistics showed that telex traffic rose by 67.6 percent between 1985 and 1986 (Datapro, PRC, 1989). International telex facilities are now available in 14 coastal cities and in four Special Economic Zones, as well as Hainan Island.

Rurl Distribution Radio: As mentioned under "SWITCHES FOR RURAL AREAS", telecommunications investment for rural areas will gradually increase and peak in the 1990s. The point-to-multi-point digital radio system is a more economical and practical alternative to copper cable in remote rural areas. With financial support from the Italian Government, Italtel succeeded in signing a joint venture with the Hebei Province to establish an R & D, installation and maintenance centre in that province. With products sold in over forty countries abroad, S R Telecom in Quebec has also had some success in marketing its TDMA radio in China.

KEYS TO SUCCESS

Corporate Objects

International corporations attempting to enter the Chinese market have had varying degrees of success. Doing business in China entails some risk, just as it does elsewhere, including the corporation's home country. Before deciding to explore opportunities for the corporation in China, a Chief Executor Officer (CEO) should ask the following questions:

1. *Is the attraction of the market size the only reason for entering China?*

A businessman once described what he termed the "China Syndrome" for many foreign corporations: "First there was euphoria in the early post-Mao years with the promise of a market of a billion consumers. After some big campaigns, they realized that the market environment was very different and business was not easy. After that, the withdrawal was as rapid as the 'invasion.' Both times I think these corporations over-reacted." This has been a frequent occurrence in all sectors of the Chinese market, not just in communications.

Corporations were often premature in their entry into the Chinese market and others will go into China without a pre-conceived strategy. Lured by an apparent market of a billion, they learned too late that it is a market with very little buying power. The only institutions that can afford to buy are those with foreign exchange allocated. Local currency (the renminbi) does not count when it comes to purchasing imports. The gestation period for most international sales is normally long, but tends to be even more protracted in China. Those who hope for a quick strike and rapid success will soon lose their enthusiasm as their resources drain away. Ninety percent of active foreign companies in China are "in the red" for the first few years. The size of the consumer market in China is an illusion.

2.   *What is the corporate goal in the China market?*

In the writer's experience with the China market, corporations that come out as winners are those with pre-conceived goals. In contrast, the corporations that failed and withdrew are those that lacked vision, analysis and strategy as to their market goals. When a corporation is unwilling to address its future in such a unique market, it succumbs to short-term situations and withdraws. Certainly opportunities exist in this vast country, but pragmatic entrepreneurs must decide where they want to establish their stepping stones before they become involved in China. They must have a clear vision of where their corporation will be in China in 10 years, which is the minimum start-up time frame in this part of the world. Executives must endorse this kind of vision and sponsor the type of mission established by their international branches. This means that corporate commitment is absolutely necessary and must be sustained because the initial pace is slow and even the customers themselves find their hierarchy too bureaucratic to move any faster. This is particularly important to Canadian corporations because Canada's scale in international business is often small and resource-limited. The crux of the matter is that corporations must be prepared to allocate sufficient resources and support for the start-up strategy to achieve their long-term goals. China is not a market for those with only short-term strategies, and this reality must be recognized at the start.

3. *Is the corporation clear about its short-term goals?*

Executives must be clear that one of their short-term goals is to secure appropriate small gains, both in profits and market share. Because they have limited foreign exchange resources, Chinese customers aim to obtain maximum return from every dollar they spend. In such a climate, any successful deal must result in a buying price that represents a win for the customer and a selling price that provides incentive for the vendor to pursue further business deals.

The Chinese have a centralized system in their national and provincial Foreign Economic Relations and Trade bureaus that provides excellent communication channels for cost comparison. They fully capitalize on vendor competition and have adopted an unremitting style of negotiation that will prove difficult for any foreign businessman. It is thus very important for Canadian corporations to stand firm on the profit margin for every deal and have no illusion that any introductory losses can be compensated for in the next deal. The next round will be worse because of precedents established. By slashing prices just to get into the market, they are unknowingly helping the Chinese to play the price game with other vendors. In such a market, the only companies that can afford to undercut prices are those that intend, once they control the market, to ask the Chinese to pay for it. In the long run, the Chinese will suffer because many companies will abandon their ventures in China, and buyers will eventually face a single vendor who controls market prices. The cost of doing business in China is high. On the international business scale, Canadian corporations which, in comparison with other competitors, have limited resources must not overlook short-term gains.

The Role of the Canadian Chinese

Having a core of Canadian Chinese among the marketing executives is one of the most effective arrangements in customer contacts in China. The advantages accrue from knowledge of the language, the remote cultural link from having Chinese ancestors, and the capability of establishing rapport with the customer. Middle and upper managers in China lack exposure in dealing with foreigners. Psychologically, there is a certain degree of doubt about the sincerity of the vendor. This alienation becomes more acute in the absence of a common language. The managers have to protect themselves from making poor commercial decisions and so prudence will sometimes lead to what might be called "hypercaution." The presence of ethnic Chinese who can demonstrate that the vendor's intentions are sincere and who can speak the customers' language often relieves their fears. Once a common bond is established, the Chinese can express their concerns.

The advantage of the presence of Canadian Chinese is that "ice-breaking" is very easy. They can help to develop trust and channel communications. They will facilitate the signing of contracts of mutual interest to both sides. By being patient and contributing viable alternative ideas, the author often found that his Chinese counterpart quickly realized that apart from wanting some gain from doing business, Canadians are also interested in helping them to solve their problems. In some ways, the Chinese are very shrewd businessmen though their style may upset Western negotiators. As a result of their previous experiences, including with the Russians, they may believe they have dealt with too many foreigners who think they understand Chinese culture and problems after only one trip or one contract. The author was told that these foreigners tend to be unsympathetic to unique Chinese problems. The Chinese are looking for a long-term relationship, and in the expatriate Chinese, they see credible associates who can more effectively build bridges for them to the West than they themselves or foreigners can do.

On the other side, we must understand the sometimes difficult position in negotiations for the Canadian Chinese who are loyal to their own companies. Although their mandate is to explore new grounds for their company, they are often pressured intentionally or unintentionally by the Chinese customers. Often, immediately conveying their concerns, the latter expect the Canadian Chinese to take their side and press the Chinese case informally. While it is preferable that the customer's desires be known, the disadvantage is that the buyer is exerting pressure on the Canadian staff. The author was once asked in a talk, organized by the Canadian Chamber of Commerce in Hong Kong, how to get out of such a situation. The answer is very simple: the company's objectives have priority. However, the Chinese expect concessions from the Canadian Chinese and the Canadian chef-de-mission should understand this and should reassure the staff that they should never feel threatened and may exercise judgement to reach a "win-win" situation.

Having a good core of Canadian Chinese managers is a sure way to expedite business. It also eliminates many problems in China on customs and transportation arrangements. There is also an element other than loyalty in the efforts of these staff. Beyond the desire for profit and achievement, they seem to have more drive and perseverance than others because of their additional feelings for this ancient country. It may be said that they are fit to be the intermediaries of such a market. Others will not be as effective. For others, it would be like walking in a cultural minefield, oblivious of the profound damage caused by their insensitivity.

Marketing to the Government of Canada

There are two reasons why it is important for Canadians to make efforts to market themselves to their own government. First, exporters to the China market need the extra prestige that government support brings. Second, assuming that the product is of good quality and price-competitive, government programmes with grants and financing may make or break a deal.

Once abroad in a country like China, Canadians soon find that "hoisting a Canadian flag" gives more credibility than operating as individuals. Political ideology and indoctrination have instilled the idea among the Chinese that governments are the highest representatives of nations, hence the most credible organizations. It is vital, therefore, that a company is well known to Canadian External Affairs and have marketed itself to the Canadian Embassy. Commercial counsellors and first and second secretaries in the telecommunications and transportation portfolios in the Canadian Embassy can provide excellent help and advice. They participate in business banquets and often reinforce their support by promoting the business relationship at the country level. This gesture is very important, particularly to the bureaucrats in Beijing.

Although the available concessional line of credit has been under-utilized, the government's good intention to take the competition head on must be recognized. Unlike the United States, Canada has a financing package. The closest U.S. equivalent is the Discretionary Financing through Eximbank, but it is not explicitly ear-marked for China. The Canadian International Development Agency (CIDA) offers the Industrial Cooperation Program and Bilateral Assistance Program to exporters. These can be used in the telecommunications market. The Export Development Corporation (EDC) offers commercial loans as well as the concessional line of credit. However, it quickly becomes apparent that the Canadian government is no less bureaucratic than the Chinese. While EDC carries on business in a manner similar to a bank, dealing with CIDA takes patience and requires considerable marketing. In short, CIDA should be regarded as another set of customers.

Understanding the motives of the Canadian government in establishing these funds is important. Domestically, they help exporters to gain sales, create employment, and fuel the industrial and financial machinery. Internationally, they reinforce Canada's long-established humanitarian image of providing assistance to developing countries, and it should be noted that the magnitude of aid programmes is often a measure of prestige in the international arena. Though China is a different and difficult country for market penetration, it is an important one in diplomatic terms. It is only natural, therefore, that the Canadian government has been extremely careful in allocating funds to the right exporters and to appropriate projects of national importance and high profile in China.

The following excerpt from Canada Task Force on China Power Sector (Billowes, 1986) best describes the ground rules for all government support:

> ... there are some criteria that are applicable to all firms:
> - they should have a demonstrable reputation for technical excellence;
> - they should have demonstrated an understanding of the particular problems of marketing in China;
> - they should be willing to invest their own resources in the project on a long-term basis;
> - they should have a well-founded plan for exploiting the China market on the successful completion of the project;
> - they should be willing to consider technology transfer and joint-venture agreements; and
> - they should be willing to consider arrangements whereby, if a project is successful, some of the government investment should be repaid or re-invested in similar marketing activities ...
>
> To the extent that the above criteria are valid, firms not meeting them should be discouraged. This is particularly true of those firms that are simply impressed by the size of the Chinese population but have not used what resources they have to research the market in any significant way ...

This excerpt clearly outlines the rationale of the philosophy of the Canadian government in supporting exports in this market. The keywords, long-term and commitment, are implicit in the message. These are appropriate criteria and are in keeping with customers' demands.

Five Crucial Links in Making a Sale in the China Market

There are five elements, given below in order of significance, that should be addressed in making a sale in China: Politics, Chinese Connections, Price, Quality, and Delivery.

Politics

Can politics be separated from business? In dealings with the Chinese since 1985, politics have never been a pivotal element in any negotiations though they might have been mentioned casually. However, the Political Bureau of the Chinese Communist Party sets all policies and direction for the whole country and the State Council under which each ministry functions must operate within such ground rules. Politics are involved even before an entry visa to China is issued for a foreign businessman. Even if entry is permitted, business talks can stall if the local Bureaus were told not to buy from this country. Good examples of this are the slow down in purchase of Japanese goods when China joined other Asian nations in criticizing Japanese history textbooks that de-emphasized past Japanese aggression in the Pacific region, causing a suspicion of possible revival of militarism in Japan, and when the late Premier Zhou En-lai's statue in Japan was vandalised by radicals. Since 1949 the leaders of the New China have shown their determination to shake off a "century of shame and humiliation" that was dominated by foreign aggression and unequal treaties. The importance of *sovereignty and independence of action* is very pronounced in China's foreign policy. No outside pressure can bend the independent will of those leaders who control China's direction. At this critical point in China's history, any negative changes introduced internally or any sanctions by the West will cost China dearly in terms of economic losses. But China can only maintain her level of self-reliance by putting politics ahead of business. As Kissinger (1989: 6) has said:

> Friends of China can only hope that the process of modernization will continue. History has shown that a weak and divided China produces instability throughout Asia. China is so enormous, its population so vast, its people so talented, that when it is removed from the scales they tip towards extremes.

Chinese Connection

This term is the closest English equivalent to what the Chinese call "guanxi." However, guanxi means more than friendship and relationship. It is a traditional concept of what one can and should do for a true friend in terms of special favours. There is implicit a sense of mutual obligation and indebtedness. The author is ambivalent about guanxi, because while it may further business transactions with the Chinese, it also promotes favouritism. It is not the Canadian style of conducting business. It can backfire on the vendor if the buyer's wishes cannot be gratified in return. Business contacts and leads all revolve around having guanxi with someone in the buyer's organization, otherwise favour may be shown to others who can establish better guanxi.

Price, Quality, and Delivery

In the West, price, quality, or delivery may be the determining factors for a purchase, depending on the buyer's criteria. In China, price is the most sensitive item. Under a tight allocation of foreign exchange, each organization strives to drive prices down to the absolute minimum. The effectiveness of communication channels on prices exceeds that of the physical telecommunications network. After a product is sold once in China, it is tagged with that price. The next organization that buys the product will want to maintain, if not obtain an even better, price, or the negotiators cannot show that they have done their job. The Chinese also emphasize "huo bi san jia," that is, comparing goods with three suppliers, and they quickly select the most competitive price. With a strategy of playing one against the other in a queue of over-enthusiastic foreign exporters who are slashing prices to increase their market share, the Chinese are in the driver's seat. It is an unfortunate situation. It hurts both honest suppliers of lesser financial resources and the Chinese as well, because it will rapidly create a situation in which no honest competition exists. The importance of the price issue may originate in a perception of having been cheated by foreigners in the past.

The concept of the changing values of time and money are not necessarily recognized either. A sale offer may include a clause "quotation valid for 90 days" but negotiators do not perceive the price quotation as time-limited. They expect that, once quoted, it will remain unchanged till negotiations are concluded even if they drag on for more than a year. In sum, exposure and education are required before the Chinese rules of business can be understood.

CONCLUSION

The Chinese market is very large and in particular the Chinese need for telecommunications is great. On the negative side, the picture is one of stiff market competition, very high operating costs, small profit margins, and often impeding bureaucracy. On the plus side, however, this may be a unique market that presents the greatest challenge to all exporters. To most Chinese, there must be more to doing business than just excellence in technology, expertise in marketing, and the relentless pursuit of profit. They may place more value on durable relationships and long-term goodwill. Understanding of this, from a limited Canadian perspective on the international marketplace, can only come about by the realization that people in different societies have differing value systems and social mores.

REFERENCES

Billowes, C., and Task Force on China Power Sector. (1986). Sector Brief for Telecommunications Sector, Ottawa.

Canada, Department of External Affairs. (1986). *Telecommunications products for world markets*. Ottawa.

Global Management Bureau. (1985). *China briefing book for SaskTel*. Toronto (unpublished manuscript).

"China's New Concessions for Foreign Investors: The 22 Points", Client Memorandum of Arthur Young International, Hong Kong, 1986.

Datapro Reports on International Telecommunications (1989), Delran, NJ.

Denny, D. (1986). China's Seventh Five-Year Plan, *The China Business Review*, 13(4).

Dymond, A., and Sector Working Committee on Telecommunications in China. (1988). *Telecommunications in China: A strategic analysis for Canadian involvement*. Teleconsult and CIDA.

The Economist, "No Order Too Small", February 18, 1989.

The Economist, "Yankee Gone Home", June 24, 1989.

The Economist Intelligence Unit, Country Report: China, North Korea, No. 1, 1988

Franco, G.L. (1987). The missing link requirements of the Third World establishment of a basic service. *World Communications*, Telecom '87, Geneva.

Gao, X. (1989). The future of Chinese Public Packet Switching Data Telecom Network. *China Telecommunications Construction*, 1(4).

Interlude. (1987). How to sell to China, Special Report, Hong Kong, February.

Kissinger, H. (1989). New forces in China will continue to the future. *Inside Guide, Synergism Marketing & Communications Inc.*, 3(2).

Lerner, N.C. (1987). Who's in control? Managing China's complex telecom industry, Part 1 - Telephony, August 24, 1987; Part 2 - Telephony, September 28.

MacDonald, T. (1986). The China concessional line of credit. Notes for a Speech to China Business Seminars, Canada-China Trade Council, Vancouver.

"Peking Agrees to Buy Nortel Phone Switches", *Globe & Mail Report on Business*, November 22, 1985.

"People's Republic of China", *Datapro Reports on International Telecommunications*, IT10-030-503, Delran, NJ. 1988.

Statistics Canada. (1988). Catalogue 65-003, 65-006, 65-202 and 65-203.

"Telecommunications in the Far East", *Datapro Reports on International Telecommunications*, IT10-30-102, Delran, NJ. 1988.

Worden, R.L., Savada, A.M., and Dolan, R.E. (1988). *China—A country study*. Washington, DC: Library of Congress, Federal Research Division.

Year Book of Peoples Republic of China, 1986.

Zhang, D. (1989). Development and modernization of telecommunications in New China. *China Telecommunications Construction*, 1(4).

Zita, K. (1987). Modernizing telecommunications in China. *Telephone Engineer & Management International*, October 15.

ACKNOWLEDGEMENTS

Particular thanks are due to Mr. Basil Pogue who reviewed the manuscript and made numerous suggestions for improvements both in content and writing style. My sincere thanks to Mrs. Susan Hope who edited the draft. Last but not least, my indebtedness to Mr. Graham Bradley for his encouragement to write this article.

TECHNOLOGY, EXPERTISE AND TRANSFER: COMPUTING SYSTEMS

R.B. Maguire and D. Lim
Department of Computer Science
University of Regina

INTRODUCTION

At present, there does not appear to be any trade in computing systems between Saskatchewan and the Chinese provinces of Jilin and Shandong. The term "computing systems" includes the hardware, that is, the actual machines on which computer programmes, especially the software, run. It was planned to describe in detail in this chapter successful trading agreements or joint ventures between Canadian and Chinese partners, but insufficient available data has militated against this. Instead, the main focus of this chapter is the view that there is much room for growth in trade in the computing sphere. Specifically, the chapter assesses the Saskatchewan computer industry and the need to promote reciprocal trade in this industry. Also, to facilitate the initial steps towards trade between the computing sectors of Jilin-Shandong, the chapter provides a list (Appendix 1,6) of Saskatchewan companies that have indicated their willingness to be contacted about potential trade and joint-venture agreements by organizations in China.

COMPUTING IN SASKATCHEWAN

The primary emphasis of the computing industry in Saskatchewan is software, especially the development of applications software for small-to-medium-size companies. There are several notable Saskatchewan enterprises which are producing hardware products for fields related to computing. For example, the Northern Telecom plant in Saskatoon produces fibre optics cable that is sold world-wide. SaskTel, the provincial telecommunications company, has installed over 5,000 kilometres of fibre in its telephone network. SED Systems of Saskatoon is actively developing control systems and satellite communication systems. Develcon, also of Saskatoon, sells its data switching systems across Canada and the United States. There are firms engaged in the design and manufacture of specialized control systems for agriculture. Duncan's Computers in Regina is the only large-scale manufacturer of microcomputers, and the Duncan's market is concentrated primarily in Saskatchewan and the neighbouring provinces of Alberta and Manitoba.

As Saskatoon has evolved into the "Silicon Valley" of Saskatchewan with the presence of Develcon and SED Systems, so has Regina become the dominant software and computer services centre in Saskatchewan. This is partly explained by the number of government offices and departments located in Regina. For example, the Saskatchewan Computer Utility or SaskComp was formed in 1973 in response to the needs of several government departments, as well as the Province's universities, for increased computer capacity. SaskComp was formed as a government-owned crown corporation. SaskComp then created a centralized, mainframe-based computer facility that satisfied most of the computing requirements of government by offering time-sharing and remote job-entry services. Although the initial objective of SaskComp was to offer primarily computer time, it became apparent quickly that there was a need and a market for more general consulting and programming services. SaskComp grew and operated profitably in this mode for 15 years.

In 1988, as part of a provincial government programme to transfer ownership of many publicly-owned corporations and service departments to private enterprise, the Westbridge Computer Corporation, an off-shoot of SaskComp, was formed. The Westbridge Corporation was really a mix of the computer division of SaskTel and two private companies (Pitsula and Rasmussen, 1990:168). Westbridge subsequently bought several other computing firms, including Management Services Limited of Regina, a firm which itself had 100 employees. In 1990, Westbridge moved into a new building on the campus of the University of Regina and brought into one location approximately $85 million of computing equipment. In 1991, Westbridge became ISM Information Management Systems Corporation of Regina after a major investment by IBM. ISM, with 2,750 employees and data centres in Vancouver, Calgary, Regina, Winnipeg, Ottawa and Toronto, is now the largest information systems management company in Canada (Regina Leader-Post, January 9, 1992: C6).

Another large computing firm in Regina is Cooperator's Data Services Limited (CDSL), a privately-owned company that specializes in insurance and banking, computer software and services. CDSL grew in size as it expanded its banking and insurance services to credit unions in Saskatchewan and several other Canadian provinces. CDSL's head office is in Regina where it operates a large data centre. There are also data centres in Ontario and British Columbia. All three data centres communicate with credit union offices and with each other over Telecom Canada's packet switched network. Both CDSL and ISM employ hundreds of computer professionals and are ranked among the largest computer service companies in Canada.

Saskatchewan also has several large computing organizations which exist as departments of companies whose primary business does not involve computer sales or services. For example, SaskTel is both a major shareholder in ISM as well as ISM's largest Regina based customer. Yet, SaskTel also continues to operate a large computer department with its own personnel. The Saskatchewan Wheat Pool owns and operates grain elevators for its farming community members. It also has a large data centre in Regina which has equipped and networked the Wheat Pool's five hundred grain elevators, each with microcomputers. Such data centres do not normally offer computer services on the same basis as ISM or CDSL. SaskTel, however, has formed a wholly-owned subsidiary, SaskTel International, to market other SaskTel technology. It is conceivable that Chinese firms currently doing business with these firms might be able to open discussions with their data centres. In the discussion which follows, only firms which normally compete directly in the computer field will be considered.

TRADE OPPORTUNITIES

In order to establish trade between Saskatchewan and Shandong and Jilin, there must, of course, be commodities of value to each area that can be offered in exchange. This is a somewhat simplistic statement, but it is unlikely and undesirable that a one-way flow of goods can exist. China has an abundance of manpower. The current level of skill of Chinese programmers has improved rapidly in the last few years, and has made for a widespread availability of microcomputers—a contrast to the lack of microcomputers in the early 1980s. At that time computer systems in China consisted mainly of mainframe and minicomputer systems accessible to limited numbers of programmers. At present, there is in China a growing number of skilled programmers and analysts. The dominant operating system there for business applications seems to be Unix; most of the applications run on minicomputers or Intel 80286 and 80386 microcomputers. The applications which have been developed to date are typically stand-alone systems, with little or no networking or data communication capabilities. For example, China's recent and rapid expansion of its tourist trade saw many computer systems installed in the new tourist hotels. With economic growth, banking became another area of rapid computer expansion. Many standard banking functions have now been computerized and current developments include the introduction of automated teller machines and the first efforts to tie bank branches together in on-line networks.

The Saskatchewan computer industry should not expect to sell computer systems directly to China. Existing systems which have been marketed by Saskatchewan firms, such as the CDSL banking or insurance systems and the ISM system for the Department of Social Services, are unlikely candidates for export to China simply because of the differences in policies and procedures. There could certainly be sales of components of Saskatchewan software, and there will be opportunities in the short term for contract development of custom software by Saskatchewan firms. Indeed, Saskatchewan firms have the experience and the resources to compete internationally for Chinese business. Hong Kong has a natural advantage owing to its geographical location, but staff turnover among programmers and analysts has been a severe problem there. However, China is developing its own computer industry rapidly. Consequently, it is more appropriate for Saskatchewan firms to offer their known experience in the management of software design and implementation rather than compete in the market for raw programming time and talent. Software development is a time-consuming process, much more so than the manufacture of hardware. China has programming resources but is in need of the type of management expertise available in Saskatchewan as the country begins to plan for the complex computer systems needed, for example, by its banking industry.

The foregoing suggests that trade should, in the main, be in the area of software rather than hardware. On the Chinese side, the manufacture of computer hardware is centred in the south of China, largely in Shanghai. In particular, computer manufacturing in Jilin and Shandong appears to be limited at present to the assembly of microcomputers which use components imported from other countries. It is unlikely that the products of such firms could compete directly in price with those that are being shipped to North America from factories in countries such as South Korea and

Singapore. Moreover, the hardware sector of the computer industry tends to be dominated by larger, established firms with extensive resources. It is clear that these firms are already developing joint-manufacturing ventures with Chinese firms. IBM, the world's largest computer company, recently opened a joint venture with the Tianjin Zhonghuan Advanced Information Products Corporation to manufacture IBM's PS/2 line of personal computers (Qu Yingpu, 1990: 2). The Tianjin Zhonghuan Computer Corporation is very well established in computer manufacturing in China with 13 factories and 4 research centres. The company had previously signed six joint-venture agreements with foreign investors. Yet, even with this previous experience and these resources, the agreement with IBM took two years of negotiations to complete.

It is certainly easier to enter the software market, although becoming and remaining successful in it is as difficult as taking the hardware route. Software development is labour intensive, although it does not require the capital plant and facilities of hardware manufacturing. In addition, there is more scope for original ideas and innovative software applications in both Canada and China than there is room to enter the hardware manufacturing market.

The Chinese government continues to stress vigorously the need for China to pursue joint-venture development both at home and abroad. In contrast to the escalating voices for protectionism, heard from the United States, Japan and Europe, the existing twinning arrangements between Saskatchewan and Jilin and Shandong indicate a fertile ground for joint-venture development (Government of Saskatchewan, 1987). Thus, the best opportunities for trade would seem to be long-term joint ventures which attempt to combine the manpower resources of China with the pool of experienced management talent in Saskatchewan in software-related pursuits. To discuss the similarities and differences between the Chinese and Canadian computing systems in more detail would be to deviate from the focus of this chapter which is to consider the potential of establishing such joint ventures.

THE SASKATCHEWAN CASE

Saskatchewan's labour force reached 495,000 in 1987, an increase of 40,000 from 1982. Approximately 24 percent or 118,000 of this work force are managerial or professional personnel (Government of Saskatchewan, 1989). Thus, Saskatchewan can offer Jilin and Shandong adequate levels of expertise in management. Although a breakdown is not available for the distribution of management personnel in the software industry, the practice of dividing programming personnel into teams and project-areas suggests at least a similar division of responsibilities in the computing profession.

Many of the computer systems developed in Saskatchewan are already marketed internationally. Such systems include the hospital and health care automation products of BDM Systems, a Saskatoon firm which markets its products across Canada and the United States, but also sells to the Middle East. Saskatchewan has been the North American birthplace of many universal systems such as universal medicare. As a consequence, there has been a need to develop large and complex systems that provide services throughout the province. The early experience in implementation of such systems resulted in a strong export market, as such policies were adopted by other provinces and states. Thus, there are firms in the computing industry in Saskatchewan with international marketing experience, although most of this experience is limited to North America. However, many of Saskatchewan's raw materials such as wheat, potash, oil and uranium are marketed internationally to a much more diverse marketplace. Thus, while little trade in the computer industry between Saskatchewan and China exists at present, the experience and infrastructure-support to facilitate such trade exist in the Province.

FACTORS AFFECTING TRADE OPPORTUNITIES

The presence of a large number of Chinese graduate students and scholars in the computer science programmes at the two universities in Saskatchewan might appear to be beneficial to the development of trade in computers. Certainly, these students have acquired a solid background in the use of computing technology and are moderately familiar with the development of computer services in Saskatchewan. But these students took their undergraduate studies in China where academic computing at the undergraduate level has little involvement with industry. There are no opportunities comparable with the co-operative work/study option which allows undergraduate students to work alternate terms in industry. The majority of these students have continued to work along generally theoretical lines after coming to Saskatchewan. The missing ingredient is the type of business computing background that is acquired, for example, by a typical computer science or administrative studies co-op programme student. The experience and, it appears, the natural inclination of these graduate students are to do the type of research that has not prepared them to participate in a joint venture. Canadian immigration laws allow visa students to take employment in Canada for a period not exceeding one year after graduation. Consequently, there is a reservoir of talent that might participate in a joint venture as programmers and analysts, and those who have experience and familiarity with both China and Canada. But, as mentioned above, it is not clear if these students desire to work in such an applied field after graduation.

There are significant differences in the education, training and background of programmers and analysts in China and Canada. For example, COBOL is not as widely used in China as in Canada. This is significant in that China's potential to supply programmers to perform maintenance on the large number of existing systems in Canada will be hampered by this lack of COBOL experience. Similar, though perhaps less severe, problems exist with respect to the use of fourth generation languages, computer-assisted, software-design technology and the types of operating systems used in the two countries. The selection of operating systems is a good example of inherent differences between the information systems of both Saskatchewan and China. In Saskatchewan, and generally across Canada and the United States, the Unix operating system is regarded as a system suitable to academic and engineering or scientific computing. In China, Unix is widely used on microcomputers with Intel 80286 or 80386 microprocessors for traditional business applications.

Another potential problem between Chinese and Canadian programmers is the difference in their perspective of the programmes they have developed. In Canada, programmers may be expected to subject their designs and programmes to a structured 'walk-through', for example. In this design practice or in equivalent processes, an analyst or programmer, as a member of a design team, must at regular intervals describe to the rest of the programming team the design or approach that he or she plans to follow. The team then criticizes the material presented in an attempt to discover weaknesses in the design during the often vigorous and heated exchanges between team members. The programmer or analyst must be able to detach himself or herself from his/her own work and understand that the 'walk-through' is intended to be a constructive process. This is not particularly easy and it may be considerably more difficult for a Chinese programmer or analyst. The Chinese educational system does not promote such confrontational exchanges in the classroom. The issue of "loss of face" may also be more important in the Chinese context. For example, Maguire (former head of the Computer Science Department, University of Regina) once asked a programmer in China why he had not translated an existing program from the BASIC programming language to the Fortran language. The Fortran language used on the computer was known to produce much faster running programmes than the BASIC language. The programmer knew that such a translation would dramatically improve the speed of calculations. His reply was that to do so would insult the original author of the program.

The Chinese approach to business also tends to contrast with the more budget- and deadline-oriented nature of information systems development in Canada. This approach is changing as more systems are developed in China on a contract basis among industry, institutions and companies that are engaged in software development as their primary business. However, at present many of the software development organizations are government supported, as are their customers. The customers are also less likely to have their own in-house computer expertise than a corresponding Western firm. Thus, due dates for delivery of software tend to be postponed with less rancour than such occurrences in Canada. This practice is changing rapidly as more Chinese businesses and industries implement their second or third generation of computer systems, and the financial stability of companies is more dependent on quick and efficient conversion between computer systems.

In Chapter 1, Dale described the differences between the centralized and decentralized approaches used in business in the two countries. This difference is compounded by the number of small companies that constitute the information systems sector in Saskatchewan. Apart from the few large organizations, such as ISM and CDSL, the majority of the remaining firms are small companies with little or no experience in the international market. It will be difficult for these firms to establish joint-venture initiatives because they lack the infrastructure and the funding to do so. There is no provincial organization available in Saskatchewan to help establish initial contacts in the field of information systems.

There are numerous other factors that will be encountered and must be considered by companies in both Canada and China that would enter into a joint-business venture. These factors range from travel difficulties, whether it be the problem of the Canadian partner getting around in China or the high cost of travel in Canada for the Chinese partner, to language difficulties and cultural background. Such issues are generic concerns for any trading relationships, regardless of the industries that are represented. Recommended reading for both sides is the *Proceedings of the Tenth Annual Canadian M.B.A. Conference*, "Doing Business with China". The papers presented at this conference came from both Canadian and Chinese business and industry representatives, and ranged from case-study reports to step-by-step plans for initiating a joint venture.

CONTACTING SASKATCHEWAN COMPUTING FIRMS

The current low level of trade and joint ventures among the provinces of Saskatchewan, Jilin and Shandong does not allow for detailed description of case studies of joint ventures. It would be preferable to provide a Saskatchewan road map to guide firms interested in initiating trade arrangements, but since this is impossible, a survey of the Saskatchewan firms located in the cities of Regina and Saskatoon was undertaken. These firms were asked if they would be interested in having their businesses listed in this chapter, and if they would be willing to respond to contacts from China. Those listed (Appendix 1,6) responded positively. The list may be used as a starting point by Chinese organizations interested in beginning a dialogue with Saskatchewan companies, with a view to co-operation in trade or a joint venture in computing.

There is no guarantee of success in this approach because the firms were simply asked if they would be interested in being approached by a company or institution in China. That is, the firms listed have not committed themselves to undertaking a project with a Chinese partner. They are, however, willing to discuss the possibilities and potentials. It is hoped that Appendix 1,6 will at least provide a starting point for initial discussions. The firms were requested to provide the following information:

- name, address and telephone number of the company,
- the name and/or the title of the person to contact,
- a brief description of the primary area of expertise of the company,
- the computer systems and languages or application packages used by the company, and
- the number of employees in the company.

The majority of the firms listed are privately-owned companies and are of a small size when compared with the staff sizes of many Chinese organizations. Readers in China should understand the difference between the number of employees in a Canadian company in comparison with that in a Chinese company. The number of employees in Canada may seem very small, compared with the number of employees in China. However, salary levels in Canada are very high in relation to the cost of equipment and services. This explains why many of the firms involved in the software industry in Canada are both small and very specialized. For an initial venture, both of these factors could be positive. It would be wise to select an application area that is narrow in scope in order to facilitate communication between the partners and allow both sides to focus their expertise on a specific problem or development area. Moreover, a small firm, although more limited in available resources, may be both more responsive to and energetic about a joint venture. Admittedly, if there is potential for rapid growth or the need for a massive marketing campaign, for example, it may be advisable to approach a larger company. A piece of information that was not requested in the survey mentioned above was the year of incorporation of the company. This information would indicate the maturity and stability of the firm. Because many firms in the computing industry are relatively young, the reader should exercise caution in exploring fully the financial strength and commitment of a potential partner, particularly in initial discussions. It must also be stated that the descriptions of software and expertise, given in Appendix 1,6, were from the companies and are restated with only minor editorial changes.

The smaller firms listed could be at a definite disadvantage, for they lack the financial resources that could make for success. These companies and their owners will need to be convinced that there is a good opportunity for success, that is, profits, in a joint venture. Moreover, limited resources means that a profitable or at least a break-even situation must be reached quickly. On a more positive note, small-sized and limited ownership means that quick decisions can be made without involving large numbers of administrators. Given available federal and provincial government programmes to help small firms expand their business internationally, these firms are frequently too impatient to take advantage of such programmes because of the delays and administrative procedures that must be followed in obtaining government funds. The Chinese partner in a joint-venture discussion should understand also that Canadian or Saskatchewan government support for a joint venture may be more difficult to obtain than similar Chinese government support. Issues of government support for private enterprises can be extremely complex in Canada. In a competitive environment, even if the joint venture is clearly desirable, the government must not be seen to be giving an unfair advantage to one firm over its competitors.

The Saskatchewan Software Directory (Saskatchewan Government, 1990) gives a longer list of software companies known to the Science and Technology Division of the Saskatchewan Economic Diversification and Trade Department. The second edition of this directory, dated June, 1990, lists eight-five companies and may be obtained without charge (see Appendix 2,6).

CONCLUSION

Viewed optimistically, trade between Saskatchewan and the Chinese provinces of Shandong and Jilin appears feasible. The geographic similarities between the areas, the twinning programmes which have been in place for several years between cities and institutions, and the growing interest in China by Saskatchewan people are precursors for bilateral trade. However, the challenge is formidable. It will certainly take much time and careful planning to develop this trade. Joint ventures could well be a reliable catalyst for trade in the three provinces, assuming that computing entrepreneurs attempt to meet this challenge in the next few years.

REFERENCES

Government of Saskatchewan. (1987). *Saskatchewan Backgrounder on Trade*, Trade Negotiations Secretariat, Regina, Saskatchewan.

Government of Saskatchewan. (1989). *The Saskatchewan Promise*, Saskatchewan Trade and Investment, Regina, Saskatchewan.

Government of Saskatchewan. (1990). *Saskatchewan Software Directory*, Second Edition, Science and Technology Division, Saskatchewan Economic Diversification and Trade, Regina, Saskatchewan.

McMaster Faculty of Business. (1989). "Doing Business with China", *Proceeding of the Tenth Annual Canadian M.B.A. Conference*, January 13-14, 1989, Hamilton, Ontario

Pitsula, J.M., and Rasmussen, K. (1990). *Privatizing a province*. Vancouver: New Star Books.

Qu Yingpu. (1990). "IBM sets up joint firm", *China Daily*, Wednesday, August 29, 1990, p. 2, Beijing

Regina Leader-Post. (1992). "ISM building in Winnipeg", *Leader-Post*, Thursday, January 9, 1992, p. C6

ACKNOWLEDGEMENT

We are grateful to those companies which responded to our survey with suggestions, comments and product literature. The Science and Technology Division of the Saskatchewan Economic Diversification and Trade Department was most helpful in providing copies of several of our references. We especially want to thank Dr. Edward Weynes, Faculty of Administration, University of Regina, for providing numerous excellent sources on the problems of international trade.

APPENDIX 1,6: LIST OF COMPANIES

(in alphabetical order by company name)

Axon Development Corporation
102 - 294 Venture Cres.
Saskatoon, Sask. S7K 6M1

Telephone: (306) 652-8202

Contact: Ken Sparrow, President

Primary area of expertise:
Software development tools and languages, object-oriented 4th generation computer languages.

Systems/Languages/Packages used/supported:
Unix, Xenix, MS-DOS, Macintosh, VMS.

Number of employees: Omitted

Note: An MS-DOS tutorial demonstration of the company's "C4" object-oriented 4GL is available by contacting the company.

Celestial Computer Systems
815 Colony Street
Saskatoon, Sask. S7N 0S2

Telephone: (306) 373-8202

Contact: Richard Mills, Owner

Primary area of expertise:
Computer accounting, point of sale software, installation support and service.

Systems/Languages/Packages used/supported:
Most major accounting systems including AccPac, Bedford and Abacus. IBM and compatible computers.

Number of employees: 3

Deloitte & Touche
Suite 400 - 122 1st Ave. South
Saskatoon, Sask. S7K 7E5

Telephone: (306) 244-8900

Fax: (306) 652-2686

Contact: Ronn Lepage, Partner, Computer Services

Primary area of expertise:
Microcomputer based accounting software. Local area networks.

Systems/Languages/Packages used/supported:
MS-DOS, OS/2, Unix. AccPac and companion products. Platinum.

Number of employees: 6,000 across Canada; 200 in Saskatchewan;
120 in Saskatoon.

Fisher + Associates
201 - 901 3rd Avenue North
Saskatoon, Sask. S7K 2K4

Telephone: (306) 664-4666

Fax: (306) 664-4746

Contact: Robert Fisher

Primary area of expertise:
Professional computer consulting: designing information systems/networks; procurement of hardware and software; installation; custom programming; training and on-going support; accounting and business management consulting.

Systems/Languages/Packages used/supported:
O.S.A.S., Man_trak, E.D.I., Unix, Xenix, AIX environments.

Number of employees: 10

Garman Software Services Ltd.
209 - 2121 Airport Drive
Saskatoon, Sask. S7L 6W5

Telephone: (306) 242-6322

Fax: (306) 244-1065

Contact: Roy Engel

Primary area of expertise:
Custom programming, application design, conversion of software between computers.

Systems/Languages/Packages used/supported:
IBM System 36: RPG II, IBM Application System 400: RPG 400, beverage bottling, distribution and financial applications.

Number of employees: 20

GDS & Associates Systems Ltd.
103 - 2629 29th Ave.
Regina, Sask. S4S 2N9

Telephone: (306) 586-7832

Fax: (306) 584-3822

Contact: Willis Groshong, President

Primary area of expertise:
Custom software development for government organizations as well as oil and gas companies.

Systems/Languages/Packages used/supported:
IBM MVS/XA: COBOL, IMS, DB2, SAS; DEC VAX/VMS: COBOL, Oracle; Prime/Primeos: Blacksmith, Information; HP/Unix: Oracle, C; IBM PC: local area networks (Novell), Dataflex

Number of employees: 25

Generation 5 Technology
575 Park Street
Regina, Sask. S4N 5B2

Telephone: (306) 721-2362

Fax: (306) 721-2472

Contact: Len Exner

Primary Area of Expertise:
Generation 5 Technology Ltd. is an industry leader in Geographic Information
System (GIS) software development. Their software is marketed under the
name "Geo/SQL (MunMAP)". Areas of expertise include CAD systems, GIS
systems, database languages and civil engineering software.

Systems/Languages/Packages Used/Supported:
The Geo/SQL (MunMAP) software operates with the MS-DOS and Unix
operating systems. Geo/SQL utilizes AutoCAD graphics and industry standard
databases which include RBase, DBase III and IV, Oracle, Gupta and other SQL
databases.

Number of employees: 20

Note: The Generation 5 Technology office in Regina is a branch office of a
company with offices in Toronto, Edmonton, Calgary, Saskatoon and
Denver. The company can provide information on how its software has
been used in an international project to map statistical information on
China.

Intelligent Transportation Systems Corp.
142 - 105th Street East
Saskatoon, Sask. S7N 123

Telephone: (306) 955-6633

Fax: (306) 374-2442

Contact: Greg Hentz, President

Primary area of expertise:
Vehicle maintenance and management software. The software is offered under
the name "Fleet Plus". It was developed by a large fleet operator to schedule
preventive maintenance activities, monitor fuel and oil performance as well as
streamline fleet administrative activities.

Systems/Languages/Packages used/supported: MS-DOS and Novell networks.

Number of employees: 4

MicroAide Services
1024 Winnipeg Street
Regina, Sask. S4R 8P8

Telephone: (306) 757-5788

Fax: (306) 757-5410

Contact: Ron Wild, General Manager

Primary area of expertise:
Consulting services; technical support including implementation assistance, custom programming and hardware support; training.

Systems/Languages/Packages used/supported:
Microcomputer end-user applications: databases, spreadsheets and word processing. All windowing environments supported. Novell network and C programming expertise.

Number of employees: 5

Professional Computer Services Inc.
5th Floor, 1821 Scarth St.
Regina, Sask. S4P 2G9

Telephone: (306) 359-0668

Fax: (306) 757-1865

Contact: David J. Wormsbecker

Primary area of expertise:
Design, development and implementation of customized computer software. Currently have one package for sale, ProMed, a medical billing software application.

Systems/Languages/Packages used/supported:
Experienced in IBM compatible systems including mainframes and mini-computers; supporting a variety of programming languages.

Number of employees: 18

Profit Systems Inc.
124 - 15 Innovation Boulevard
Innovation Place
Saskatoon, Sask. S7N 2X8

Telephone: (306) 975-3737

Contact: Wayne Lambie, President

Primary area of expertise:
Custom software for business and industry, provincial and federal government departments and agencies, education and health care institutions as well as the manufacturing and transportation sectors.

Systems/Languages/Packages used/supported:
MS-DOS and Unix environments; C programming.

Number of employees: 7

Sage Consulting Group
2169 McIntyre St.
Regina, Sask. S4P 2R8

Telephone: (306) 525-5265

Fax: (306) 525-0584

Contact: Clare Kirkland, Director

Primary area of expertise:
Technology management consulting; custom software for on-line transaction processing systems; systems integration; local area networks; image processing systems.

Systems/Languages/Packages used/supported:
IBM, DEC, Data General and Bull. MS-DOS lans (OS/2 and Novell). Unix lans.

Number of employees: 20

Software 2000 Inc.
Strathdee Centre
402 - 2206 Dewdney Ave.
Regina, Sask. S4R 1H3

Telephone: (306) 777-0850

Fax: (306) 565-8505

Contact: Bonnie Jackson

Primary area of expertise:
Office information systems. Unix technology in networking solutions. OS/2 Lan Manager in local area networks. Application development in PROGRESS. Training and support accompany all installations.

Systems/Languages/Packages used/supported:
C, Basic, Pascal, Datatrieve, Cobol, dBase, Fortran/77, Imlac Assembler, GPDS, Snobol, Ingres, Oracle, Powerhouse. WordPerfect/WordPerfect Office and an extensive list of microcomputer packages. Operating Systems: Unix, VAX/VMS, VM/CMS, MS-DOS, RT-11, RSTS, CP/M. Hardware: DEC, IBM, Apple, Sun, Commodore and Sperry.

Number of employees: 16

Standard Computer Limited
15 Innovation Blvd.
Saskatoon, Sask.   S7N 2X8

Telephone: (306) 975-1208

Fax: (306) 975-0636

Contact: Jack Lazariuk, General Manager

Primary area of expertise:
Image processing and databases. Experienced in the attachment of Apple Macintosh microcomputers to various input devices such as cameras and microscopes and the processing of the resultant images.

Systems/Languages/Packages used/supported:
Apple Macintosh and A/UX operating systems, MS-DOS, Pascal, C, Hypertalk and assembly language programming.

Number of employees: 4

Umbrella Accounting Group
448 Witney Ave. South
Saskatoon, Sask. S7M 3K7

Telephone: (306) 978-1877

Contact: Tony Cabral, President

Primary area of expertise:
Computer consulting for small businesses, specialization in property management.

Systems/Languages/Packages used/supported:
Lotus 1-2-3, Dbase III and IV, Pascal.

Number of employees: 1

Uptime Laser Products
501 - 4010 Pasqua St.
Regina, Sask. S4S 7B9

Telephone: (306) 586-4678

Contact: Brian Smyth, President

Primary area of expertise:
Laser printer toner cartridge and photoreceptor assembly. Sale of laser printer supplies. Maintenance of laser printers.

Systems/Languages/Packages used/supported:
IBM and Apple products are supported.

Number of employees: 5

Vercom Systems Ltd.
910 - 1867 Hamilton St.
Regina, Sask. S4P 2C2

Telephone: (306) 757-3510

Fax: (306) 525-0824

Contact: Paul Verhelst

Primary area of expertise:
Business application software with a specialization in utility billing systems.
Software applications are also developed for clients on a custom basis.

Systems/Languages/Packages used/supported:
Hardware familiarity: IBM 3090, DEC VAX, IBM PCs and clones, local area
networks. Software: COBOL, SAS, Easytrieve, C, PC Tools. Databases: DB2,
Adabas, Oracle, SQL Server, IDMS, VSAM.

Number of employees: 20

APPENDIX 2,6: GOVERNMENT OF SASKATCHEWAN CONTACT

Science and Technology Division
Saskatchewan Economic Diversification and Trade
206 - 15 Innovation Boulevard
Saskatoon, Sask. S7N 2X8

Tel: (306) 933-7200

Fax: (306) 933-8244

FOREIGN INVESTMENT IN CHINA: A GENERAL GUIDE

Edy L. Wong

Grant MacEwan College, Edmonton, Alberta

INTRODUCTION

China has been undergoing a process of economic transformation ever since economic reform was implemented in late 1978. The objectives of economic reform were to modernize an inefficient, technically-backward industrial base, to overcome the weaknesses of an overly centralized economy, and to enhance the material well-being of the Chinese people. Since then, important institutional and structural changes have occurred in virtually all sectors of the Chinese economy. The policies most responsible for these changes include expansion of the private economy, financial and fiscal reforms, greater enterprise autonomy, labour market reform, and liberalization of external commercial relations. Although many difficulties remain extant, the effects of economic reform to date are seen in a Chinese economy that has grown in market orientation and prosperity as a result.

The foreign dimension of China's reform policy is called the opendoor policy. The essence of this policy is to de-emphasize the principle of economic "self-reliance" and to promote foreign trade and investment as a new vehicle of economic development. This change in development strategy was motivated by both internal and external considerations. Externally, the economic success of the Asian Newly Industrialized Countries (NICs) through export promotion was at once a reminder of China's own economic inferiority and a lesson in the benefits of foreign trade and investment. If China was to keep abreast with the economies in the Asia-Pacific region, it must become a member of the international economic community. Meanwhile, low levels of income and technological expertise at home meant that the investment capital and modern technology required for China's modernization were unavailable domestically and could only be obtained abroad. Increased exports and foreign investment thus became important sources of the additional resources required for capital formation and technology imports.

The potential contributions that the foreign trade and investment could make to China's modernization drive were recognized as early as 1975 by some of China's top leaders, including Deng Xiaoping. Subsequently, the need for Chinese economic development was magnified in the 1977 post-Mao economic adjustment period. During this time, China's effort to modernize its economy through large-scale importation of foreign plants and equipment not only resulted in a foreign exchange crisis, but additionally demonstrated the need for a sustainable source of foreign exchange and long-term financing for its development programmes. China must increase her foreign exchange earnings through increased exports and foreign investment if modernization of its economy was to become a reality. Therefore, a series of measures were later adopted to encourage foreign trade and investment, thereby giving rise to the open-door policy.

The introduction of the open-door policy was greeted with much excitement outside China. Given its vast consumer market and abundance of low-cost manpower, the opening-up of China was seen by many as the birth of a new market and a new source of low-cost production facilities. However, other than Hong Kong investors, who were quick to take advantage of China's open door, Western capital did not enter into China in any significant quantity until the mid-1980s. By 1987, the level of direct foreign investment in China had reached $2.3 billion US. The top three investing nations in China were Hong Kong, the United States, and Japan, each accounting for 68.6 percent, 11.4 percent, and 9.5 percent, respectively, of the total. Canada's share of the total was 0.4 percent in that same year (ACFERT, 1988: 682). Clearly, there is room to increase Canada's share in foreign investment in China.

The aim of this chapter is to promote a better understanding of China's open-door policy and foreign investment environment in Canada by providing a brief history of foreign investment in China and a general guide to China's foreign investment approval process. The subsequent sections of this chapter will begin with an overview of foreign investment and attendant development in China since the inception of the open-door policy. It will be followed by a discussion of the three principal types of foreign investment in China. A description of China's foreign investment approval process will then be given before the concluding section of the chapter.

A BRIEF HISTORY OF FOREIGN INVESTMENT IN CHINA

The decision to encourage foreign investment in China was a bold, new experiment in the history of the People's Republic of China (PRC). It began with the establishment of four Special Economic Zones (SEZs) in the southern provinces of Guangdong and Fujian. These economic zones were special because foreign investors were granted special incentives and privileges and were allowed to operate relatively freely in an environment friendly to market forces. The SEZs were also intended as an economic laboratory where Chinese officials and enterprises could learn about the working of a market economy. However, given their lack of a mature industrial base and geographical isolation from other Chinese industrial centres, the SEZs were never successful in meeting expectations of the Chinese authorities and had merely become low-cost production centres for Hong Kong manufacturers (Wong, 1987). By the early 1980s, it had become apparent that, if China was to harness effectively the benefits of foreign investment, greater efforts would have to be made to encourage foreign investors elsewhere in China.

Outside the SEZs, foreign investment in China was initially allowed only as Chinese-foreign joint ventures and was subject to a rather rigorous regulatory regime. The "Law of the People's Republic of China on Joint Ventures, Using Chinese and Foreign Investment" or the "Joint-Venture Law" was promulgated by the National People's Congress in July, 1979 to regulate activities of Chinese-foreign joint ventures in China. The joint-venture law represented the rudiment of a legal foundation for foreign investment that has since continued to evolve and develop to create a better investment climate in China. However, because of the immaturity of the legal system, the initial inflow of foreign capital was less than expected and totalled $1,769 million US between 1979 and 1982 (Moser, 1984: 106). Most of this investment, which was contributed in labour-intensive, small-to-medium industrial projects and hotel construction, originated mainly from Hong Kong rather than from western sources (Chai, 1983). Therefore, additional reforms and incentives were announced in 1983 to enhance China's appeals to Western investors.

The measures mentioned above began with more flexible forms of foreign investment and legislative changes aimed at strengthening the legal system and protecting the rights of foreign investors. The implementing regulations of the joint-venture law were also announced, however belatedly, to clarify the intents of this law, and greater freedom was accorded provincial and local authorities in conducting foreign trade and investment negotiations. The response to the above changes was a 41 percent rise in foreign investment to $916 million US in 1983 (Harding, 1987: 154). Concomitantly, 1983 also saw a change in the character of foreign investment from mainly relatively small, low-technology ventures to include some large, technologically sophisticated, industrial projects, such as the American Motors Corporation's venture for the production of Jeep vehicles in Beijing.

Further impetus was given to the open-door policy when special trading areas and development zones were established in 14 coastal cities in 1984. Like the SEZs, special incentives and advantages were made available to attract overseas investors to these 14 cities where relatively developed industrial and trading facilities were found. These same privileges were later extended to the Yellow River, and Pearl River delta areas, making most of China's population and industrial centres special target areas for foreign investment. Subsequently, in 1985, 11 less prosperous western provinces were given permission to receive foreign investment (TKP, 1989). Today, virtually every region of China is eligible for foreign investment and, according to former premier Zhao Ziyang, plans were afoot to open up China's entire seaboard as a special investment zone (Economist, 1988).

While foreign investment steadily increased between 1983 and 1986 in response to the further opening-up of China, many remaining obstacles had conspired to prevent China from becoming an even larger recipient of foreign investment. The list of complaints commonly cited by foreign investors included the high cost of many inputs such as land, housing, labour and office space; a lack of adequate training and discipline of Chinese workers; low quality and insecure supply of some raw materials; difficulties in obtaining Chinese currency loans; an immature legal system; an overburdened communications and transportation infrastructure; and convoluted lines of authority in the Chinese bureaucracy (Harding, 1987: 160). In addition, because foreign joint ventures were required to maintain their own foreign exchange balance, any local profits not matched by an inflow of foreign exchange through exports or new investment could not be easily repatriated. The effect of those constraints was to reduce the attractiveness of China's domestic market to foreign investors. The above problems were further aggravated by China's balance of payments difficulties in 1985 and early 1986, which led to the devaluation of the renminbi and a rise in the cost of imported inputs. As a result, there was increased dissatisfaction with the investment climate in China.

In an effort to improve the investment environment, a number of new policies were adopted by the State Council in 1986. The promulgation of the Law of the PRC on wholly foreign-owned enterprises in April formally extended the practice of wholly foreign-owned enterprises beyond the SEZs. Although only ventures intending to introduce advanced technology or to export most of their production would be allowed to operate as wholly foreign-owned enterprises, this law has nevertheless provided a legal basis for such enterprises, for the first time, in a socialist country.

Later in 1986, this law was followed by other initiatives undertaken by the State Council to address the concerns of foreign investors (Cohen et al., 1987: 11-14). First, the cost of doing business in China was decreased through reduction in taxes, land use and utilities fees, and in the wages of workers of foreign ventures. Second, foreign ventures were promised better access to crucial state-controlled inputs, such as water, electricity, communication, transportation, and renminbi loans. Third, the foreign investment review process was made more efficient by establishing deadlines for government approvals and by creating local agencies that could expedite the approval process. Fourth, foreign ventures were granted greater authority over production plans, enterprise and personal management, and import and export decisions. Fifth, special tax incentives were made available to foreign joint ventures which either produced for exports or used advanced technology in their production.

At the local level, these incentives were matched by additional concessions by some provincial and municipal governments. For example, cities such as Beijing, Guangzhou, Shanghai, and Tianjin undertook to establish foreign-enterprise materials and equipment-supply companies for the express purpose of producing for foreign ventures at the same cost as local state enterprises. Despite the significance of these changes, it was the Chinese authorities' willingness to learn from past difficulties that was considered by many to be the most encouraging developments that year (Sullivan, 1987: 8).

The consequence of these changes were a 30.7 percent increase in foreign investment commitment and a 23.5 percent rise in actual foreign investment in 1987 (Cheng, 1989: 59). The result of China's efforts at enhancing its investment climate during the last decade is a set of foreign investment incentives that compares very favourably with those of other Asian countries today. For example, in addition to various tax concessions, China's restrictions on foreign-equity holdings are less stringent than those of South Korea, or the Philippines, or Thailand; while its corporate tax rates are comparable with those of the Philippines, Thailand, Singapore and Taiwan (Dean, 1988: 49). However, despite such investments, other problems have continued to detract from China's foreign investment policy. For example, although existing problems such as strict limitation on conversion and repatriation of renminbi earnings, inadequate patent and trademark protection, and barriers to domestic market are slowly being resolved, a shortage of skilled workers and retrenchment in capital spending have emerged as new dampers on foreign investment (Cheng, 1989: 59-60). An austerity programme instituted by the Chinese government in October 1988 to combat spiralling inflation has not only reduced the domestic credit supply to existing Sino-foreign joint ventures but also has led to a re-centralization of decision-making power.

Consequently, some sectors previously open to foreign investment are now discouraged or are required to obtain approval by the Ministry of Foreign Economic Relations (MOFERT) irrespective of size, location, or type (Cheng, 1989: 59).

Instead, the most important impact on investment conditions in China will likely remain the pace of general economic development in the foreseeable future. The constraints on opportunities for foreign investment in developing nations, such as China, are always closely influenced by its macro-economic performance. And as a developing nation, the risks confronting foreign investors in China are not common for foreign investment in developing countries which often offer excellent profit opportunities for those who are able to manage such risks effectively (Brewer et al., 1986). For example, the many Hong Kong investors have reaped considerable returns on their investments in China in the last decade.

TYPES OF FOREIGN INVESTMENT IN CHINA

There are four types of foreign investment that have been undertaken in China: compensation trade, co-operative investments, equity joint ventures, and wholly-owned foreign investments. Of these, only the last three necessitate a direct foreign investment.

Compensation Trade

Compensation trade is the simplest form of foreign investment in China and was first employed by Hong Kong investors to invest in neighbouring Guangdong and Fujian provinces in the mid-1970s. In its pure form, compensation trade may be defined as "any transaction involving the purchase by a Chinese entity of foreign capital equipment and technology" (Moser, 1984: 109). As such, compensation trade is fundamentally a loan transaction with the agreed purchase price of the equipment being the loan principal. This loan principal and the attendant interest charges are to be repaid in fixed instalments of goods produced with the equipment purchased. Because of the two-way flows of equipment and goods necessitated by this arrangement, compensation trade may also be combined with a processing or assembly operation agreement. Under a combined procession and compensation trade agreement, the foreign investor, in addition to the equipment he purchased through compensation trade, will also supply raw materials to the Chinese enterprise. The cost of this will then be deducted from the instalment payments on the purchased equipment. Similarly, when an assembly operation agreement is added to the compensation trade transaction, the Chinese will undertake partly to assemble a product with parts provided by the foreign investor. The modification of direct compensation trade to allow for the foreign equipment to be paid in goods, other than those produced by these equipment, is called counter purchase or comprehensive compensation.

Compensation trade is an attractive way to invest in China for several reasons. First, the risk is generally small because of the relatively short duration and low dollar value of compensation trade agreements. Typically, the terms of these agreements are between three and five years with an investment of less than $1 million US (Moser, 1984: 110). Second, compensation trade agreement are highly flexible and do not require direct managerial participation by the foreign investor. This means that the foreign investor is free from the frustrations and difficulties that foreign businesses usually experience when operating in China. Third, incomes generated by compensation trade to date are not yet subject to Chinese taxation. However, because of the trade element in compensation trade, the foreign investor must be prepared for the problems usually associated with trading with China, such as defective goods and lateness in delivery.

Co-operative Investment Arrangements

Co-operative investment arrangements have been an important vehicle of foreign investment in China to date. Even with the rise in equity joint ventures, such arrangements still accounted for 40.3 percent of direct investment in China during the period from January to September 1988 (Cheng, 1989: 59). This type of investment comprises a variety of arrangements whereby foreign businesses may co-operate with Chinese enterprises in jointly producing certain goods or services for a specific period of time. These arrangements may be broadly classified into two categories: joint-development agreement and contractual joint ventures.

Joint-development Agreements

The main aim of joint-development agreements in China is usually the exploration and development of offshore oil and gas reserves. In this type of agreement, the financial burden of exploration is shouldered entirely by the foreign investor who, for this contribution, will be given the right to develop jointly any oil and gas finds for commercial purposes. The initial exploration costs will then be taken into account in determining the foreign investor's share of any future incomes generated by the resources. Because of their unique character, joint-petroleum development activities in China are governed by a regulatory regime consisting of rules and regulations specifically designed for them. They include, among others, the National Petroleum Regulations, the Model Petroleum Contract, special customs rules, and the tax and registration regulations.

Contractual Joint Ventures

Contractual joint ventures, also known as co-operative joint-ventures or co-production agreements, are by far the most prevalent mode of co-operative investment arrangement in China. These ventures may take two different forms. In its first form, no legal entity, separate from the contracting parties, is created for the purpose of the joint venture. Rather, the parties will enter into a contractual relationship to operate the venture through a joint-management body led by a foreign-appointed director. The obligations, rights, profit shares, and liabilities of each party vis-a-vis the joint venture are defined in the underlying contract. Because of the absence of a distinct business entity, contributions made by each contracting party, which may be in cash or in kind, are not treated as equity capital in the joint ventures. This allows the contracting parties to determine the distribution of profits or products of the ventures as they choose instead of in proportion to specific ownership shares. As a result, an agreement on a precise valuation of their contributions is not needed, thereby removing a problem frequently encountered in equity joint-venture negotiations.

Alternatively, a co-operative joint venture may be operated through a legal entity separate and distinct from the contracting parties. The business entity thus created is essentially a partnership arrangement (which does not automatically enjoy "limited liabilities" status) under the co-operative joint-venture law. The highest authority over the joint venture is invested in a board of directors led by a foreign-appointed chairperson. Although contributors to the venture and profit shares remain matters of contractual negotiation, valuation of each partner's contribution to the joint venture is now necessary to establish a registered capital. This is because, in order to obtain the legal person status, a registered capital and its amount must be stated at the time the joint venture registers with the State Administration for Industry and Commerce (SAIC). Furthermore, if "limited liability" is desired by the joint venture, it must publish its registered capital and declare itself to be a limited liability company as provided under the General Principles of Civil Law (GPCL) (Cohen, 1988: 15-16). A non-legal person joint venture is not endowed with limited liability under the GPCL.

In addition to their flexibility, co-operative joint ventures also enjoy other advantages embodied in the co-operative venture law. First, unlike the equity joint-venture law, which requires a 25 percent minimum for the foreign investor's contribution to be registered capital, no such minimum exists for co-operative joint ventures. Second, a 45-day maximum is set on the approval process but 90 days for equity joint ventures. Third, while reductions in registered capital during the contract period are prohibited for equity joint ventures, early recovery of capital by foreign investors in co-operative joint ventures is permitted. Fourth, investors in co-operative joint ventures are accorded great flexibility in the management of their ventures which may include third-party management through management contracts.

Equity Joint Ventures

Despite a slow beginning, equity joint ventures have emerged as the most important vehicle of foreign investment in China in recent years, accounting for 52.8 percent of all direct investment in the first nine months of 1988 (Cheng, 1989: 59). These ventures are highly favoured by Chinese legislation and are governed by the most developed legal regime on foreign investment in China. According to the equity joint-venture law, equity joint ventures are separate, legal entities with the status of Chinese legal persons, fully subject to and protected by Chinese laws. They must assume the form of limited liability companies, with a maximum life of 50 years. Although foreign investors are required to hold at least 25 percent of the registered capital, no maximum is specified, and this makes it theoretically possible for a foreign investor to own up to 99 percent of an equity joint venture. In practice, however, distributions of ownership between foreign investors and their Chinese partners have usually been 50/50. The management responsibilities are also fairly shared by the venture partners through a board with a Chinese-appointed chairperson.

Furthermore, a great degree of flexibility exists in the capital contributions of venture partners. Their equity contributions may assume the form of cash or in-kind contributions such as equipment, technology, trademarks, and other intangible assets. Ownership of the registered capital may also be transferred or assigned to a third party with the consent of the other party and the original approval-granting authority. However, unlike the co-operative joint venture, reductions in the registered capital of an equity joint venture is not allowed during the term of the contract, though permission may be granted for an increase.

A key advantage of equity joint ventures over other forms of joint ventures is the special tax regime that allows lower tax liabilities for foreign investors. Because the venture is responsible for all income taxes arising from its activities, the foreign investor is not required to pay any further income taxes which will presumably be characterized by higher tax rates. Clearly, the benefit of a limited liability is also significant in confining the foreign investor's risk exposure to his original investment.

Wholly Foreign-Owned Enterprises

The right to operate a wholly foreign-owned enterprise in China was first granted to foreign investors in the Special Economic Zones (SEZs) in 1979. The early history of such enterprises consisted primarily of small manufacturing establishments set up by Hong Kong investors. It was not until the promulgation of the Law of the PRC on Wholly Foreign-owned Enterprises in April 1986 that the same right was extended to cover all of China. However, unlike foreign investment in the SEZs the opportunity to establish a wholly foreign-owned enterprise elsewhere in China is available only to foreign investors who will either introduce advanced technology to China or export most of their production. The response to this policy change has been an increase in wholly foreign-owned investment from 1.1 percent of total direct foreign investment to 6.3 percent of the same between January to September, 1988 (Cheng, 1989: 59), and the numbers of wholly foreign-owned firms has also risen from 16 in 1986 to 1,800 in 1990 (Barale, 1991: 8).

Although the essence of the law on wholly foreign-owned enterprises is similar to regulations governing such enterprises in the SEZs, this law, nevertheless, offers foreign investors greater autonomy and protection than those on joint ventures. For example, assurance of the long-term rights of foreign investors are provided for in several provisions of this law, guaranteeing the right for profit remittance, protection from state expropriation, and autonomy in enterprise management and operation. The status of a Chinese legal person (though not that of a limited liability company) is also accorded wholly foreign-owned enterprises.

Despite the advantages mentioned above, two drawbacks of wholly foreign-owned enterprises must be mentioned. First, since a specific tax regime applicable to those enterprises has yet to be developed, wholly foreign-owned enterprises established to date have been subject to the Foreign Investment Income Tax on their net income and to the Consolidated Industrial and Commercial Tax on their gross business revenues (Moser and Zee, 1987: 115-116). Because the Foreign Enterprise Income Tax was designed for companies incorporated outside China, many tax advantages available to joint ventures in China are therefore, presumably, unavailable to wholly foreign-owned enterprises. Second, unlike joint ventures which are merely encouraged to maintain a foreign exchange balance, wholly foreign-owned enterprises are required to do so without formal assistance from the Chinese authorities.

CHINA'S FOREIGN INVESTMENT APPROVAL PROCESS

The mechanics of foreign investment in China are closely related to economic planning of the Chinese economy. Because foreign investment is viewed mainly as a remedy for deficiencies in the Chinese economy, foreign investment in China is subordinated to the national economic plan which spells out the types of direct foreign-investment projects desired by China. Consequently, the approval process is designed to enhance China's control over foreign-capital inflows and to ensure compatibility between foreign-investment projects and the national plan. Given the complexity of China's planning system, however, this process is cumbersome by Western standards and may be affected by varying local practices. Therefore, the description of the procedures and organizations involved in the investment approval process presented in this chapter can only serve as a general guide to the process of foreign-investment approval in China.

Moreover, this discussion is characterized by several limitations. First, foreign investment rules in the SEZs are excluded because of their economic autonomy and the relative lack of restrictions on foreign investment. Second, because no direct foreign investment is necessitated by compensation trade, the foreign investment approval process is not applicable to compensation trade activities. Third, description of the approval process, as attempted here, is largely based on regulations promulgated for equity joint ventures because these regulations are the basis of direct investment rules in China. Although these regulations are applicable also to co-operative joint ventures and wholly foreign-owned enterprises, not all steps are pertinent to these latter types of investment. For example, wholly foreign-owned ventures and some co-operative joint ventures are exempt from having to conduct a detailed feasibility study; while a joint-venture contract is clearly not relevant to wholly foreign-owned ventures.

The process by which direct foreign-investment approval may be obtained in China may be described in five stages: approval of project proposal, preliminary feasibility study, detailed feasibility study, preparation of the joint-venture contract, and final approval and registration.

Approval of Project Proposal

Before proceeding with any investment proposal, irrespective of its origin, the foreign investor must ensure that it has the approval of the appropriate authorities. Any investment proposal involving foreign participation, be it Sino-foreign joint venture or wholly-owned foreign investment, must be approved and included in either the local or national income plan before they are eligible for implementation.

The level of approval required generally depends on the nature and size of the project. For example, investment projects in sectors of national importance and those with a total investment of 10 million Rmb or more must receive approval from the Ministry of Foreign Economic Relations and Trade (MOFERT). Should the life of a project exceed 50 years, approval from the State Council would also be required. Otherwise, approval from the ministry, under whose authority the project is undertaken, or provincial authorities through their local planning commission would suffice. Exceptions to the above rule, however, exist for the investment undertaken in the 14 open coastal cities and the municipalities of Beijing and Shanghai, and the provinces of Guangdong and Fujian. Because of their special status, the local governments of these areas are able to approve foreign investment much larger than the usual $3 million US limit. For example, although the provinces of Guangdong and Fujian are given the power to approve independently projects worth up to 100 million Rmb, the limit in Shanghai and Tianjin is 30 million, and is decreased to 10 million in each of Beijing, Lianoning, Palian and Guangzhou. For other provinces, municipalities, autonomous regions, ministries or commissions of industry, communications, agriculture, and forestry, as well as enterprises located in Zhongqing, Shenyang and Wuhan, the limit is $5 million US (Chu, 1987: 7). It must be pointed out that, even when MOFERT approval is not needed, investment proposals approved by local authorities are nevertheless required to be submitted to MOFERT "for the record". This is because of MOFERT's responsibility to ensure project compliance with applicable regulations.

The above general rule notwithstanding, the austerity programme, instituted in October 1988 has created temporary exceptions. Twelve sectors previously open to foreign investment are now being discouraged or must receive MOFERT's approval regardless of size, location or type. These sectors include electronic goods, household appliances, motor vehicles, tobacco, alcoholic and other beverages for domestic sale, and products in which manufacturing capacity is nearly or already saturated (Cheng, 1989: 59). The intent of this new policy is to stop production activities that have contributed to China's inflation and foreign exchange difficulties.

When the need to ascertain the official status of a project arises, a foreign investor may do so through MOFERT's Foreign Investment Administration or, in the case of a local project, the local Foreign Economic Relations and Trade Commission.

Preliminary Feasibility Study

For projects which are large ($100 million Rmb) or those that involve manufacturing of a product on MOFERT's list of controlled imports, a preliminary feasibility study is required to justify their viability before project approval may be granted. In cases of Sino-foreign joint ventures, this is usually conducted by the Chinese partner, at its own expense. He provides documented support for the project. Then, only rough estimates are needed to determine potential costs and returns. However, for wholly foreign-owned investment ventures, a much more detailed and precise study is mandated.

No strict rules exist on the timing of submission of preliminary feasibility studies. In fact, these studies may be submitted in lieu of project proposals in most cases. The only precise rules that exist pertain to large services sector and manufacturing projects. The studies must be submitted at the same time as the proposal for the former and before the proposal for the latter.

Detailed Feasibility Study

Subsequent to a project being approved, a more detailed feasibility study is required by Chinese law for a majority of Sino-foreign joint ventures. Only wholly foreign-owned ventures, which have fulfilled this requirement in an earlier stage of the project, oil-exploration joint ventures, processing and assembly arrangements, and small projects are exempt from this rule.

Aside from the usual focus of a feasibility study, studies undertaken in the present context must also address two additional issues. First, they must ascertain if support from suppliers of key inputs is forthcoming, a question of extreme importance in the Chinese economy where key inputs remain under the control of government departments. In the case of Sino-foreign joint venture, the Chinese partner must submit reports to each local department whose co-operation will be required for successful implementation of the project. These reports should identify clearly what the project will need from each department. The departments must then reply in writing, stating whether they agree to supply the goods and services requested. A favourable response from these departments is vital because their decisions are generally not reversible by higher authorities, such as the local planning commission. Second, for projects anticipating a foreign exchange problem, a plan for solving profit repatriation difficulties must be included as a part of the study. Should countertrade be involved, the venture must actively seek out a supplier of the product it wishes to export and, if an export licence is required for this product, obtain the necessary consent from MOFERT's Import-Export Department.

The importance of a thorough feasibility study has been made increasingly apparent by recent difficulties experienced by many joint ventures. Without a proper examination of international demand and domestic-supply conditions, many joint ventures have encountered severe foreign exchange difficulties and suffered significant losses. These problems have also been exacerbated by insufficient co-ordination between decision-making departments, and this has resulted in unexpected input shortages and unnecessary delays in project implementation. In viewing these studies, MOFERT usually pays particular attention to projected product quality, general competitiveness and foreign exchange earnings of the venture, factors that are most likely to affect the viability of the product. Moreover, feasibility studies conducted for joint ventures, and requiring State Planning Commission approval (for those involving technical renovation of $30 million US or more at collective or state-owned enterprises) must be appraised by the China International Engineering Consulting Corporation at the expense of the venture partners.

Joint-Venture Contract and Agreements

Before application for the final approval of a Sino-foreign joint venture, a joint-venture contract must be finalized for submission to MOFERT or to the local Foreign Economic Relation and Trade Commission.

According to the 1983 Joint-Venture Implementing Regulations, the joint-venture contract is a legally binding document, signed by all partners to the joint venture that clearly identifies the rights and obligations of each partner. It is a document that will profoundly affect the interests of the foreign partner during the course of a joint venture and must therefore be negotiated carefully.

It has been suggested that this contract should be fashioned closely after the sample joint-venture contract published by MOFERT. The reason is that the familiarity of MOFERT officials with its format should help to expedite the approval process (Lee and Ness, 1986: 16). However, this approach is not without shortcomings. For instance, the sample contract has been criticized as "vague, simplistic, and at point inconsistent with China's laws regulating joint ventures" (Chang, 1987: 9), and may not necessarily reflect the needs and particular circumstances of a given joint venture. Therefore, despite the usual reference of Chinese negotiations to adopt the sample contract as the basic format of Sino-foreign ventures, the foreign partner should ensure that it is indeed in his interest to do so.

As well as the joint-venture contract, any agreement between the joint-venture partners must also be submitted to the approving authorities. These agreements may include a joint-venture agreement, which formalizes the key points and principles governing the joint venture and is usually drawn up before the contract, or a labour-management contract. Though these agreements may be negotiated separately from the joint-venture contract, they must be approved along with the latter.

Final Approval and Registration

After the conclusion of a joint-venture contract, an application for final approval of the venture may be submitted to MOFERT or to the local Foreign Economic Relations and Trade Commission if the project is within local approval limits. The documents that are required to support the application include a copy of the approved project proposal, the preliminary feasibility study (if applicable), the detailed feasibility study, the joint-venture agreement (if any), the joint-venture contract, the articles of association, a list of the joint-venture board members, and supporting statements from the department in charge of the Chinese partner and those whose support is necessary to the joint venture. The approving authorities are then responsible for co-ordinating a review of these documents by other relevant authorities, such as tax and customs, before final approval of the contract.

Once final approval is obtained, a joint venture has one month within which to register and apply for a business license at the local Administration for Industry and Commerce. This process is outlined in and governed by the Joint-Venture Implementing Regulations and the regulations on the registration of joint ventures. Once registered, the joint venture, whether jointly or wholly foreign-owned, becomes a part of China's planned economy. As such, all ventures are subject to supervision by a bureau within an industrial ministry that supervises Chinese enterprises (Lichtenstein, 1987: 39). Although the supervisory unit is formally empowered to approve each enterprise's annual and long-term plans, technical improvement projects, and high-level managerial appointments, enterprises with foreign participation do enjoy a high degree of autonomy in these areas under China's various foreign-investment laws.

CONCLUSION

Despite the many difficulties associated with foreign investment in China, the Chinese economy represents a repository of opportunities that simply cannot be ignored.

China has emerged in the last decade as an increasingly important trading nation, particularly in the Asia-Pacific economy, of which Canada is a member. The total volume of China's trade has increased from 4.9 percent of its domestic output to 13.8 percent in 1986. Almost 70 percent of this trade is conducted with countries in the Pacific Basin. As a member of the fastest growing region in the world, China and its expanding economy offer unparalleled opportunities to foreign investors who are patient and not easily daunted. Canada is in a favoured position to explore the many opportunities China has to offer because of its close trade ties with China. These opportunities will likely expand as the Chinese economy continues to grow and develop. For Canadian investors who are interested in China, enquiries about opportunities in China may be made at government organizations in charge of foreign economic relations and trade. These are located in the various Chinese provinces, municipalities, autonomous regions (all three are directly under the State Council), or provincial and local investment and trust companies that maintain lists of projects for which foreign investment is welcome.

REFERENCES

Almanac of China's Foreign Economic Relations and Trade (ACFERT) (1988). *Statistics: Utilization of foreign capital* (pp. 681-682). Hong Kong: China Resources Trade Consulting Co. Ltd.

Barale, L.A. (1991). The new WFOE implementing regulations. *The China Business Review*, 18(4), 8-11.

Brewer, T.L., David, K., Lim, L.Y.C., and Corredera, S. (1986). *Investing in developing countries*. Lexington, Mass: Lexington Books.

Chai, J. (1983). Industrial co-operation between China and Hong Kong. In A.J. Youngson (Ed.), *China and Hong Kong: The economic nexus* (pp. 104-155). Hong Kong: Oxford University Press), .

Chang, T-J. (1987). The great battle of the forms. *The Chinese Business Review* (Washington, D.C.), 14(4), 7-10.

Cheng, E. (1989). Credit squeeze puts brakes on joint ventures, *Far Eastern Economic Review* (Hong Kong), 143(9), 59-60.

Chu, B.T. (1987). The effectiveness of China's adsorption of foreign investment. In Richard D. Robinson (Ed.), *Foreign capital and technology in China*. New York: Praeger.

Cohen, J.A., and Chang, T-K. (1987). The investment climate; China attempts to restore confidence, *The China Business Review* (Washington, D.C.), 14(1), 11-14.

Cohen, J.A. (1988). The long-awaited co-operative venture law. *The China Business Review* (Washington, D.C.), 15(4), 14-18.

Dean, G. (1988). Investment incentives throughout Asia, *The China Business Review* (Washington, D.C.), 15(2), 49-51.

Economist. (1988) China throws open its seaboard. March 12, pp. 61-62.

Harding, H. (1987). *China's second revolution: Reform after Mao*. Washington, D.C.: The Brookings Institute.

Lee, S., and Ness, A. (1986). Investment approval, *The China Business Review* (Washington, D.C.), 13(3), 14-18.

Lichtenstein, N.G. (1987). Law and the Enterprise, *The China Business Review* (Washington, D.C.), 14(2), 38-42.

Moser, M.J. (1984). Foreign investment in China: The legal framework. In Michael J. Moser (Ed.), *Foreign trade, investment, and the law in the People's Republic of China* (pp. 106-142). Hong Kong: Oxford University Press.

Moser, M.J., and Zee, W.K. (1987). *China tax guide*. Hong Kong: Oxford University Press.

Sullivan, R.W. (1987). New foreign investment provision, *The China Business Review* (Washington D.C.), 14(1), 8-10.

Ta Kung Pao (Chinese Language), (San Francisco, CA), American Edition, August 25, 1989.

Torbert, P.M. (1986). Wholly foreign-owned enterprises come of age, *The China Business Review* (Washington, D.C.), 13(4), 50-52.

Wong, E.L. (1987). Recent developments in China's special economic zones: Problems and prognosis, *The Developing Economics* (Tokyo), 15(1), 73-86.

8 SHANDONG'S AGRICULTURE AND ITS NEEDS

Chen Longfei and Yan Aihua

Shandong Teachers' University, Jinan, Shandong

INTRODUCTION TO SHANDONG PROVINCE

Of the 31 administrative areas at the provincial level of the People's Republic of China, Shandong best reflects the country as a whole; it could well be regarded as a microcosm of the Republic. Thus an understanding of Shandong makes for a ready understanding of China as a whole.

Shandong Province lies in the eastern part of China. It has the vast hinterland of east Asia at its back and the Huanghai (Yellow Sea), the western edge of the Pacific, at its front. The province is situated in eastern China, a location similar to the province of New Brunswick in Canada, or to the state of Virginia in the United States. What may be said of the geographical location of China in the eastern part of the Eurasian continent and on the west coast of the Pacific may also be said of Shandong Province. More specifically, the province lies between 34°22'52"N and 38°15'02"N, and 114°19'53"E and 122°43'E. The greatest distance from north to south is 420 kilometres, and east to west 700 kilometres; thus the physical differences are greater east-west than north-south. In summer, it is hot and rainy; in winter it is cold and dry—the main characteristic features of the monsoon climate.

Like most of China, Shandong has many resources. For example, some 97 different kinds of minerals have been discovered in the province, equivalent to 64 percent of the 150 minerals so far discovered in China. Deposits of such minerals as petroleum, coal, iron and gold, all vital to the national economy, make Shandong one of the richest provinces in the country. The water resources in the province are also fairly good. However, because precipitation varies from year to year and is unevenly distributed, drought usually threatens the province in early spring. Varieties of plants include almost all the deciduous fruit trees in the temperate zone, but the area of land covered by forests is no more than 14 percent of the total area of the province, which is a little higher than that of the whole country.

Again, similar to the whole country, Shandong may be divided into the relatively developed east, the moderately developed middle, and the fairly backward west. From the eastern coastal areas to the western hinterland, the level of national economy and social development declines gradually. The three municipalities of Qingdao, Yantai and Weihai, located along the Shandong Peninsula, have always taken the lead in economic development. Food processing is the main industry, but secondary and tertiary industries have also been developed. The economic level in the middle part of the province is lower than that at the coast but higher than that in the west. Coal, petroleum, iron and steel, and chemicals are the chief industrial activities. In the west, agriculture dominates. Although this part of the province has made some progress since China adopted new reform measures in 1978 and opened the country to the outside world, relatively backward conditions remain unchanged. Altogether, the regional economic features closely resemble those of China proper.

With respect to the Gross National Product (GNP), at present Shandong's is the second highest of all the provinces, but its per capita GNP takes tenth place. Compare this with that of the whole country, which in 1979 took eighth place in the world and the per capita GNP took 120th place. This amounts to only $300 US, which has changed little since 1979 when it was $299 US. In much the same way, Shandong's agricultural output value tops those of the other provinces, the average value being equal to that of the whole country.

In terms of demographic weight, by the end of 1979, Shandong's population had reached 81.59 million, which is 7.3 percent of the nation's total population, and the third highest of all the provinces, next to Sichuan and Henan Provinces. But the area of Shandong is only 156,700 square kilometres and the agricultural density 440 persons per square kilometre (1989). The percentage of the urban population (city and town), 20 percent, is a little lower than that of the nation's. Thus, rich as the province is in natural resources, the amount is small in relation to the large population. This is also the problem faced by the whole country.

Shandong Province lies along the valley of the Yellow River, one of the four cradles of world civilization (the others are the Tigris-Euphrates, the Indus and the Nile Valleys). The lower reaches of the Yellow River are filled with mud and sand. In this valley are the ruins of the Dawenkou and Longshan cultures which flourished some 6,000 or 7,000 years ago (Shandong Provincial Party Committee, 1986: 56). The valley is really the cradle of the Chinese nation. Indeed, the province, like the rest of China, contains many relics and abounds in places of historical interest. The long history partly accounts for the heavy population density and intensive cultivation of the area. Here are Qufu and Zouxian counties, former residences of Confucius and Mencius, two founders of Confucianism. In the 2,000 years of China's feudal history, Confucius has been respected as the supreme sage, and Mencius as the second sage. Although Confucianism has never appeared as a typical religious form, it has exercised much influence on China and the whole of Southeast Asia. For thousands of years, the value system, ethical and moral concepts, and the patterns of thinking have been influenced to a great extent by Confucian culture. This culture has dominated the life-style of scores of generations. It is owing to this fact that Confucius has been listed among the 10 great thinkers of the world. His great image still hovers over the country. Whether he is or is not liked, he has been constantly and repeatedly studied.

With windows (Qingdao, Yantai and Weihai) to the outside world, Shandong is a fairly developed province. There are rich resources to be exploited and used, many industrial enterprises to be updated with modern technology, and conditions for agriculture, communication and transportation, and tourist facilities to be improved. Shandong looks forward eagerly to enhancing contacts and co-operating with peoples and friends from various countries, and compatriots from Hong Kong and Macao in developing these facilities. It seeks to promote its own advantages and abide by the principles of equality and mutual assistance. It strongly believes that far-sighted, overseas enterprises will be interested in the potentialities of the province and find it profitable to transfer their advanced technology to help in its development.

INTRODUCTION TO SHANDONG'S AGRICULTURE

It is well known that the Chinese economy is faced with two great problems: the one is its agriculture, the other its population. Once these two problems are solved, that is, agriculture is greatly improved and the population is well controlled, China should do well.

The development of agriculture as the basis of the national economy is now one of China's fundamental policies. Though a major element in the national economy, agriculture is greatly restricted by physical conditions, including topography, soil, climate and hydrology. In the history of human civilization, the productive activity first introduced was agriculture.

The physical environment is the spatial reality that supports people, and understanding of this is a prerequisite for making rational decisions about the development of agriculture. This is the main concern of this chapter.

THE GEOGRAPHICAL CONDITIONS AND DISTRICTS FOR AGRICULTURAL PRODUCTION

The Physical Conditions

The general relief of Shandong Province shows an elevated central portion, the highest part of the province, which inclines in all directions. It divides the province into three topographic areas. The southern and middle areas are the highest and are dominated by Mount Tai, Mount Yi, Mount Meng and Mount Zulai. From these mountains rivers drain in all directions and dissect the mountains. The alluvial plains in front of the mountains comprise loose sediments from the Quaternary Period of geological history. The soil is thick and fertile and supports grain production (Figure 1,8). The hilly area, mainly in the Shandong Peninsula, became land in an earlier period. As a result of long years of weathering and erosion, the surface is undulating and has a thick layer of soil. Surrounded by the sea on three sides, and with a humid climate, the plains and basins among the mountains are important agricultural areas. In the northwest of the province, the great plain of the Yellow and Huai Rivers is semi-circular in shape, low and flat for the most part, and about 50 metres (16.5 feet) above sea level. Fertile, it has a great potential for grain, cotton, and livestock production, also for forestry development

The climate of Shandong Province is temperate and has four distinct regimes: hot in summer; cold and dry in winter; dry, sandy and windy in spring; and fine, clear and warm in autumn. The average annual temperature of the province is 11 to 14°C (52 to 57°F). Its frost-free period of 180 to 220 days and an annual accumulated temperature of 3800 to 4500°C are suitable for growing crops. The average annual illumination hours of the province are 2,300 to 2,890 hours. The average precipitation is 550 to 950 millimetres (22 to 38 inches) and decreases from the southeast to the northwest. Rainfall is highly concentrated, from June to August, when the temperature is high. This is the growing season. Sometimes, however, this high precipitation causes flood.

For 617 kilometres (382 miles) of its total length of 5,432 kilometres (3,395 miles), the Yellow River flows through the province and enters the

Bohai Sea. The river carries much mud and sand, some 38 kilograms per cubic metre, and its constant sediments raise the river bed yearly. Consequently, the river becomes higher than the land surface and forms a "river above the land". Some 600 million to 800 million cubic metres of water can be drawn off each year. This is enough to irrigate 25 million mu (nearly 4.2 million acres) of land. The mouth of the river supports the cultivation of 34,000 mu (5,667 acres) each year.

The total area of Shandong Province is 156,700 square kilometres (61,320 square miles), 55 percent of which is plains, 15 percent hills and 10 percent marshes, rivers and lakes. By 1988, the most valuable part of the farming land of the province comprised 690,000 hectares (1.7 million acres), that is, every hectare (2.47 acres) of land had to provide food for 12 persons.

The Structure and Development of Farming

As the cradle of Chinese civilization, Shandong Province has a long history of development. Whether we are dealing with the slave or the feudal society, this area's economy was fairly well developed. The earliest or primitive way of farming was to fell the trees, burn the wild grass, sow the seeds in holes dug in the ground with stone hoes, and then wait for the harvest, hence the term "farming with hoes." With the improvement of tools, the Shandong area, typical of oriental agriculture, reached the highest level of development in the country during the Qin and Han dynasties. The custom was to grow a crop in a plot year after year with the application of fertilizer. The "land fertility renewing" theory adopted during the Southern Song Dynasty was opposite to the principle of "reward decreasing" which was the basis of Western European crop rotation.

Generally, Chinese traditional farming did not include livestock farming or forestry. If Western farming was the combination of farming with animal husbandry and forestry, Oriental farming was a type of discretion. Management of the typical Chinese farm was by a single family unit, that is, "a household of five" on a plot of land, growing a variety of crops, sometimes interplanting. Accordingly, family cotton and hemp spinning and weaving were very popular. Simultaneously the production of food crops for family needs, and the sale or exchange of the remainder for what was needed characterized the farming structure, as were farming by males and weaving by females. Emphasis was always laid on grain production. This was the nature of China's agricultural practices for the past 2,000 years. Though some farming households may have raised livestock, the operations were small in number, and this explains why livestock farming has been underdeveloped in China.

In Shandong at present, and even in the vast rural areas of China, the old farming practices are still strong. Farming tools, such as hoes, spades, sickles and draught animals, are still being used as they were thousands of years ago (Figure 2,8). But combine-harvesters and spraying-irrigation techniques have now come into use in some areas, as well as new farming tools. This change has to be taken into consideration before a new agricultural policy is introduced.

The Chinese revolution and reconstruction were based on the nature of the economy and have wrought changes in the thinking of the people. "The great production campaign" in the Yan'an area in the 1940s, based on manual labour, succeeded in breaking the blockade of the Japanese army. After the founding of the People's Republic, Shandong Province completed its land reforms in accordance with the socialist transformation of agriculture. The structure of agriculture and agricultural production then underwent considerable change and development. However, after the end of the 1950s, and owing to "leftish" ideological guidance and the one-sided emphasis on grain production, the structure of agriculture and agricultural production suffered adversely. Since the end of the 1970s, a series of decisive policies have been introduced to incorporate the initiative of the peasants, and agriculture is now undergoing rational development.

Division of Agricultural Districts

Given the varying physical conditions, the unevenly distributed agricultural resources, and the great difference between economic levels and traditional modes of management in various parts of the province, an effort is made here to divide the districts arbitrarily to show their differences.

The Peninsular Area. This area is located along the coastline. Good conditions exist for an overall development of farming, fishery, forestry, and the raising of livestock. It is intensively farmed; grain yields are high, and commodity prices are rising. With concentrated growing and high-unit output, this area produces half of the total output of peanuts in the province, and high-quality apples and pears. In fact, the area has become the national base for fruit production (Figure 3,8). With a favourable location along the Bohai and Yellow Seas, it also produces aquatic products. Besides, it has developed rural industry and commercial services. In short, this is the most developed agricultural area of the province.

Northwest Shandong: Farming, Forestry and Livestock. This is a vast area, located on both banks of the Yellow River. It is the alluvial or flood plain of the river, with thick soils and an annual temperature high enough for

Figure 1,8 A Good Wheat Harvest in Sight *(Photo by Pang Shouyi)*

Figure 2,8 Rural Agriculture, Shandong Province

cotton growing, the dominant activity. The total area given to cotton is 80 percent of Shandong's land area, and the output of cotton constitutes 80 percent of Shandong's total cotton output. The output value exceeds that of grain crops. Historically one of the 12 poorest areas in the country, the area has been subjected to great changes since the introduction of rural reforms. However, forestry and livestock are fairly undeveloped, owing to a poor beginning.

Central Shandong, a Suburban Agricultural Area. Situated along the Jinan-Qingdao and Beijing-Shanghai Railways, this area is the political, cultural and economic centre of the province. Here, economic levels top those of the province proper. There are eight cities in the area, all of which are supported by mines and industry. The high urban population density and the high consumption of agricultural and related products support the local specialization in high-yielding grain and a high output of meat, poultry, eggs, milk and vegetables. Most of the enterprises are owned by the townships.

Southern Shandong—a Lake Area. This includes the four southern lakes, chief of which is Lake Weishan, the main source of fresh-water aquatic products. It has sufficient heat and rainfall for growing rice (Figure 4,8) and wheat.

The Mountain Area of the Yi and Meng Mountains. This area suffers from soil erosion as a result of the many rivers descending from the high mountains. The soil is poor and farming is backward. In addition, transportation is inconvenient and its distance from economic centres combine to keep the level of economic development fairly low. Some villages have difficulty even in obtaining drinking water.

REFORM OF THE ECONOMIC SYSTEM IN RURAL AREAS

China's economic reforms were initiated at the rural level, where, so far, they have been most successful. A description of these economic reforms follows.

Reform in Land Management Rights

Since the introduction of the "People's Communes System" in 1958, the so-called three-level ownership system, based on production teams, has been practised in China's countryside. This gives both the ownership and management rights to the collective. Commune members were

Figure 3,8
Sweet Apples in the Apple City of Weihai
(Photo by Liu Zhenging)

Figure 4,8 A Paddy Harvest in Yutai County *(Photo by Liu Zhenging)*

assigned to do all kinds of farm work according to the arrangement of the production team. The team recorded each member's "working credits" on which the distribution is based. As individual labour was not directly reflected in the profit distribution, all the disadvantages of the system were exposed, for example, giving the same credits to workers who worked and to those who did not work, though present. With low productivity, many rural areas could not solve the problem of inadequate food supply.

At the beginning of the 1960s, economic difficulties began to appear. To solve the basic problem of food, it was advocated that the land should be allotted to the farmers to farm. This policy, called "salvation through production," did solve the urgent need for food, but was later criticized widely for "taking the capitalist road." Nevertheless, towards the end of the 1970s, this became the primary reform measure. Soon the idea spread across the country and was most successful.

Under this land reform, all lands, fertile and infertile, are given the same rating and allotted to each farming household according to the number of its family members. The annual production from the land belongs to the farmers, except that part which is given as agricultural tax for the land received, and a quota which must be sold to the state. At the same time, the State raises considerably the buying price of the product. By so doing, the productive initiative of the peasants has greatly improved, hence the unexpectedly great increase in the output and value of China's agricultural production between 1978 and 1984, as Table 1,8 shows.

Table 1,8   Increase in the GNP in Rural Areas, Between 1978 and 1984

	1978	1984	Annual Rate of Increase (%)
GNP in rural areas (billion RMB)	19.93	49.63	16.5
Agricultural Output Value (billion RMB)	14.48	26.66	10.7
Total Output of grain (million tons)	22.88	30.40	4.8
Total Cotton Output (million tons)	0.15	1.72	27.1

Source: Shandong Provincial Statistics Bulletin, 1978 and 1984.

Reform in the Buying and Selling System of Agricultural Products

The second reform was in the buying and selling system of agricultural products. This was introduced simultaneously with that just mentioned. During operation of the People's Communes, the policy of unified buying and selling of agricultural products operated throughout China: all agricultural products were bought and sold only by the State. The great increase in output of agricultural products, brought about by the first reform, resulted in a surplus of products for which the state had to pay a large subsidy. It was then necessary to consider the role of the market. Beginning in 1984, the policy of contracted buying of agricultural products was implemented in the countryside. This was the first step toward a market economy. But a decrease in the amount the state was to buy and a drop in the price of economic crops led to a decline in farming in 1985.

Readjustment of Industrial Policy in Rural Areas

During operation of the People's Communes, the peasants, but not the few industrial or miscellaneous businesses run by the commune (township) or brigade (village), were strictly forbidden to engage in business of any kind. All businesses operated by factories, construction teams, transportation or services, even the raising of oxen and horses, were banned; they were regarded as the "tails of capitalism." With the introduction of the reform policy, farmers may now raise livestock and poultry, buy farming machines like tractors, and engage in construction, transportation and the service industry. Peasants are also allowed to run private business with hired hands. This was impossible in previous years.

The feasibility of the policies has increased prosperity in rural areas. Table 2,8 shows the increase of rural industry between 1975 and 1987.

Table 2,8   Rural Industry, Between 1975 and 1987

	Percentage Increase
Rural Industry	24.3
Rural Construction (Business)	9.7
Rural Transportation (Business)	30.3
Rural Commercial Services	21.7

Source: Shandong Provincial Statistics Bulletin, 1978 and 1984.

Also, the proportion of the output value of rural construction and rural transportation in the rural GNP increased from 43.7 percent in 1978 to 52.6 percent in 1987 (Shandong Provincial Statistics Bureau, 1978 & 1987). Equally, the output value of non-agricultural products surpassed for the first time in history that of agricultural products. This improvement is of historic significance. It marks a definite upgrading of the rural industrial structure.

The new flexibility of the rural industrial policy has released the peasants from the land and made it possible for them to grow or produce whatever is beneficial for them. The general orientation is undoubtedly correct, but a series of problems have emerged as a result, such as the decline in farming output because of inadequate material input, poor management, the nation-wide migration of labour from rural to urban areas since 1989, and competition in getting materials between township-owned enterprises to key enterprises in big cities. The Central Government is now committed to finding solutions for these problems.

The Status Quo of Shandong Agriculture

Whereas the agricultural output value of the province has been increasing within the past few years, the output of major crops is stagnant and could be improved, according to official data, shown in Table 3,8.

Table 3,8 Agricultural Production, Shandong Province, 1989 and 1990

	1989 (million tons)	1990 (million tons)
Grain	32.5	35.7
Cotton	1.0	1.0
Oil-bearing crops	1.5	2.1
Fruit	2.5	2.4

Source: Shandong Statistics Yearbook, 1990 & 1991

During the period of the Seventh Five Year Plan (1986 to 1990), the total output value of agriculture in Shandong was expected to increase at an annual percentage rate of 2.9, grain at 1.02, cotton at 2.47, tobacco at

6.97, fruit at 6.97 and meat at 6.35. The output value of township-owned enterprises increased at an annual rate of 30 percent (Shandong Statistics Yearbook, 1991).

After the past few years of stagnation, it became clear that the present comprehensive capacity for agricultural production in the province was 3.2 million tons of grain and 1.2 million tons of cotton. Given favourable climate, the production of grain could be increased by one million tons, but struck by natural calamities, it might decrease by one million tons or more (Shandong Provincial Statistics Bulletin, 1989). With no further improvement of the present conditions for production, it is very difficult to obtain the quick, favourable increases of the past few years.

The truth of the matter is that Shandong's agriculture is not mechanized. Available for agricultural production in 1989 were only 625,600 tractors, i.e. one tractor per 11 hectares (27 acres); 2.27 million tons of fertilizers, equivalent to 22 kilograms (54.3 lbs) per mu (1/6 acre) of land; and 7.34 billion kilowatt hours of electricity (Shandong Provincial Statistics Bulletin, 1989). Except for such basic technical measures as tilling, sowing and irrigating, which have been mechanized, all other measures of administering the farming land are done either by manual labour or with draught animals. Such intensive farming is typical of concentrated labour. This and the mechanized farming in North America are perhaps models of two different modes of agriculture. Because of the lack of energy, China's agriculture might never equate with that of mechanized agriculture, nor would the small parcel of land produce enough for both local consumption and extra for export on a large scale. And there seems no radical change of this state in the foreseeable future.

Problems Respecting the Rural Reform Programme

Five reform measures were attempted during the past few years. The first is in the system of management. The system of "ownership on three levels," based on the production team, has been changed to one with household responsibility. Each household undertakes to produce a quota. The system combines unified with individual management. The second reform is in the circulation system. The former system of unified distribution and purchase has been changed for one with contracted purchase of agricultural products, such as grain, cotton and oil-bearing seeds. The surplus may then be sold in the free markets. In the third reform, adjustment is made in the industrial structure. Apart from farming, the peasants are engaged in industrial and miscellaneous business activity.

The fourth reform permits the coexistence of a variety of economic activities, and allows individual peasants to own some means of production. Here the individual or private business is considered necessary supplements to the state-owned business. In the fifth and final reform measure, the state exercises macro control to prevent erratic fluctuations in price.

These five reforms appear both rational and practical. In recent years, special emphasis has been placed on establishment of a service system on the two levels of county and township to realize the socialization of agricultural service. This is in conformity with global reforms in agriculture.

CONDITIONS RESTRICTING AGRICULTURAL PRODUCTION

Since the extraordinary increase in agricultural production from 1979 to 1984, China's agriculture has stagnated. This is due to many factors. Foremost is the insufficiency of water resources. The total amount of fresh water resources in the province is 34.5 billion cubic metres (44.8 billion cubic yards) (Shandong Provincial Statistics Bulletin, 1980-1989). The per capita amount, 448 cubic metres (582 cubic yards), and the average amount per mu, 326 cubic metres (424 cubic yards), are less than one-fifth of the average for the whole country. In an ordinary year, water insufficiency amounts to 10 billion cubic metres (13 billion cubic yards) (Ibid.). As a result of successive droughts and increased use of water in recent years, the storage of surface water has decreased markedly; also, the level of underground water has dropped considerably. Therefore the lack of water resources has become a critical factor. It restricts the development of agriculture in the province. Since 1978, the province has suffered a loss of 600,000 mu (100,000 acres) of farm land, resulting from an annual population growth of 900,000. For the three years from 1986 to 1988, the decrease of farm land was 2.12 million mu (353,000 acres) and the increase in population 3.14 million, that is, an annual growth rate of 1.04 million. The per capita farm land had decreased from 1.37 mu in 1985 to 1.28 mu (0.23 to 0.21 acre) or nearly two-thirds of what it was in 1949 when the People's Republic was established. In four cities and prefectures, and in 38 counties, the per capita farming land is less than one mu (1/6 acre) (Ibid.).

Still another problem is soil erosion. The total area of erosion in the unprotected mountain area and the windy and sandy area of the plains of the province is 43,000 square kilometres (17,200 square miles) (Ibid.). Equally, there is soil erosion by human means. It is reported that the land area in the province which becomes desert every year is 1.8 million mu

(300,000 acres); the rate of increase of naked rocks is 0.28 percent; the loss of soil is 0.33 billion tons; the loss of nitrogen, phosphorus and potassium that could be converted to chemical fertilizer is 3.5 million tons; the soil deposit in the lakes, reservoirs and riverbeds is 70 million cubic metres (91 million cubic yards) (Ibid.). Factors like these severely damage the ecological environment and adversely affect production.

The next serious problem is pollution. With the development of rural industry, the displacement of three wastes (gas, liquid and solid) has increased enormously. Across the province, the yearly displacement of waste water amounts to 1.3 billion tons, 90 percent of which flows into natural reservoirs without any treatment. At present, the quality of over 50 percent of the water stored in the rivers, lakes and reservoirs of the province is below the minimum standard set by the State (Ibid.). The water in some places is not only undrinkable but unfit even for irrigation.

Again, a tight budget and insufficient funds for agricultural construction have decreased greatly since 1980. Throughout the Fifth Five Year Plan, and especially between 1986 and 1988, the annual capital investment in agricultural construction dropped from Y226.4 million to Y164.12 million, a decrease of 27.5 percent. The total provincial investment in water conservation also dropped, from Y175.3 million to Y74.47 million, a 57.5 percent decrease, as was the provincial total investment in capital construction, from 7.8 to 0.94 percent (Ibid.). The present water conservation facilities that are still serving agriculture were mostly constructed in the 1960s and 1970s. Their service period has almost expired. Deteriorating badly, they are unable to function properly. Altogether there are 167 big and medium-sized reservoirs, 163 of which are in a critical, if not dangerous, state. The ability of the rivers to resist floods has generally been reduced by 30 to 50 percent. Because of this, the total area which needs to be irrigated has increased to 3.7 million mu (0.6 million acre) since 1986 (Ibid.). As new projects cannot be supplied with water, agricultural production is retarded. Clearly, for increased agricultural production there must be an increase in agricultural investment.

Price structure is another inhibiting factor in agricultural production. In the years immediately following the founding of the Republic, the State took, without repaying, a part of the income created by agriculture to develop industry, which was then backward. Between 1953 and 1985, China's budget showed a fixed assets investment of Y767.8 billion annually, Y24 billion of which equalled approximately to the absolute amount of every year's price differential. On the other hand, the big differential apparently weakened the power of agricultural production and restricted improvement of the life of the peasants. From 1952 to 1977, calculated at a fixed price, China's output value of heavy industry increased by 33 times, light industry by 7.7 times, but agriculture by only 1.1 times. It was by using the returns of agriculture to finance industry that caused urban growth and rural decline during that period. Towards the end of the 1970s, the adjustment of the prices of agricultural products reduced considerably the price differential (Ibid.).

LANDMARK IN THE DEVELOPMENT OF AGRICULTURE

Economic upheavals in the development of the new China since its founding have invariably been related to agriculture. Difficulties with agriculture, as mentioned earlier, will necessarily cause a chain reaction involving all sectors of the economy. When this occurs, attention is immediately drawn to agriculture, but no sooner are the difficulties overcome and agriculture improved than negligence returns. The National Conference on Rural Work (Vice-Premier Tian Jiyun, November 29,1989) pointed out that in the past 40 years, China has experienced several re-adjustments in its economy. It states clearly that on each occasion the re-adjustment was aimed at improving agriculture and promoting the improvement and development of all other sectors of the economy; that this is now law and that present adjustments must abide by this law. It shows further that on several occasions since 1949, industry has experienced over-heating which agriculture could not support because of agriculture's weak base. Thus an imbalance would occur and steps would be taken to correct it, but with the removal of the difficulty, agriculture would be neglected again. The National Conference on Rural Work declared that this was the main reason for repeated re-adjustments; and that agriculture must be strengthened, must be given priority and support, put on a sound foundation if it is to support the steady development of the national economy. The Conference concludes that in order to solve the problem of food for the 1.1 billion people, it is absolutely vital that urgent attention is given to improving agriculture.

The direct response of the Central Government to the Conference's recommendations was a decree that the Farming Land Possession Tax for land development and construction, later named the Agricultural Comprehensive Development Fund, was to be used to develop agriculture comprehensively. Accordingly, 11 vast areas of development have been selected along the plain formed by the Yellow, Huai, and Hai Rivers, bordering the five provinces of Hebei, Shandong, Henan, Jiangsu and Anhui; the Three-River Plain in Northeast China; the Song-Liao Plain; and Zhejiang, Guanxi and Xinjiang. The central part of the Yellow-Huai-Hai River Plain, on which Shandong stands, is one of the key areas for development. The aim is to improve the middle and low-yielding land and increase the output of grain, cotton and oil-seeds, while comprehensively developing farming, forestry, livestock, fishery and miscellaneous activities. In general, the aim is to make this area the largest base of agricultural production of grain, cotton, oilseeds and meat in the country. The area for development in Shandong occupies about two-thirds of the province's farm land, except the East Shandong Peninsula and a few counties and cities in the Yi and Meng Mountains. It will employ most of the province's labour force.

Since reform measures were introduced, this area has witnessed much development. Albeit the base of agriculture here is weak. It is necessary to start almost from scratch. The restricting factors include drought, flood, saline-alkaline soils, an incomplete system of water conservation, and the difficulty of resisting natural calamities. Besides, there are insufficient investment funds for production of essentials, such as chemical fertilizer, diesel, and pesticides; backwardness in education, science and technology; a low level of technological expertise; a monotonous industrial structure with an undeveloped economy; and 60 million mu (10 million acres) out of 70 million mu (11.6 acres) of middle- to low-yield farm land. Yet this land has great potential for increasing output. The period of development will extend over 13 years, from 1988 to 2000 (Shandong Provincial Agricultural Bureau, March 1988).

Initial estimates show that the development envisaged will require some Y5,000 million—Y2,800 million to be provided by the local government, and Y2,200 million by the national government. Altogether, Y3,400 million will be provided by the financial organs of both the Central Government and the local governments, Y1,000 million from loans, and Y600 million raised by the collective or the farmers themselves. The loan includes a $100 million US special loan from the World Bank. The state has to arrange in the proportion of 1:1, another $100 million US (Y472 million) loan (Ibid.). The projects selected to receive the World Bank loan have been selected in Heze and Jining Prefectures in the western part of the province. After inspection, the World Bank Evaluation Delegation was satisfied with the submission by the province, including the preliminary research on the feasibility of the project and the measures to be taken to pay back the loan when the projects are completed.

The details of the proposed development may be briefly summarized. First, a series of relatively large-scale projects are planned to convey water from the Yellow River to farm lands that suffer from drought, and to use the mud and sand to form new land and thus reduce the alkaline content in the soil. Also wells and reservoir-irrigated areas are to be supplied with electric machinery and facilities.

Second, emphasis will be put on improvement of middle or low-yield soils, such as the saline-alkali soil, sajong black and yellow moist soils. The measures to be taken include deep ploughing, increasing the application of organic fertilizer, and applying chemical fertilizer scientifically. The amount of the chemicals applied to each mu of land will increase from the present 80 to 110 kilograms (176 to 242 pounds). The total amount of chemicals, containing phosphorous, potassium and other trace elements, will also be increased.

Saline-alkali soil covers a large area of this development area, and the harshness of this soil is a universal problem. Thus at the beginning of the 1960s, UNESCO established an experimental area for transforming the alkaline soil in Yucheng County, Shandong Province, and scientists from many countries of the world have since been working there. They have acquired valuable information about the area, and some of their practical techniques will be useful for the project.

Livestock production and processing is another of the proposed developments. The goal is to establish a base of high-quality livestock products for export. Also planned is the rebuilding and introduction of some fine breeds of livestock and poultry from abroad. A bull farm kept for artificial insemination, located in the eastern suburbs of Jinan, has decided to introduce two bulls from Canada. Owing to the 1989 turmoil in Beijing, the Canadian side refused to implement the contract, and it was aborted. Besides, the facilities for epidemic prevention, the equipment, and the professional personnel are not only inadequate but need to be improved. Developing feed-processing is also one of the key projects, consequently the construction of plants for condensed fodder facilities is planned.

Plans have also been made to afforest windbreak forests, timber forests, economic forests and forest networks over an area totalling 24 million mu (4 million acres). Thus a considerable amount of high-yielding and quick-growing seeds and seedlings is needed.

Nor is aquaculture ignored. Every year large quantities of aquatic products, especially prawns, are exported. Now it is planned to introduce some fine breeds of fish from abroad to increase production and exports.

Agricultural machinery is also to be developed and popularized, especially small-size, multi-purpose, high-quality and energy-saving machines to suit the present household management system. Large machines, such as tractors, excavators, bulldozers and forklifts will be purchased. It is planned that by the end of this century, the level of mechanization will be increased from the present 30 percent to over 60 percent.

It is Shandong Province that will be responsible for agricultural development in the Yellow-Huai-Hai River Plain. It has established an office which is in charge of registering, examining and checking before accepting development projects. Similarly, the Shandong Provincial Development Investment Corporation has been established for rural agriculture. It is responsible for State investment, and the management and utilization of foreign investments.

Besides agricultural development, Shandong Province has evolved a "Bumper Harvest Plan" and a "Plan for Kindling the Great Prairie." It has popularized extensively advanced technology in relation to new strains of grain, fine breeds of livestock and poultry, the model cultivation of crops, plastic sheet-covering, water-saving irrigation, cultivation under drought conditions (dry-land farming), the prevention of pests and diseases, the application of fertilizer with set prescriptions, fresh ammoniated fodder, quick-growing timber forests, fine cultivation of aquatic products, food processing and preservation, and, not least, agricultural machinery. It is required that agricultural research topics and the funds needed be emphasized, and that scientific agricultural research funds be mainly used to subsidize agricultural research projects. It is also required that the equipment of agricultural research units and agricultural universities be strengthened and the means of research improved in order to support agricultural development. Science and technology personnel are encouraged to go to the countryside to demonstrate and popularize new techniques, and help to train farmers.

In summary, the detailed plan seeks to renew the breeds of the main crops; to index the cultivation of such crops as wheat, corn, cotton and peanuts; to increase the projected area of farming by plastic sheets or plastic shelters from 2.5 million to 8 million mu (0.4 million to 1.3 million acres); to popularize prevention techniques in dealing with pests and diseases, and high-quality, energy-saving, low-consumption techniques in ecological agriculture; and to introduce projects for storing, processing and preserving agricultural products. To support the plan, the Shandong Provincial Government (1990) decreed that governments at the two levels of province and municipality are expected yearly to arrange for a certain amount of foreign exchange and RMB to be used for the introduction of new techniques, new breeds and key instruments and equipment so as to improve scientific research in agriculture.

Another measure taken by the government is to develop vigorously industries closely associated with agriculture. During the past year, the economy of Shandong Province, like that of the rest of the country, has witnessed steady progress as a result of the reforms introduced by the Central Government. Industrial production is increasing, inflation is being checked, and prices have become stable. At a time when funds, materials and energy are in short supply, the province is paying much attention to the production of chemical fertilizer, pesticide, and plastic sheeting. The result is that production has generally improved. It is not surprising that Li Peng, Premier, in his Report on Government Work (March 21, 1990) emphasized at the Third Session of the Seventh National People's Congress that agriculture must be the first of 10 tasks to be accomplished in 1990. Declaring that agriculture is the basis of the political, economic and social stability of the nation, he urged governments at all levels to give priority to agriculture and to mobilize all walks of life to give it full support.

Li Peng's Report stated also that in 1990 the state would increase investment in agriculture, and banks at all levels should give more loans for agriculture. As to state-controlled investment for capital construction projects, the funds for agriculture would be increased by 30 percent, the largest increase in the past 10 years, as would funding for water conservation, construction and the production and supply of chemical fertilizer, pesticide, plastic sheeting and agricultural machinery. The Report stated further that increasing the buying prices of cotton, oil-bearing seeds and sugar cane would begin in 1990.

Overall, the national government is paying much attention to agriculture and is determined to improve this sector of the economy. It is expected that, with the transference of government funds to agriculture and its associated activities, this action will contribute to foreign trade.

Co-ordination of Planned Economy and Market Regulation

In a country like China where the essential elements of a commodity economy are in short supply, and central planning has dominated the economy for so long, it is very difficult to change the socialist economic mechanism and develop a marketing mechanism. Experience in China and in other socialist countries has shown that a centrally-planned economy tends to strangle the vitality of enterprises and become the protection umbrella for low efficiency and high consumption. Admittedly, the market will not disappear. But the aim of reform must be to establish a freer commodity economy, and the market will make a valuable contribution to the whole national economy.

Regulating the market has been the aim of most socialist countries since the 1950s and 1960s. Although conditions and the time of beginning the reforms vary from country to country, these reforms have much in common. First is the necessity to alter the sole State-ownership and allow more economic elements and modes of management to co-exist. The second is to transform the management system which is too rigid and results in a weak market. Third, it is necessary to transform the concentrated power of the Central Party and government organs and transfer more power to the local organs. Finally, the control of the State over all enterprises needs to be changed and an attempt made to unify the economic benefits of the Central and local governments, the state and enterprises, the collectives and individual concerns in order to establish a satisfactory system of distribution, distinct responsibility, power and benefits.

The chief aim of the reform is to incorporate the market element into the economic mechanism, and to find a permanent socialist method of coordinating a planned economy and a commodity economy to suit China's needs, in short, to alter the tight control of centralized planning. The plans adopted over the past 10 years have brought considerable economic changes.

The introduction of a responsibility system, a significant feature of the rural reform, soon improved the relationship between commodity and money, and, in turn, the whole economy. With remarkable speed, the market saw, first, a surplus not only of agricultural but other commodities. Then, toward the end of the 1980s, intensive farming, commodity and money were infused into the economic mechanism in the rural areas. By 1984 when the price of agricultural and miscellaneous products had increased, the market forces began to lead the way. However, owing to miscalculation of the potentiality of the rural areas and the reduction of state investment in agriculture, agricultural production declined. The contradiction between the demand and supply of agricultural and miscellaneous products became sharper, as were the contradiction between administrative orders and the nature of the new system. Therefore the degree and scope of the co-ordination of planned economy and market economy must necessarily be adjusted if a solution of the problem is to be found.

The Gradual Transference of Agriculture from a State- to a Market-Controlled Activity

As China is a developing country, commodities for export have a high profile, that is, agricultural and miscellaneous products, as well as semi-manufactured products which take precedence over high-value manufactured products. In contrast, the structure of imported commodities show the opposite. Shandong Province is no exception.

In 1980, the total value of all the commodities imported into Shandong was over $100 million US, increasing to $640 million US in 1989, that is, an annual rate of increase of 22.2 percent. As Table 4,8 shows, the total value of all the commodities exported from the province in 1979 was $1.3 billion US, and in 1987 nearly $3 billion US, the yearly rate of increase being 8.8 percent. The kind and proportion of the commodities imported will be discussed in the next section.

Table 4,8   Value of Commodities Exported From Shandong, 1979 to 1987

| Year | Absolute Value ($ million US) | Percentage | | | |
		Agricultural & Misc.	Light & Textile	Arts & Crafts	Industry & Mineral
1979	1,305.7	28.3	22.6	10.2	38.9
1980	1,763.1	25.9	19.2	9.3	45.6
1981	1,891.2	30.9	18.6	9.4	41.1
1982	1,658.4	24.4	22.2	8.4	45.0
1983	1,807.8	26.9	21.1	8.5	43.5
1984	2,288.2	35.8	16.8	4.5	52.9
1985	2,666.7	22.6	15.3	5.4	56.7
1986	2,135.1	33.1	24.7	8.3	33.9
1987	2,975.8	29.8	24.7	8.0	37.5
1988	2,980.2	31.4	27.5	10.5	30.6
1989	3,063.1	32.3	31.8	11.7	24.3
1990	3,496.7	31.1	33.0	14.3	21.6

Source: Shandong Statistics Yearbook, 1980-1991

From Table 4,8, it is clear that the value of agricultural and miscellaneous goods exported from Shandong Province between 1979 and 1988 was between 24 and 36 percent of the total value of all commodities, most of which was produced in the province. Moreover, the supply of goods was steady. Traditional commodities for export, such as corn, peanut, vegetable oil, goatskin, blue fox-skin, rabbits' hair, vermicelli, small dates, cotton, tobacco and even articles made from grass, willow branches and reed can earn annually over $10 million US and enjoy a good reputation in the international market.

Shandong is most certainly a huge agricultural province, and this results in a relatively small importation of agricultural products, chief of which is wheat, imported to regulate the supply of food. The output of wheat in the province in 1989 was 15.8 billion kilograms, that is, 193 kilograms per capita. Some of the wheat produced in the province must be sent to Beijing and Tianjin, but generally, since wheat flour is the main food, there is still need to import wheat, largely from Australia. This means that if Canada desires to sell wheat to Shandong, Canada must compete with Australia.

It is worth noting that co-operation between Shandong Province and the World Bank in agricultural development has produced good results. More specifically, a World Bank loan of $106 million US has been devoted wholly to developing three comprehensive agricultural programmes in Shandong, including that mentioned previously, for transforming the middle and low-yielding soils along the Tuhai River. This involves 12 counties in the three Prefectures of Dezhou, Liaocheng and Huimin. Some Y88.5 million have been used for developing livestock farming in the Yi and Meng Mountains, involving eight counties in Linyi Prefecture and the two municipalities of Tai'an and Zaozhuang. Another Y64 million have been used for developing agriculture along the coastal area of the province, involving four counties in the municipalities of Yantai and Weifang, and in Huimin Prefecture. The World Bank loan is to be matched by a similar amount from the province for the same purpose of developing agriculture in the province.

The World Bank has made another loan of $100 million US for an irrigation programme for 28 counties in four municipalities and prefectures of Heze, Jining, Zaozhuang and Tai'an. An evaluation of the programme was to be made in 1990.

In addition, the World Bank has lent $22.5 million US for the construction of quick-growing forests, while the Federal Republic of Germany has invested 20 million marks for providing drinking water for people and livestock in the Yi and Meng Mountains (Shandong Provincial Finance Bureau, 1989). The attitude of Shandong Province towards utilizing foreign investment to develop agriculture has all along been positive.

Potential Areas for Co-operation
Between the Provinces of Shandong and Saskatchewan

It would appear that the potential for co-operation between Shandong and Saskatchewan is promising. Saskatchewan, one of the three prairie provinces of Canada, is an important wheat-producing area, a part of the so-called "bread basket of the world." Whereas Saskatchewan produces 60 percent of Canada's wheat, Shandong's comparatively small farmland produces only a small amount of wheat, and its population, which is 82 times that of Saskatchewan, makes it imperative for Shandong to import wheat yearly. Also, frequent, destructive natural calamities reduce yield and cause a shortage of grain, which is overcome by importing wheat. Therefore, Shandong Province should undoubtedly be a target area for Saskatchewan's wheat. On the other hand, Shandong's soils and climatic conditions permit the growing of specialized crops that Canada could consider importing. These include fine-quality rice, millet, Chinese sorghum, dates, chestnuts, garlic, hawthorn, pomegranates, and Chinese yams, all of which are in demand by a certain section of the Canadian population.

Again, in contrast to Shandong, Saskatchewan produces turkeys and chickens, breeds which are large and yield more meat than those produced in Shandong. Here, then, are two other commodities that could enter the Shandong-Saskatchewan trade.

Co-operation in Agricultural Science and Technology

As an agricultural province in Canada, Saskatchewan is said to have one of the most up-to-date means of production, transportation and marketing facilities. It also has excellent varieties of grain, fodder, livestock breeds; advanced technology for soil testing, monitoring instruments for crop growing, equipment for plant protection, water-saving-irrigation technique—in short, technology and technological expertise required for Chinese agriculture. And because the Shandong Provincial Government has decided to increase its expenditure on agricultural scientific research, the possibilities for co-operation and mutual exchanges appear considerable. The quick-growing poplar trees imported from Canada grow well in the province and rightly earn their popular nickname "Canada Poplar."

True, the investment, labour and material that Shandong has so far given to agricultural scientific research in the province has achieved some successes, for example, a fine breed of corn that yields 900 kilograms per mu, and a strain of wheat that yields 400 kilograms per mu. And, as mentioned above, the province has also taken steps to improve its alkaline soils. These are endeavours in which both Saskatchewan and Canada could invest profitably.

Now that China's agriculture is intensively done on a household basis, the scope of management is very limited. Usually the management of 5 to 20 mu (about 3 acres) of land, what were the large-scale State or collective farms, and the forest and livestock farms are small in number. They do not require large agricultural machines. What is in great demand are light, energy-saving, small-size, agricultural machines for cotton-picking and for taking stalks back to the fields. Large machines are needed for opening wasteland, for seeding and harvesting. The level of management also needs improving. Thus new techniques and joint development are urgently required.

The great need in Shandong, especially in agricultural production, indeed, in the whole of China, is the application of modern technology and modern methods to farming. There is an urgent need to improve Shandong's agricultural production by applying more chemical fertilizer (especially nitrogen and pesticide for cotton pests), and by supplying weed-killer. Whereas the demand for pesticide is 50,000 to 60,000 tons, the province can produce only 42,000 tons. Again, the shortage of plastic sheeting is about 60,000 tons. In each case, the shortage must be replaced by imports from other provinces or from abroad, in particular from Japan which monopolizes this market. This is very much an area in which Canada could compete. Apart from supplying technology, Canada could well consider establishing enterprises to produce chemical fertilizer, pesticide and plastic sheeting. Shandong is ready to welcome such a venture.

Between 1975 and 1989, Canada and Shandong Province signed contracts for six projects, the value of which was only $1.37 million US, but the contracts have yet to be implemented. Japan, on the other hand, has invested some $310 million US in Shandong. Perhaps Canada is overly cautious and willing to take only small steps.

CONCLUSION

Shandong is determined to improve its agriculture, and to a high degree. It aims to develop large water conservation projects and wastelands, to improve poor soils, forest networks, animal husbandry and processing. However, the province lacks the essential ingredients to effect speedy development: modern technology, technological expertise and development capital. On the other hand, Shandong, like the rest of China, has a considerable potential for trade which should be attractive to Saskatchewan and all Canada. Strong links, mutual co-operation and trust have already been established between them. It is to be hoped, therefore, that the transference of Saskatchewan's technology and capital to help in the development of Shandong's agriculture will be profitable to both provinces.

REFERENCES

Shandong Provincial Agricultural Bureau. (March 1988). Research for the Planning for Agricultural Development of the Yellow-Huai-Hai Plain in Shandong Province, Jinan.

Shandong Provincial Finance Bureau. (1989). *Conditions of utilizing foreign investment by Shandong Province.* Jinan, Unpublished.

Shandong Provincial Party Committee. (1986). *Conditions of Shandong Province.* Jinan: Shandong People's Press.

Shandong Provincial Statistics Bureau. (1978, 1987, 1980-89). Bulletin on National Economy and Social Development, Jinan, an annual publication.

ACKNOWLEDGEMENTS

The authors are greatly indebted to Professor Hou Mingjuin for his painstaking translation of the text from Chinese to English and for the edited version from English to Chinese so that they could see and approve what changes were made.

INDUSTRIAL DEVELOPMENT, SHANDONG

Chen Longfei and Yan Aihua

Shandong Teachers' University, Jinan, Shandong

INTRODUCTION

As a developing country, China has fully realized, especially since the past decade or more, that the industrial sector of its economy is inefficient, partly as a consequence of underdevelopment of its resources, outdated technology and techniques, and inadequate investment capital, among other militating factors. What is true of the nation is also true of Shandong Province. Yet, Shandong has very favourable conditions for industrial development, including an abundant supply of energy and raw materials, a favourable geographical location within easy reach of Beijing and Tianjin in the north, and Shanghai and Nanjing in the south, a frontage on the sea, a large population, and a huge labour force which also provides a considerable market. Together, these offer much scope for industrial development.

According to official statistics, the total industrial output value of Shandong Province in 1989 was 8.76 percent of the national total, taking fourth place after Shanghai, Liaoning and Jingsu. Of the 260 major industrial products included in the national plan, 68 from Shandong ranked third in output, among them gold, diamonds and crude salt. Another 20 products ranked first, including petroleum, tractors and leather. Some 23 other products ranked second, including synthetic ammonia and cotton cloth. Still others ranked third. Table 1,9 shows the differences between Shandong's major industrial products and those of the nation. It reveals that machine and electronics, textile and sewing, crude oil and petroleum products were the chief.

Table 1,9   Output of Selected Major Industrial Products (1988)

Products	Unit	Nation's Output	Shandong's Output	Percentage of Nation
Cotton yarn	mil.tons	4.7	0.6	12.5
Cotton cloth	bil. metres	18.6	1.9	10.2
Wood fibre	mil. metres	270.0	19.0	7.0
Machine & Paper	mil. tons	12.8	1.0	7.5
Crude salt	mil. tons	28.0	6.0	20.0
Cigarettes	mil. boxes	32.0	2.3	7.4
Synthetic detergent	000 tons	1430.0	115.2	8.1
Bicycles	million	36.7	2.5	6.9
TV Sets	million	27.0	0.7	2.6
Home refrigerator	million	6.6	0.2	3.1
Cameras	million	2.3	0.1	6.2
Crude Oil	mil. tons	137.0	33.3	24.3
Raw coal	bil. tons	1.0	0.6	5.5
Electricity	bil. kwh	582.0	41.7	7.2
Steel	mil. tons	61.2	2.1	3.4
Rolled steel	mil. tons	48.6	1.5	3.1
Cement	mil. tons	207.0	18.8	9.1
Sulphuric Acid	mil. tons	11.4	0.7	6.4
Sodium carbonate	mil. tons	3.0	0.5	16.8
Chemical fertilizer	mil. tons	18.8	1.4	7.7
Chemical pesticide	000 tons	227.3	12.3	5.4
Machine tools	000	165.3	11.8	7.1
Trucks	000	573.7	13.4	2.3
Tractors	000	43.3	7.2	16.6

Source: *State and Shandong Annual Statistics Report*, 1989

As Table 1,9 shows, Shandong's industries are many and varied. They make up 38 of the 40 categories listed in the National Standard Industrial Department Classification. The chief are textile, machine-building, food processing, chemical fertilizers and pesticides, building material and energy. Village industry is also important. It makes up 26 percent of the total value of the industries of the whole province and nearly 17 percent of the whole country. This means that industry in the rural areas of the province is developed to some extent even higher than the average industrial output of the country. The ratio of light industrial output value to that of heavy industry in Shandong is slightly over 1:1, and to that of the whole country slightly under 1:1, an indication that Shandong's industrial base concentrates more on light industry than that of the nation.

On the whole, the technical level of industrial equipment in the province is backward. About 10 percent of it is on par with that of the developed world; 31 percent equates with the advanced level, 42 percent with the average level, and 17 percent with the backward level of the country (Shandong Economic Research Centre, 1989: 214-216). In respect of the technical equipment used in the whole country, only 18 percent of it is equal to that of the advanced world; 8 percent higher than Shandong; 14 percent regarded as backward; and 3 percent lower than that of Shandong (Ibid.). In the local industrial fixed assets of Shandong, both the rate of depreciation and the rate of drawing from the heavy repair fund are lower than those of the municipality of Shanghai and the provinces of Jiangsu and Liaoning. Clearly, backward technology has adversely affected the economy. The tax from the industrial enterprises in Shandong Province in 1987 was low, only 16 percent of all taxes, lower than the average tax (16.6 percent) from the country. The profit from the sale per Y100 was only Y9.2, again lower than that of the whole country. The fixed production cost in Shandong, compared with that of the whole country, was higher. The rate of utilizing the fixed assets is lower. Some 15 to 20 percent of the equipment and assets is estimated to be idle or semi-idle.

For some time, a leading industry that could contribute significantly to Shandong Province has failed to emerge, unlike Japan, for example, where in the 1960s the chemical industry dominated. In the 1970s, it was the motor car industry; in the 1980s, it was new technology, such as micro-electronics, new materials, biological engineering, all of which at different times played an important role, and at different times made a contribution to the Japanese economy. Although Shandong has decided to concentrate on textiles, machine-building, food processing, chemicals, building materials and manufacturing of non-ferrous metal products, these activities are unlikely to play a significant role because they are still backward and occupy an inferior position in the whole industrial structure.

For various reasons, new industries develop very slowly, and tend to hinder the upgrading of the industrial structure. Consider the electronics industry, for example. Although it has a history in Shandong of more than 20 years, its output is less than that of other provinces, no more than 2 percent of the provincial total industrial output value in 1987. It seems that in China it is difficult to develop high-value industries, an obvious result of the backward technology and industrial techniques used, which in turn affect the level of economic development.

The requirements of a planned commodity economy, as it relates to Shandong's industry, are officially stated: to take market demand as a guide; to adopt technical reforms; to place emphasis on basic industry, technique-intensive machine building, and the electronics industry; to upgrade the equipment of all the economic departments, and guarantee the supply of raw materials; to pay much attention to high-tech equipment and new industries; to establish bases for exporting textile and food products which utilize agricultural sideline or miscellaneous products as raw materials; to produce more high-quality products and products to earn foreign exchange; and to realize a high efficiency in output (Shandong Provincial Overall Plan, 1991). The Plan, prepared by Shandong Province, states that by the year 2000, the industrial output value of the province should reach Y248.2 billion, the annual rate of increase being 9 percent (Table 2,9). The output value of the five industrial departments of energy, raw materials, machine-building and electronics, textiles and food should make up 89 percent of the total industrial output value, higher than that of 1987. The Plan states further that the present export of raw materials (60 percent) and manufactured goods (40 percent) should be reversed.

Table 2,9   Shandong's Planned Industrial Development by 2000

	Output Value (billion Y)	%	Output Value (billion Y)	%	Rate of Increase (%) 1988-2000
Total Output Value	89.2	100.0	27.4	100.0	9.0
Village Ind. & below	19.4		6.7		10.0
Township Ind. & above	69.8		20.7		8.7
Coal, Crude Oil & Electricity	7.4	10.7	18.0	8.7	7.0
Food, Drinks & Tobacco	8.6	1.2	28.0	13.5	9.5
Textile & Sewing	13.7	19.7	42.0	20.3	9.0

Table 2,9   continued

	Output Value (billion Y)	%	Output Value (billion Y)	%	Rate of Increase (%) 1988-2000
Petro-Chemical Medicine, Synthetic Fibres & Rubber Products	9.2	13.2	30.0	14.5	9.5
Building Materials & Non-metal Mines	4.1	5.9	12.0	5.8	8.7
Mines & Electronics	16.1	23.0	55.0	26.5	10.0
Crude Salt	0.3	0.4	1.5	0.7	13.0
Plastic Products	1.4	2.0	4.0	1.9	8.4
Metal Mines & Smelting	2.4	3.4	7.0	3.4	8.0
Others	6.6	9.4	9.8	4.7	3.0

Source: Shandong Provincial Overall Land Plan, 1991.

At this point, it might be helpful to discuss the industries separately in order to highlight their individual characteristics, needs and potentialities.

THE ENERGY INDUSTRY

Generally, Shandong Province has a variety of energy resources—coal, petroleum, natural gas—which are widely distributed and easily exploited. These accord the province a far greater economic advantage, compared with those provinces along the southeast coast of China, which are economically developed but short of energy. It is, however, ironic that every year Shandong has to import 7 million tons of coal from other provinces, and finds itself short of over one million Kw of electricity. The shortage clearly reduces the productive capacity of factories, mines and labour force in both rural and urban centres. At the same time, the generating equipment of the province is over-loaded and often breaks down. The serious shortage of energy has thus become the major factor restricting the economic development of the province. So while there are distinct advantages to Shandong's energy industry, there are some drawbacks.

The Energy Resources

Deposits of the major energy resources in the province are considerable. By the end of 1987, the known coal deposits were estimated at 20 billion tons, 60 percent of which is concentrated in the four mines of Tengnan, Tenabel, Yanzhou and Jining. Altogether, 15 billion tons of the total output of these mines are reserved for industry and 5 billion tons must be saved for further exploration in the area north of the Yellow River and Jining Prefecture (Shandong Provincial Land Planning Office, 1991: 72). Again, in 1987, a large-scale coal reserve, estimated at 5 billion tons, was discovered in the Heze Prefecture. The prediction is that even if it is exploited at the present level of output in the province, its life is likely to be some 300 years.

Equally advantageous is the variety of Shandong's coal, bituminous or coking coal being the chief. The mines are mostly located in areas where the economy is relatively well developed and supported by a dense population and easy transportation. The peninsular area, however, is poor in coal reserves.

Petroleum and Natural Gas

Since the 1960s oil exploration has been carried out in the five sedimentary basins of Jiyang, Changwel, Jiaolai, Linching and southwest Shandong, as well as in the continental shelf fronting the delta of the Yellow River. The total exploration area is about 65,000 square kilometres. The expected output from this area is over 6 billion tons of crude oil. The reserves rank second in the country. The second largest, in Shandong, Shengli oilfield, has an annual output of more than 30 million tons.

Natural gas in Shandong is also associated with petroleum. It is estimated that some 150 billion cubic metres are concentrated in the Shengli Oilfield.

Increase in the production of energy in Shandong has developed rapidly, more so since the exploitation of the Shengli Oilfield in the 1960s. In contrast, the output of raw coal has increased annually by only 3 to 4 percent in the past few years, much lower than the annual rate of oil output, which is 18 percent. As the petroleum industry is administered by the central government, and oil has to be exported to other provinces, the consumption of coal, which is 70 to 80 percent of what is produced, continues to increase. From the data assembled in Table 3,9, calculation will show that the annual rate of energy production in Shandong for the decade 1980 and 1989 was 5 percent, much lower than the annual rate of increase of the GNP (16.8 percent) for the same period. As the production of energy lagged far behind economic growth, the shortage of energy is unavoidable.

Table 3,9   Energy Output in Shandong, 1980 to 1989

	Raw Coal (million tons)	Crude Oil (million tons)	Natural Gas (million tons)	Total Output Standard Coal (million tons)
1980	26.1	30.6	1.9	58.7
1981	23.0	29.5	1.4	53.9
1982	23.3	30.4	1.3	55.1
1983	26.2	31.3	1.4	58.9
1984	32.8	32.5	1.4	66.9
1985	38.6	35.1	1.5	75.3
1986	42.1	36.4	1.8	80.4
1987	45.1	37.9	1.9	85.1
1988	47.5	39.7	1.8	89.1
1989	47.6	40.6	2.0	90.3
1990	47.8	42.8	1.9	92.6

Source: Shandong Statistics Yearbook, 1991

By the end of 1987, the capacity of the generating equipment owned by the Province was 5.7 million kilowatts (Shandong Provincial Land Planning Office, 1991: 81). Major power plants have been built in the west and southwest parts of the province, close to the coal bases. The present proportion of the power generated by coal is 81 percent and that by oil 19 percent. Thus the province appears to be sending the power from west to east. The amount of electricity generated in 1989 was 41.7 billion kilowatt hours, and the annual rate of increase in the past 10 years was 9.4 percent. But as industrial and other power-consuming activities developed rapidly, the shortage of power continued and has now become even worse. Production of power from the networks is critical. Disconcerting also is the fact that the generating units cannot be repaired on time, consequently the power system is unreliable.

Energy production is crucial for the basic industries. Whether the development plan of the national economy can be implemented will depend upon energy production. The forecast of energy supply and demand in Shandong Province is shown in Table 4,9.

Table 4,9   Forecast: Demand and Supply of
Energy in Shandong Province, 1990 to 2000

	1990	*1995*	*2000*
Total demand (million tons std. coal)	73.6	92.2	106.5
For sections of material production	61.0	77.4	89.5
For sections of non-material production	7.5	8.5	9.7
For transformation and loss	5.0	6.3	7.3
Converted to: Raw coal (million tons)	77.3	96.9	111.9
Crude oil (mil. tons)	15.9	19.9	22.9
Natural gas (billion c.metres)	1.8	2.3	2.8
Others (1000 tons std. coal)	14.7	18.4	21.3
Demand for electricity (billion kwh)	50.0	70.0	100.0

Source: *Strategy for Economic and Social Development of Shandong Province*, 1989.

According to the forecast, beginning 1990 coal production should have increased at the annual rate of 7 percent, but the annual rate of increase in recent years was 3 to 4 percent. For crude oil the annual rate of increase should remain at 4 percent, the level that it is at present. This appears possible and may even surpass that level. For power produced from coal and natural gas, the annual rate of increase should be 9 percent, close to the rate of increase in the past few years. Clearly, it is necessary for the coal industry to improve its rate of production.

Future Development of the Energy Industry

For the provincial economy to develop and operate at an increasing speed, the energy industry must develop even more speedily. To this end, the Planning Section of the Shandong Government has evolved its development plan of the industry, referred to above.

In respect of coal production, the plan aims to increase and maintain output, depending on the progress of science and technology; to speed up the construction of new and improvement of old mines; and to make maximum use of the resources of the province in order to satisfy demand. By the end of the century, it is planned to open 50 to 60 new mines, each to produce 50 million tons annually. These will be located in Tengbei, Yanzhou and the north Yellow River area. The plan also aims to improve the old mines—Yanzhou, Zaotang, Xinwenand Feicheng—and increase their production capacities by 11 million tons. The estimated investment will be Y17 billion, that is, an annual investment of Y1.3 billion.

In the case of oil and natural gas, production in the province has always been fairly smooth. The plan estimates that there will be no difficulty to attain a goal of 50 million tons annually by the end of the century. But it states that attention should be paid to improving the methods of prospecting, to increase the storage capacity, and maintain a balance between exploiting and conservation. The Shandong part of the Zhongyuan Oilfield is to be developed into a new complex which will focus on the production of oil and natural gas.

Next, for electricity generation, the plan calls for the installed capacity to reach 7.6 million kilowatts in 1990, 12 million in 1995, and 17 million in 2000. The planned power plants (including newly built and rebuilt) are to be in Zouxian, Dezhou, Heze, Shijiu and Weihai. In addition, two 500 kilowatt extra high voltage transmission lines from Jinan to Weifang and from Zouxian to Zibo will be built. The capacity of the Zouxian Power Plant will be increased to 2.6 million kilowatts. The construction period is set for 1991 to 1995. The whole requires a total investment of Y2.76 billion, a part to be provided by foreign investment.

To meet the requirements of the plan, the Province has devised detailed policy measures. Some that are likely to be implemented by cooperation between China and Canada include:

- the introduction of advanced technology to replace old machines and equipment, including modern production lines, a wide application of computers, monitoring of the key links in production, and high energy-consuming equipment.

- developing urban heating and gas-supply systems by replacing the low-efficiency boilers and coal stoves of the residents with large-scale boiler-generating units to produce both heat and electricity.

- directing foreign investment to exploit the coal mines and build power plants. It is planned to utilize over $1.5 billion US of foreign investment and to repay foreign loans by exporting local coal, conducting comprehensive compensation trade, and by the foreign exchange earned within the province;

the building of nuclear power stations. At present, 80 percent of the power in the province is generated from coal. As the coal deposits are concentrated in the middle and western parts of the province, and as the Shandong peninsular area (which is relatively developed) is poor in coal and must import it from other areas, much pressure is exerted on coal production, its transportation, and on environmental protection. It would seem rational, then, to develop a domestic nuclear-power plant in the peninsular area, but the problem is not whether a nuclear power station is needed, but whether the Province can afford the cost of establishing it, and whether the advanced nuclear-power technology is fully understood. There are already plans to build a 900,000 kilowatt nuclear power plant in the eastern part of the province before 2000.

Also planned is the development of other energy sources, including solar, wind, tide, marsh gas, and geo-thermal. As Shandong is in the warm temperate zone, with long hours of sunlight and high accumulated temperature, it has a high potentiality to develop technology to utilize solar energy. This is still at the research and experimental stage. Once economical and practical products, which are easy to popularize, appear, their prospects should be promising. Besides, Shandong has operated wind-power and tide-power stations for years, but their progress has been limited by natural conditions and the lack of advanced technology. Canada has developed these power stations along its coasts with advanced technology, and Canada's experience, shared with Shandong, would be of considerable help in this endeavour.

THE METALLURGICAL INDUSTRY

The metallurgical industry in Shandong and throughout China is both old and young. In Shandong the industry has had a long history, but development of the modern metallurgical industry there is relatively new; it began only in the last 30 years. During the industrial upsurge in the whole country, beginning in 1958—the Big Leap Forward—"going in for steel in a big way" was the official aim, and Shandong mobilized three million people in building thousands of small blast furnaces. It established a group of metallurgical enterprises with fairly high technical level, such as the Jinan Iron and Steel Works, and later the steel works of Laiwu

(Figure 1,9), Zhangdian and Qingdao. But the output of steel was just a few hundred thousand tons. The metallurgical industry in Shandong remained somewhat stagnant until 1984 when the Province established a corporation of metallurgical industry and reformed the management system. By 1987, the output of steel, rolled steel and pig iron produced in Shandong ranked first, fourth and second, respectively, among those of other provinces, municipalities and autonomous regions. The output of gold, for example, rose to 25 percent of the nation's total output.

Ascribing age and youth to Shandong's metallurgical industry may be considered in another way. Now that industrialization in China has increased rapidly during the last two decades, demand for iron and steel is much greater than the supply. Yearly, much foreign exchange has to be spent in importing rolled steel. Shandong province produces no more than 50 percent of its needs. This means that much emphasis will be placed on the industry in the next few decades.

Natural Resources for the Metallurgical Industry

Apart from coal, the major raw materials for the smelting of steel are refactory clay, limestone for flux, magnesite and gangue, deposits of all of which are found in Shandong Province. The total deposit of iron ore, for example, is estimated at two billion tons. These local raw materials make for the development of a promising iron-smelting industry The iron ore is found in the middle-southern, northern and western parts of the province. The whole area is advantageously located, convenient for transportation and close to cities like Jinan, Zibo and Tai'an. Moreover, the area is a good technological base. But although the supply of iron ore is good, the ore is low-grade. More than 60 percent comprises other constituents. Deposits of rich ore are mostly very deep underground, difficult and expensive to mine because of local hydrological and geological conditions

Demand and Supply of Metallurgical Products

The level of consumption of metallurgical products, particularly steel, is the index of measuring the level of development of the industry. Especially in a developing country, the level of consuming rolled steel is always in indirect proportion to the increase of material production in the national economy. From 1980 to 1987 the consumption of rolled steel in Shandong increased from 1.76 million tons to 3.84 million tons. The annual rate of increase was 11.8 percent, equivalent to 210,000 tons of steel. The annual rate of increase for the total output value of industry and agriculture in the same period was 12.4 percent (Shandong Economics Research Centre, December 1989: 264-266). It is evident that the increase of both should be in step.

Of the different kinds of products consumed, rolled steel accounted for about 40 percent, wire or rod 16 percent, and tube, plate and belt 44 percent. This consumption is similar to that of the whole country.

At present, the disparity between demand and supply is very sharp. The national total output of steel in 1989 was 61.24 million tons and rolled steel 48.65 million tons; the shortage was 40 million tons. Some 20 million tons of this was imported, requiring more than $6 billion US every year (Ibid.). It is estimated that the demand for steel and rolled steel will be 100 million tons and 90 million tons, respectively, by the end of this century (Ibid.). The shortage of rolled steel is also troubling. The output of steel in Shandong in 1989 was 2.1 million tons, and rolled steel 1.5 million tons, both of which were far from meeting the demand. Thus in recent years, Shandong's annual importation of rolled steel (0.3 million tons) required some $100 million US (Ibid.). From 1980 to 1987 the rate of increase in steel production in Shandong was only 7 percent, which was 4.8 percent lower than the rate of increase in the consumption. This made for a shortage of 44 percent in 1980, 33 percent in 1985, and 32 percent in 1987 (Ibid.). Also, it has necessitated the importation of rolled steel, the foreign exchange for which will, in the long run, adversely affect the provincial budget.

A conservative prediction of the consumption of rolled steel in Shandong by the year 2000 may be attempted. Given the combined total output value of Shandong's industry and agriculture as Y144.6 billion, and assuming that the annual rate of increase remains at 5.5 percent, it is more than likely that there will be a doubling of the total output value by 2000. Again, the consumption of rolled steel in 1987 was 3.8 million tons; if this were to increase annually at the same rate of 5.5 percent, it would reach over 7.7 million tons by 2000. The 5.5 percent annual rate of increase is a very conservative one, therefore the consumption should be over 8 million tons by 2000. Even if a large-scale iron-and-steel-works complex were to be put into operation and were to produce 3 million tons of steel yearly, the disparity would still have to be rectified.

Future Development of the Metallurgical Industry

The aim of developing Shandong's iron and steel industry is to produce 2.5 million tons by 1992, 3 million tons by 1995, and 5 million tons by 2000; the annual rate of increase would then be about 9 percent, which would be 258,600 tons of steel. In 2000 the output would be expected to reach (in million tons): steel 4, pig iron 4.5, iron ore 8, and refactory materials 0.45. The exported products would earn $400 million US—a goal that is worthy of achieving and for which certain measures should be taken.

First, the existing plants would need to be upgraded to increase output without heavy input. This is not altogether impossible, for between 1980 and 1985, the Province improved the two steel works at Laiwu (Figure 1,9), and Qingdao, increasing their steel-smelting capacity by 0.46 million tons, at a production cost of no more than Y1,000 per ton of steel. Backed by foreign investment, the Laiwu steel works increased steel production from 0.3 million to 0.7 million tons at a production cost of only Y1,700 per ton. However, a newly-built steel plant, operating under normal conditions, produces a ton of steel at a cost of Y3,000 (Ibid). For this reason, it was decided to utilize foreign investment in the present iron and steel works.

Table 5,9 indicates the present and projected production capacity for steel, pig iron and rolled steel in the Laiwu General Iron and Steel works and the Jinan Iron Plant. In the former, the coking plant will be improved and complete production sets completed. Between 1990 and 2000 the plant is expected to produce one million tons of steel and 0.24 million tons of electric steel with an investment of Y1.3 billion. Similarly, the Qingdao General Iron and Steel Works will enlarge its workshop facilities to produce 0.7 million tons of steel and 0.6 million tons of rolled steel. No less, the Jinan Iron Plant will extend its iron ore mine, build up its production line of centrifugal nodular cast-iron tubes by joint investment, transform and enlarge its blast furnaces and increase its capacity, as shown in Table 5,9, and eventually become the provincial cast-iron centre.

Table 5,9   Planned Production Capacity, 1990 to 2000 (million tons)

	1990	2000
Laiwu General Iron & Steel Works:		
Steel	0.30	0.70
Pig Iron	0.30	0.80
Rolled Steel	0.24	0.63
Jinan Iron Plant:		
Pig Iron	0.2	0.5

Source: Strategy for Economic and Social Development of Shandong Province, 1989.

The second means of achieving the development aims of the metal-lurgical industry is to build new, large-scale iron and steel works. The Jining General Iron and Steel Works, which the Province plans to build, is to produce 3 million tons of steel by 2000. The project is at present under examination.

The third means is to import good quality iron ore since, as mentioned previously, Shandong's ore is not easily-mined, and underground water poses a problem, especially in Laiwu and Jinan. It is cheaper to import foreign ore. Present world production of iron ore has reached 1.3 billion tons and the consumption of iron and steel in major developed countries is nearing saturation point (Ibid.: 275-277). It is estimated that about 300 million tons of iron ore will be available for the world market (Ibid.). The countries that export most are Australia, Brazil, Canada and India. Their total export is 60 percent of the world's total. The main sources of China's imported iron ore are Brazil and Australia. There is none from Canada, possibly because of higher Canadian prices. But whatever the reason, the shortage of iron ore in Shandong Province makes for importation of the ore. There is certainly a necessity for both China and Canada to co-operate in China's importation of Canadian iron ore.

Yet a fourth means of increasing industrial capacity is increased ex-ports to maintain the balance of foreign trade. Shandong's import of iron and steel may be compensated for to a degree by the export of non-ferrous metals, rare-earth metal, rare-earth alloy, fluorite, high-quality magnesia, hard clay and fine-quality limestone—all products which may earn for-eign exchange. Bartering could also be considered.

Miscellaneous Metallurgical Industry

In respect of aluminium, the Shandong Aluminum Plant produces 650,000 tons of aluminum oxide and 50,000 tons of aluminum ingots annually. But this plant is under the control of the State, and its products are distributed by the State. In contrast, the aluminum plants at Pingyin and Zibo (annual output 4,000 and 2,000 tons, respectively) are operated by the Province, but their total output is insufficient to meet local demand. It is planned to enlarge the production capacity of the Pingyin plant to 12,500 tons and the Zibo plant to 10,000 tons to cater to the demand (Ibid.).

Also, gold is produced in the Shandong peninsula at some ten mines; their total output exceeds 400 tons (Ibid.). It is obtained from alluvial deposits. In fact, Shandong Province now ranks first in the annual output

Figure 1,9 Laiwu Steelworks *(Photo by Liu Zhenging)*

Figure 2,9 Qilu Petrochemical Refinery *(Photo by Liu Zhenging)*

of gold. The annual output from the Zhaoyuan and Laizhou mines alone has exceeded 10,000 kilograms. In addition, lead, zinc and copper are smelted. Their combined output, 2,000 tons, however, takes a minor position in the provincial metallurgical industry.

THE CHEMICAL INDUSTRY

The chemical industry serves both heavy and light industries, various sectors of the national economy and various areas of social life. It is one of the most important means of production and source of valuable materials in Shandong. It tops the list of industrial input and output, and interacts with and influences other industries. It also contributes directly to the development of agriculture, the textile industry, machine-building, electronics, building materials, construction, and national defence. Japan regards this industry as indispensable to its development; without it Japan could not have modernized its industries as quickly as it has.

As the key industry in any country's development, the chemical industry should be the premier industry in Shandong Province, and modernization of it should be the goal of Shandong industrial planning. The reasons are quite obvious. First, the present value or importance of the industry will increase with progress in science. For example, new chemical products have replaced the reinforced steel bar; cement has become economical, and construction material and super-strong plastics have replaced iron and steel; automobiles made of plastics are now being manufactured—all indicate that the range and application of chemical products have increased. Thus supply and demand should be the motivating factors in the redevelopment of the industry.

Second, Shandong has ample resources for the development of the chemical industry, including coal, petroleum, natural gas, iron ore (with both sulphur and phosphorous), bauxite, natural sulphur, raw salt, serpentine, barytes, gypsum and talc. Indeed, the industrial raw materials of Shandong Province are far in excess of those of other provinces, municipalities and autonomous regions.

Third, Shandong's experience in the chemical industry, together with its capacity for producing a variety of chemical products, makes for further development of the industry. At present, Shandong produces chemical fertilizer, pesticide, petro-chemical products, organic chemical raw materials, inorganic salt, basic chemical raw materials, dyes, paint rubber, chemical reagent, pharmaceutical products—as many as 1,300 different kinds of products and more than 15,000 models, types or standards. Moreover, scientific research, design experience, education and prospecting knowledge are also available.

The level of production and technology of Shandong's chemical industry, compared with that at the national level, is high, even higher than that of other industries. The output of many chemical products not only tops the national list, but the products themselves enjoy a high reputation. In 1987, the total output value of Shandong's chemical industry ranked fourth among the nation's chemical industry and the income earned topped the national list of industrial earnings.

Fourth, the external conditions for developing the chemical industry in Shandong are also favourable. The geographical location and adequate transportation facilities (highways, railway, sea), mentioned earlier, are advantageous for the chemical industry, which relies on collection of raw materials and distribution of chemical products. But further development of the industry, especially at the already established industrial bases like Beijing, Shanghai, Tianjin and Nanjing, will be restricted by environmental policies. Thus Shandong could well become the ideal base for the chemical industry, based primarily on the availability of adequate raw materials.

The petro-chemical industry is the catalyst of the chemical industry. As much as 85 percent of the present chemical products produced are organic chemicals from petroleum refining (Ibid.). At present, the amount of petroleum used in the chemical industry is only 4 percent of the total consumption, while that in developed countries has reached 10 percent (Ibid.). The more consumption of oil in the industry, the greater will be the degree of processing and the more beneficial it will be for the province.

Shandong's chemical industry, developed soon after the discovery and exploitation of the Shengli oilfield in the 1960s, is now firmly established. The crude oil processed by the Qilu Petro-chemical Corporation (Figure 2,9) has reached 7 million tons annually. The annual output of synthetic ammonia from the Number 1 Chemical Fertilizer Plant is 80,000 tons, that of the Number 2 Fertilizer Plant is 300,000 tons, and rubber from the Rubber Plant is 15,000 tons. Also, the annual production of crude oil at the Jinan Refinery (1.5 million tons), the annual output of lubricating oil (50,000 tons), and the eight small-size refineries (with a total capacity of 1.34 million tons)(Ibid.) offer a certain degree of permanency.

The petroleum industry aims to process up to 30.5 million tons of crude oil by the year 2000, as well as 660,000 tons of ethylene. This will be a means of gauging the petro-chemical industry. A 300,000-ton ethylene project will be enlarged to produce 360,000 tons. Major large-scale projects planned for 1990 to 2000 include:

(a) the Dongying Ethylene Plant, to be jointly funded by the Province (Y5.5 billion), and by foreign investment ($600 million US). It will have a capacity of 140,000 tons in the first phase and 300,000 tons in the second phase;

(b) the Dongying Refinery, to be funded by foreign investment ($200 million US), to produce 5 million tons of high-sulphur oil, 1.09 million tons of gasoline, 0.8 million tons of kerosine, and 1.24 million tons of diesel annually;

(c) the Shijiu Refinery, planned as a joint venture to produce finished oil, the crude oil coming either from the province or from abroad;

(d) the Jinan Refinery, which will utilize foreign investment ($70 million US) to build a synthetic ammonia plant to produce 300,000 tons (Ibid.).

The Chemical Industry: A Prop for Agriculture

Since Shandong's agricultural land is inadequate for its large population, increase in the output of grain will mainly depend on raising the output per unit; this means added input. The province has 144 fertilizer factories, with an annual output of 1.4 million tons (Ibid.), which is far from meeting the demand. Previously, 58 percent of this annual output met local requirements, but the amount is likely to get bigger. But note that development of local supply is slow, resulting in the importation of phosphate fertilizer, and all the potassium fertilizer required. It is estimated that by 2000 the demand for nitrogen fertilizer will be 1.7 million tons, phosphate fertilizer 0.8 million tons, and potassium fertilizer 0.34 million ton (Ibid.) The demand and supply of nitrogen fertilizer will be balanced, but the shortage of phosphate will be 0.1 to 0.2 million tons, and there will still be a need to import potassium.

In the coming decade, it is planned to establish a number of chemical projects to support agriculture. The Shandong Composition Fertilizer Plant will annually produce 0.2 million tons of synthetic ammonia, 0.48 million tons of diammonia phosphate, and 0.13 million tons of carbamide by utilizing a loan of $200 million US from the Asian Bank. The Heze Natural Gas Fertilizer Plant will produce 0.2 million tons of synthetic ammonia annually at a cost of $10 million US (Ibid.). In the meanwhile, efforts will be made to enlarge the production capacity of the existing plants.

As for agricultural chemicals, efforts will be made to regulate the kinds and types of preparations and to develop high-efficiency pesticide, bactericide and weed killer. It is planned to establish in Ningyang a pesticide-production base to produce amino methanoic fat which should enable the total output of agricultural chemicals to reach 30,000 tons.

Fine Chemical Industry

The fine chemical industry of Shandong produces pharmaceutical products, dyeing materials, paint, cosmetics, detergent, chemical reagent and printing ink. Fine chemicals have a high value, serve directly industrial and agricultural production, and are closely associated with public life. Generally, fine chemicals are various and are produced in small quantities with more composition elements, and are of different uses. They are a specialized production and demand an adequate work force. As a labour-intensive industry, it also needs a high quality of technical service.

The three largest of Shandong's fine chemical industries are agricultural chemicals, dyeing materials and paint. They comprise one-third of the total output. Compared with those at the national level, the fine chemicals produced in Shandong are poor in quality and the variety is limited. The industry is also slow to develop new products.

In future, the main products of Shandong's fine chemical industry will be fodder and food additive. It will use the processing of agricultural and miscellaneous products. It is also planned to use the Jinan Chemical Factory as the nation's chief base for the production of fluorine. Similarly, it is planned to build in Shandong a Tallow Chemical General Plant at a cost of $20 million US (Ibid.).

Oceanographic Chemical Industry

The coastline of Shandong Province is roughly one-sixth of the 18,000 kilometre-long coastline of China. Thus the crude salt output of Shandong's coastal area is impressive, actually one-fifth of the national total. Because Qingdao is the national centre of oceanographic scientific research, developing an oceanographic chemical industry there would seem rational. The provincial output of salt is 5 million tons, and is planned to reach 15 million tons by the end of the century. It is planned also to develop the two salt-producing areas of Laizhou Bay and Bohai Bay, and increase the production of sodium carbonate and caustic soda—Qingdao and Weifang to produce 0.7 million and 1 million tons, respectively, annually—to build a sodium-carbonate factory at Bohai Bay to produce 1.2 million tons of salt annually; to transform technically the existing factories and build a new salt chemical factory in Tai'an; to increase the output of bromide to 20,000 tons; and to produce serial products, such as fire-extinguishing and fire-resistant chemicals.

The wide spread of the seashore, the dry and warm climate, and the fairly adequate and convenient transportation of the province should make for a better development of the salt chemicals. There is much to suggest that salt chemicals should be the key products of Shandong's chemical industry.

Coal Chemical Industry

With the rapid rise of China's petro-chemical industry in the 1950s, coal, as a chemical raw material, has lost its importance. Although there was an oil crisis in the 1970s, the demand for coal for the chemical industry has not increased. However, it is estimated that exploitation of petroleum deposits will last for only 30 years, whereas exploitation of the coal deposits could continue for the next 200 if not 400 years (Ibid.). It is expected that in 20 to 30 years coal will undoubtedly resume its important role as a chemical raw material.

The present coal-chemical industrial bases in the province include the southern areas around Zaozhuana and Jining, for which two projects are planned, an 800,000-ton coking plant, and a 200,000-ton tar plant. These will produce synthetic ammonia by the coal gasification method, as well as 480,000 tons of composition fertilizer and 130,000 ton of caramide annually. Also a coal-pit gas-making factory will be built in Longkou and three factories in Jinan—the Jinan Iron and Steel Works, the Jinan Chemical Fertilizer Plant, and the Jinan Number 2 Petro-chemical Factory—all will combine to establish a multi-purpose coal chemical base.

Rubber Processing

The rubber processing industry of Shandong Province is located mainly in Qingdao and Weihai. In recent years the output of synthetic rubber in the province has topped the nation's output ,and the production of rubber tube, rubber tyre and rubber-conveying belt ranks first in the country. The material and technical force of Qingdao Rubber Processing Factory ranks second in the country, next to Shanghai.

The Shandong rubber processing industry aims to establish itself as the production base of rubber tyres, rubber tube, rubber conveying belts and rubber shoes in Qingdao and Weihai; to increase exports; and to produce annually one million sets of Ziwu tyres, four million square metres of conveying belt, and 8 million pairs of shoes for export. Weihai, on the other hand, will produce 20,000 sets of engineering tyres and 3 million pairs of chemical shoes. Also, the Rongchene Rubber Factory in Weihai, a rubber product base, will be built to cater to both the national and international market (Shandong Provincial Land Planning Office, 1991: 88). According to the plans, the output value of Shandong's rubber processing should reach Y3 billion.

THE BUILDING MATERIAL INDUSTRY

Either in industrial and agricultural production or in transportation, or in rural and urban construction, building materials are indispensable. In the industrialization of developing countries building materials take on an even greater significance. In China, the building material industry is the "pillar" of construction. With good conditions for developing a building material industry, this industry should make a valuable contribution to Shandong's economy.

It was mentioned earlier that Shandong Province has an abundance of natural resources which give the province industrial potential. Certainly the variety of resources and their wide distribution have given the province a considerable advantage over the other coastal provinces of China. By 1987, the total prospected mineral deposits that could yield building materials was 40.5 billion tons, the potential economic value of which was estimated at Y421 billion. This is equivalent to 36 percent of the potential value of all the mineral resources in the province (Ibid.: 94-95).

Limestone, which can be used for making cement, is widely distributed in the mountains of the southern part and the hilly areas of the province. Altogether, limestone deposits are estimated at 260 billion tons. Gypsum, which accounts for 70 percent of the nation's total amount, is found in the areas of Pingyi, Tai'an and Zaozhuang. All three centres are qualified to become a gypsum production base and meet national standards. The quartz sandstone found in Linyi Prefecture is adequate and of good quality for making fufa glass. The local deposits of graphite and talc rank second and third places, respectively, in the country. They are found in Lizhou, Laixi and Haiyang on the peninsula. Scaled graphite, talcum blocks and talcum powder are produced for export. In addition, some one billion cubic metres of decorative building materials, such as marble, granite and terrazzo are exploited. They are of first grade, especially the "Mt. Tai Blue" granite which is quarried in Jinan. It was selected as the base material of the Memorial Hall of the late Chairman Mao Zedong and has enjoyed a good market in Japan. The "Snowflake White" marble in east Shandong peninsula is also a famous building material; it also enjoys a good market abroad.

Special non-metals, like diamond, are also of considerable importance; the total amount of diamonds produced in the province amounts to as much as half of the national total. It may be of interest to note that the famous "Changlin Diamond" was discovered in Linshu in 1977, weighs 158,786 carats, and is a rare, very large, natural diamond in the world.

Shandong has also a great amount of gangue and industrial residue that can be used. This is not only of economic benefit, but it can play a great role in improving the environment.

Present and Future Demand and Supply of Building Materials

In 1987, the total output of building materials of the province reached Y4.1 billion. This took the second place in the value of the nation's total, contributing with cement, plate glass, wall-body-material, construction porcelain, and non-metal minerals to a comprehensive industrial system, and catering to the needs of rural and urban construction.

The cement industry is the main branch of the building-material industry. The output in 1989 reached 18.8 million tons and had a value close to one-third of the total of the building-material industry. The quality and quantity take first place in the country. The disadvantage is that more than 500 cement factories across the province are comparatively small in size, the average annual total output of them is 29,000 tons. The output of large factories is only 8 percent of the total amount of cement produced in the province, nor is the grade high enough for key construction projects and export. At present, in developed countries the total capacity of projects is usually more than one million tons. According to forecast by the Provincial Bureau of Building Material Industry, the demand for cement in Shandong by 2000 will be 30 million tons, 16 million tons of which will be used for capital construction, 3 million tons for export, and 10 percent will be a special kind of cement. Because of a strong demand, Shandong's cement output will need to increase at the annual rate of over 4 percent; equally the production of high-grade cement, building cement and a special kind of cement should increase

The production of plate glass began in 1965. By 1987 there were 11 plate-glass factories, producing 4.35 million standard cases of ordinary window glass and basically keeping the balance between demand and supply. But the variety of glass produced in Shandong is limited and cannot meet the multi-purpose and multi-level needs. Besides, glass production in the province mostly adopts the plain-drawing technique, which accounts for the poor quality of the glass. In contrast, in developed countries, the fufa technique is widely adopted. It is estimated that by the end of this century, 8.5 million standard cases of glass will be needed, and special glass will account for 25 percent of this (Shandong Provincial Bureau of Building Materials Industry, 1989).

With regard to the construction- and hygiene-porcelain industry, in 1987 the province produced 564,000 pieces of hygiene porcelain, 5.4 million square metres of glazed bricks and 1.1 million square metres of bricks for walls and floors (Ibid.). In recent years, great progress has been made in production technology, technique, and in the quality of the product. Apart from local or provincial needs, a great part of the product has been exported. The production of hygiene porcelain is still backward; it lacks middle- and high-grade products. It is estimated that by 2000 the demand for construction porcelain will be 2.5 million square metres, of which 10 million to 20 million square metres will be for export (Ibid.). The demand for hygiene porcelain will be 1.5 million pieces. The products must be upgraded, the variety improved and the ability to form series sets of production strengthened.

The production of new kinds of building materials in Shandong is almost negligible. As much as 98 percent of the building materials comprises traditional clay bricks. By contrast, between 60 and 90 percent of the construction in foreign countries use building materials other than bricks (Ibid.). The use of a large amount of clay bricks affects not only the weight and cost of the buildings, but requires large areas of farm land. Thus it is imperative to develop high-intensity, low-weight, energy-saving construction materials. It is estimated that by the end of the century, the total floor space of the buildings completed in the province will be 135 million square metres, requiring 55 billion to 60 billion standard bricks (Ibid.). Only 35 to 40 percent will use other materials, as demonstrated in Table 6,9. This is a challenging task for the province.

Table 6,9   Output and Demand of Building Materials, 1987 and 2000

Materials (Unit)	Output 1987	Demand 2000
Cement (000 tons)	15.6	30
Plate Glass (000 std. cases)	4353.5	8500
Hygiene Porcelain (000 pieces)	564.8	2500
Glazed Bricks (000 metres)	5457.0	10000
Bricks, Wall & Floor (000 sq. metres)	1130.4	9000
Asbestos Products (tons)	7821.0	13000
Graphite (000 tons)	83.3	75
Talcum (000 tons)	168.6	600
Gypsum (000 tons)	1614.0	2500
Marble Board (000 sq. metres)	518.4	2000
Granite Board (000 sq. metres)	126.4	1800
Terrazzo (000 sq. metres)	176.6	1000

Source: Strategic Research on the Development of Shandong's Building-Material
Industry, 1988

In respect of the non-metal minerals industry, the total output value in 1987 was Y1.13 billion; foreign exchange earned from exports was 90 percent of the provincial total, ranking first in the country. But these industrial enterprises are small in scale and spatially scattered; most of them are poorly equipped, and the products for export, mostly primary products, such as graphite, gypsum, talcum, and sandstone, have little value.

Future Development of the Building Materials Industry

The general plan for Shandong's building-material industry is to adopt advanced technology, encourage and support large and medium-size backbone enterprises, transform or cancel some small enterprises, protect farm land, recognize the synthetic process and increase quality and improve grading. According to the plan, by 2000 an important national production and export base will be established for cement, construction and hygiene porcelain, glass, graphite, talcum, gypsum and stone materials.

In the development of products, labour will be increased, techniques improved and the undertaking of foreign projects enlarged. Efforts will be made to invite foreign investment to establish joint ventures and co-operative or private enterprises. At present, the building material industry in developed countries appears to be declining, and their operations are being transferred to developing countries. This promises well for Shandong Province.

For the cement industry, two measures are to be taken simultaneously. The first is to add new, modern technology to existing large enterprises and at the same time install new, large complexes at locations where available raw materials and convenient transportation warrant. The existing cement factories at Zibo, Sighui and Yantai eminently qualify for modernization, because they are large enterprises and satisfy the requirements just mentioned. The combined production capacity of these three would be increased to about 4.35 million tons (Ibid.).

The plans for the development of the plate glass industry are to transform and improve the present shaping-technique of up-drawing and plain-drawing, to develop the fufa-shaping technique, and gradually realize large-scale, automatic production. This is to be achieved by a joint-venture enterprise called the Shandong Plate Glass Factory, which should produce annually 2.7 million standard cases of plate glass, including a fufa-technique production line. Also planned is the Yinan Sandstone Factory as the raw material base for plate glass production. The factory will be located close to Shijiusuo, a new seaport, where high-quality sandstone for making glass is available.

There are also plans to develop high- and medium-grade hygiene porcelain of various kinds at Zibo and Fushan, new building products, and gas-filled concrete and hollow building bricks in major cities like Jinan, Qingdao, Yantai, Zibo, Weifang and Jining. Other plans are to increase the export of non-metal materials and adopt advanced techniques and equipment to build up the production base for graphite, talcum, stone materials, gypsum and sandstone mainly in east Shandong.

Implemented, these plans would increase the total output value of Shandong's building-material industry to Y32 billion by the year 2000, at an annual rate of increase of 11.3 percent. This would be higher than that of the total industrial output value of the province.

THE TEXTILE INDUSTRY

The textile industry, the second largest industry in the province, shows a constant output value, equivalent to one-fifth of the total industrial output value of the province and second only to that of the machine-building and electronics industry. In recent years, the output value of Shandong's textile industry has taken fourth place in the country, next to those of Jiangsu, Shanghai and Zhejiang. The output of major products, such as yarn and cloth, has taken second place, that of dyed cloth and knitwear converted to yarn fourth place, and knitting wool and wool fabric fourth place.

The large supply and variety of raw materials, the wide distribution and their relative concentration are most advantageous; they make for a great variety of fabrics made from cotton, wool, rabbit's hair, bluish dog-bane and silkworm cocoon. Large quantities of cotton are exported to other Chinese provinces and abroad. The synthetic fabric industry is still weak, however, but when the Zibo Dacron Factory, the Jinan Polyester Factory and the Zibo Polypropylene Factory—all at present under con-struction—come into operation, the output of synthetic fabric will in-crease considerably.

The textile industry is highly labour-intensive, but the additive value of its products is low compared with those of new industries. Globally, there has been a significant shift in the industry, from developed coun-tries to developing countries. In Japan, for example, the textile industry formerly played a significant role in the country's economy, especially in the 1950s and 1970s. Since then, the industry has shifted to the newly-emerging industrial countries of Asia, such as South Korea, Taiwan, Hong Kong and Singapore. In the 1980s, owing to the high cost of labour and a strong desire in Asian countries to develop new industries, there has been a tendency to shift the textile industry outward from the countries men-tioned above to backward regions and countries, and the part of the inter-national market which it had previously occupied is now vacant. Now in the process of industrialization, China should be able to fill the vacancy.

In China, and especially in Shandong, the present average consump-tion of fabric per capita is only 4 to 5 kilograms, far lower than that of developed countries, which is 18 kilogram (Shandong Economics Research Centre, 1989: 400). It follows that expansion of the textile market is desirable, if not inevitable.

On the whole, a relatively solid base for the textile industry has been established in Shandong. Qingdao, Jinan and Weifang are the chief cen-tres. Qingdao is in fact one of the three national textile bases; Shanghai and Tianjin are the other two. They enjoy a high reputation. In the north-western part of Shandong where cotton is grown, small-size cotton mills have a considerable production capacity. In a word, Shandong is a major textile producer.

Nevertheless, the textile industry in Shandong is burdened with prob-lems. It has strong competition from Shanghai, Hangzhou, Beijing and Tianjin. Its equipment is out-moded; its products are low-grade; and 70 percent of its exports are primary products. The out-dated equipment makes for slowness in technical transformation and in introducing new spinning and weaving techniques. Other militating factors are poor management, the high consumption of energy and raw materials, and low economic returns. All tend to hinder production and expansion of the market. There is thus an urgent need to upgrade quality, and enlarge the market, especially foreign trade.

Further development of the textile industry in Shandong will depend on the consumption market. According to official statistics, by 2000 the per capita yearly expenditure in Shandong will reach Y1,472, while urban areas will reach Y2,000, and that of rural areas Y1,060. Although forecast of clothing consumption is most difficult because of differing customs, aesthetic tastes, fashion trends, among other whims and fancies, it is believed that the consumption of clothing will remain stable. As society progresses, the industry will be affected by sophistication and the need for comfort. This general trend is certain.

In the coming decade, plans for the further development of Shandong's textile industry include the introduction of new technology, which will focus on the famous brands of cotton for export, the development of dense, light and thin products, especially in Qingdao. The production of yarn and grey cloth will shift gradually to the cotton-growing areas in the west of the province, which will become a distribution area. Dyeing and straightening technical equipment will also be introduced.

In short, much effort will be given to a more modern development of textiles. Apart from the development of dacron in Jinan and polypropylene in Zibo, and a dozen other projects elsewhere, attempts will be made to orient the industry to cater to the needs of the public. The real test will be to achieve the goals of the plans for the industry, that is, to increase its output value to Y17.2 billion and the foreign exchange it earns to $800 million US; to raise the per capita clothing from the present 2.5 articles; and to increase the total output to 200 million articles, with a value of Y2 billion (Ibid.).

THE MANUFACTURING INDUSTRY

Much is dependent on the manufacturing industry, which is the catalyst for technical reform in all sectors of the national economy. This industry covers a wide field, but in Shandong it refers only to machine building and electronics. These were merged in the 1980s to produce high-tech products which in turn serve to equip the industry. In 1987, the output value of the industry in Shandong was Y16.06 billion, equivalent to 23 percent of the total industrial value of the province. Compared with other industrial branches, such as energy, textile, chemical and building-materials, the manufacturing industry of Shandong takes a lower place on the national list of industries. The machine-building and electronics industry depends not so much on natural resources but on technology. The level of education, culture, science and technology of Shandong province is far lower than that of the country as a whole. Thus the machine-building and electronics industry does not a contribute significantly to the advanced development of the economy of Shandong.

It is now planned to give priority to developing transportation machines, light-industry machines, electronic products, and to research in order to strengthen the basic technology, techniques, basic parts, basic raw materials, basic elements and basic machines.

The additive value of the machine-building and electronics industry is the chief motivating force in the development of the industry. Market demands for tape recorders, colour T.V. sets, refrigerators, VCRs, air conditioners and a very wide range of consumer products must be taken into consideration in the modern development of the industry.

CONCLUSION

In sum, the plans for the improvement and further development of the various industries in the province, as in the case of agriculture, invite foreign co-operation, capital, technology and technological and managerial skill, now made possible by the national government's "open-door" policy. Canadian, and especially Saskatchewan, entrepreneurs are invited to be partners in the development of these projects—undertakings which should be of mutual benefit.

REFERENCES

Shandong Provincial Bureau of Building Materials Industry. (1989). *Strategic Research on the Development for the Building Materials Industry in Shandong Province*. Jinan, Unpublished.

Shandong Economics Research Centre. (1989). *Strategy for Economic and Social Development of Shandong Province*. Jinan: Shandong People's Press.

Shandong Provincial Land Planning Office. (1991). *Shandong Provincial Overall Land Plan*. Beijing: China Planning Press.

Shandong Statistics Yearbook. 1991.

ACKNOWLEDGEMENTS

As in Chapter 8.

10 EPOCH-MAKING CHOICE

Chen Longfei and Yan Aihua

Shandong Teachers' University, Jinan, Shandong

After 10 years of reform and opening up to the outside world, China has made spectacular gains in foreign trade, foreign exchange, exporting labour, establishing Special Economic Zones (SEZs), and opening no less than 14 coastal cities to foreign investors. The province of Shandong has vigorously supported the national policies, and although not as well-placed as the province of Guangdong, with three SEZs, or the province of Fujian, with Xiamen as a rapidly developing SEZ, Shandong has taken measures to utilize its advantages and potentialities, improve management, and adjust its industrial and commodity structures towards the development of foreign trade.

THE EXPORT TRADE

Apart from its two designated open cities of Yantai and Qingdao, Shandong has 6 municipalities, 43 counties (districts), 4 airports and 7 ports (Figure 1,10), all of which are open to the outside world. In addition, the province has a strong economic base and facilities to support radical reforms; for example, in 1989 Shandong's exports earned $3.05 billion US, and the province signed 485 new contracts which had a total value of $553 million US. Also, from 1987 to 1989, the accumulated foreign exchange made from Shandong's exports was $24.5 billion US. During the same period, $2.5 billion US foreign investment went into establishing 496 different enterprises. One-third of the enterprises and Y15 billion of the industrial output value was directly or indirectly associated with the export trade; Y3 billion of agricultural and sideline (miscellaneous) products

Figure 1,10   Yantai Port *(Photo by Zhou Bendong)*

were exported; and Y1 billion had been earned as income from foreign trade. But this improvement, impressive though it is, does not represent the real gain that could be made from foreign trade. In 1989, Shandong's export trade brought in only Y10.1 billion, representing no more than 4 percent of the total industrial and agricultural output value and 8.5 percent of the provincial gross national product (GNP).

The characteristics of Shandong's export trade are first, primary products which make up the greater part of the exports. But increase of foreign exchange earned from exports depends mainly on increase in quantity. In 1987, the province earned $2.97 billion US from exports. Of this amount raw materials and primary products valued $1.8 billion US, manufactured goods, machine-building and electronics products made up $189 million US and accounted for 6.4 percent of the total exports. This classification follows international practice, but according to China's national classification, they would be classified as shown in Table 1,10. Included under "industrial and mineral products" is petroleum, which accounted for 28.3 percent of the total exports and was valued at $840 million US.

Of the small quantity of machine-building and electronic products that were exported, hardware products such as accessories, parts and

Table 1,10   Export Trade, Shandong, 1987

Products	% of total	Value ($ million US)
Agriculture & Sideline	29.8	880
Light Industries & Textiles	24.6	730
Handicrafts	8.0	230
Industries & Mineral	38.0	113
TOTAL	100.4	1,953

Source: *Strategy for Economic and Social Development of Shandong Province*, 1989.

elements were chief, while machine-building and electronic products accounted for the remainder. Of the manufactured goods, raw materials and semi-raw materials were the chief exports. The conclusion is that the main exports were primary products, and the small quantity of low-order manufactured goods do not generate a great deal of foreign exchange. They are insignificant in the international market as well as beside those of the coastal provinces of Zhejiang and Jiangsu and the Municipality of Shanghai.

Next, increase in Shandong's foreign trade depends mainly on increase in the subsidy from the central government. But the price of agricultural and miscellaneous products such as cotton, corn and fodder, has kept rising in the home market while falling in the international market. Consequently, the government departments that are engaged in foreign trade have suffered losses and deficits from year to year.

The future goal must be to expand exports, especially those of light industry and textiles, handicrafts and machine-building and electronic products. All are in demand in the international market, and Shandong has a marked potential for their development. The export goal of the Province is stated in the *Overall Plan of Development*, shown in Table 2,10.

Admittedly, present international, political and economic conditions are both favourable and unfavourable for the development of Shandong's foreign trade. The relaxation of tensions between East and West and the integrated pattern of world economy are definitely favourable factors. However, the low prices offered for commodities on the international market as well as trade protectionism are certainly unfavourable factors.

Table 2,10 Value of Planned Exports by 2000

Products	Value (US$ million)
Petroleum	1,200
Agricultural & Sideline	990
Chemical	510
Light Industrial & Textiles	2,070
Handicrafts	850
Machines & Electronic	810
Processed Raw Materials & Compensation Trade	210
TOTAL	6,540

Source: *Strategy for Economic and Social Development of Shandong Province*, 1989.

The key markets for Shandong's foreign trade are Japan, North America, the European Economic Community, and Southeast Asia. When the United States cancelled its preferential tariff with "the four little dragons" of Asia (South Korea, Taiwan, Thailand, Malaysia), and South Korea and Taiwan devalued their currencies, an opportunity was created for Shandong to export its light industrial products and textiles, handicrafts, primary machines and electronic products. But recently Canada and the U.S. signed a Free Trade Agreement, marking a rise in regional protectionism in foreign trade. It poses an obstacle for China to establish trade with both Canada and the U.S. Owing to improvement in relations between China and the former Soviet Union, on the one hand, and China's relations with European countries, on the other, China's expansion of foreign trade with all these countries appears promising, for the short run at least. China's light industrial products and textiles, hardware, food, handicrafts and labour-intensive products are well received in the Soviet Union and East Europe. It is expected that China's foreign trade will shift to these areas, in which case trade with these areas should grow.

The introduction of advanced techniques and equipment into Shandong is primarily for the expansion of exports to earn foreign currency. Simply stated, importation of technology leads to improvement in the quality and export of manufactured goods. Of course, local supply of some goods such as rolled steel, chemical fertilizer and wheat cannot meet demands, and such goods are imported. It is and will be difficult to reduce the importation of these commodities.

It is hoped that by the end of this century Shandong Province will realize its goal toward the second stage of the development of its economy and social life, that is, raising its per capita GNP from $309 US in 1989 to $800 US in the year 2000 at an annual rate of increase of 6.6 percent. It may not be difficult to reach this goal, but economic and social development are expressed not only by economic growth. The upgrading of education and cultural activities, and the general improvement of life must also be considered. It is clear that for China to develop fully, it must continue to open to the outside world, but this is Shandong's stated policy.

EXPORT OF LABOUR—POTENTIALITIES

The international labour market is a newly-emerging institution for international economic co-operation. According to the World Bank, there are 20 million mobile people in the labour market, mainly from developing countries, and their accumulated income is over $30 billion US.

The 19th century policy of China to export labour was renewed at the beginning of the 1980s. So far, various corporations in the country have been engaged in development programmes in construction, industry, water conservation, electricity, the petro-chemical industry, machine-building, agriculture, urban construction, transportation, education, culture and public health in almost 100 countries. The construction projects include highways, railways, bridges, seaports, airports, factories, hydraulic power plants, hospitals, physical culture facilities and fishery projects. By the end of 1987, Shandong had signed about 4,000 contracts valued at $8.26 billion US, and dispatched more than 270,000 workers, among them engineers and technical personnel. In 1984, five corporations won international awards. The China General Corporation of Construction Projects is listed as the 21st largest project-undertaking corporation in the world.

Shandong Province established the Shandong Branch of China General Corporation of Construction Projects in 1981, the Shandong Corporation for International Economic and Technical Co-operation in 1984, and began to export labour. Among the dozen completed projects undertaken are the 18-storey commercial building in Brunei Darussalam, residential houses in Guam, the USA and elsewhere. The total area of construction is 560,000 square metres, and the total capital outlay is more than $30 million US. In addition, Shandong has dispatched abroad a large number of seamen, cooks, agronomists, and construction and textile technicians.

The fact is that Shandong has a huge reservoir of labour which can be exported. As much as 57 percent of the 82 million people in the province is a huge labour force which, it is predicted, will increase to 65 percent when the population reaches 90 million. Always the province carried out its contracts for labour to the letter, and guaranteed quality. Always the workers and staff were conscientious and hard-working. Also, Shandong has had an advanced technical work force in agriculture, industry and science and technology. In crop breeding, for example, Shandong's technicians have proved themselves competent. The prospecting technicians in hydrology and geology are highly trained and are able to adapt themselves to difficult and trying conditions. They have also undertaken water conservation projects and geological prospecting in Asian and African countries where flood and/or drought are frequent occurrences. The manufacturing enterprises can undertake the technical design and manufacture of equipment for small-size hydraulic power plant, heating plants, cold storage plants, light industry and textiles, cement and mining operations. Further, Shandong silk, having its own unique features, enjoys a high reputation both at home and abroad. The same is true of Chinese cuisine. It has become an art par excellence. Wrongly or rightly, it has been said that oriental culture is a food culture. In Chinese culture its importance cannot be denied. Shandong dishes are one of eight categories under which Chinese food is classified. Having more than 3,000 trained cooks, the province is quite able to send them abroad to establish Chinese food outlets.

Beginning in the 1980s, the international market for labour has been adversely affected. There is hardly any need for foreign workers in North America and Europe. The largest world market for labour has been the Middle East, but that market is now closing because the price of oil keeps falling. Middle East oil producers are being forced to reduce their production in order to keep the price up. Political instability has further reduced the undertaking of new projects. In general, many countries have introduced various restrictions to foreign workers. The problem is compounded by recourse to a high degree of automation in the design of projects in order to reduce the number of workers, and strict control is exercised by all countries over the immigration of foreign workers; even if a foreign company could make a bid in the construction of a project, it would not be allowed to. Thus competition has become increasingly acute, and conditions of acceptance harsher. Worse still, a foreign company undertaking a project has to face delayed payments, payment in the form of goods exported, increasing prices of materials and increasing workers' wages. These have conspired to reduce the export of labour. Nor is there much demand for manual or unskilled labour in our present highly-technical world. All these factors are unfavourable for Shandong province.

The aim of the municipal government of Shandong is to garner from the export of labour some $170 million US between 1991 and 1995, and $240 million US between 1995 and 2000. It is planned that labourers would undertake construction projects on the one hand and on the other serve better their country when they return. In choosing the market, many factors are taken into consideration. In the Middle East it is construction work that was considered; in Africa and Southeast Asian countries, agricultural work, and in the developed countries of Europe and North America, the building of highways, lumbering, mining and environmental protection projects. The young people of many developed countries are not inclined to take such work and, consequently, foreign workers are sought.

To undertake projects in foreign countries is to explore the international channels. Shandong desires to establish offices in foreign countries to collect information. Canada could do the same in Shandong; that is, send its experts to teach and give guidance, while opening its own labour market to China. This would be mutually beneficial.

UTILIZING FOREIGN INVESTMENT

At present, the economic growth of China is experiencing a shortage of capital. To develop the market economy; to take part in the international division of labour, exchange and competition; and to compete in the international market are major tasks for China. The sources of foreign investment that China must contemplate are the international financial organizations, including the International Monetary Fund, the World Bank, the International Development Association and International Finance Corporation; government loans; and loans from commercial banks and private sources. In recent years, the scope has widened greatly. By the end of 1989, foreign investment in China had exceeded $40 billion US (*Shandong Statistics Yearbook*, 1990).

In Shandong, foreign investment is drawn from entrepreneurs who invest in enterprises, compensation trade, processing and assembling, joint ventures, China-foreign co-operation enterprises engaged in production by high-tech equipment, and from foreign funds or loans. The cost of the imported equipment, or of the technical skill, and the interest on the loans are paid from export revenue. In processing and assembling, the foreign entrepreneurs provide the raw materials, parts and elements with the models of the finished products or design, while Shandong is responsible for the processing and assembling. But the finished products must be sold by the foreign entrepreneurs. Likewise the provincial corporations purchase the equipment from abroad and rent it to the enterprises in the province. It was by these means that Shandong Province, during the decade from 1978 to 1988, could approve 1,347 contracts valued at $1.01 billion US. The amount used so far is $480 million US (excluding government and commercial loans). In those 10 years, foreign entrepreneurs from 23 countries and regions have invested in Shandong. Hong Kong, for example, has contracted $510 million US worth of projects and has spent $175 million US so far. Both figures represent 50 and 36 percent, respectively, of the province's total foreign investment. To date, Hong Kong has established in Shandong 212 joint ventures, co-operative corporations and private enterprises (Shandong Statistics Yearbook, 1989).

Japan, on the other hand, has signed contracts which are valued at $311 million US and has spent $210 million US already, largely on processing, assembling and in hiring through the Qingdai Huahe International Hiring Corporation (Ibid.).

Those countries and regions that have invested more than $20 million US in the province include Macao, United States, the Federal Republic of Germany, Austria, Switzerland and Singapore. Since 1987, Taiwan and South Korea have also invested heavily in Shandong. Canada has invested in only six enterprises, the contracts totalling $1.37 million US, a small amount compared with the other sums just mentioned. It could be that Canada is not yet fully aware of the investment opportunities in Shandong that may be exploited, in which case this book is timely.

Between 1978 and 1983, the total foreign capital invested in Shandong was $711.86 US, increased to $947 million US between 1984 and 1989, and involved 1,101 signed contracts, 485 of which were signed in 1989 despite setbacks in relations between China and other countries in that year. They were valued at $315 million US (Ibid.).

It is the policy of Shandong Province to continue its open policy to the outside world during the 1990s, indeed even more vigorously than before. The province has planned to increase exports through foreign investment and introduce advanced technology, so as to upgrade the quality and level of the provincial economy. It will give priority to enterprises which export goods; earn foreign exchange; and introduce capital, advanced technology and equipment. It will give attention to obtaining foreign loans and to direct investment by foreign businesses. Similarly, it will place more emphasis on enterprises that are oriented to profitable high-tech programmes.

Further, the Province has plans to organize and conduct the Qingdao Commodity Fair, commodity exhibitions, and to negotiate trade with the USA, Italy, Germany and Singapore. The Hualu Corporation, a Shandong overseas institution, will be strengthened; more trading locations and "windows" will be established to expand the market with North and South America in respect to foreign projects and the export of labour (Governor Zhao Zhihao, 1990).

The Province is also aiming to improve the environment for foreign investment. Priority will be given to improving the infrastructure, especially transportation and communication facilities. These include the construction of first-grade highways from Jinan to Qingdao and Yantai, and Rushan to Weihai, and railway from Taocun to Weihai. Also a programme-controlled telephone system in the provincial postal system is to be put into operation soon. Likewise, it is planned to create an association of, and a service centre for, foreign investment to help to solve possible investment difficulties (Ibid.). Existing institutions that are in charge of foreign investment are committed to simplify their procedures in the examination and approval of projects, and in improving work efficiency. The Province is determined that its laws, regulations and existing preferential policies will be carried out to the letter.

In opening the coastal cities of Qingdao and Yantai to foreign investors, the Province is attempting to speed up development while implementing regulations concerning hiring and transfer of employees, and payment on the land in order to attract more foreign investment.

Shandong's favourable economic conditions and potentialities have attracted and will continue to attract foreign economic co-operation, as indicated in Appendix 1,10, which lists the large number of business branches that are already registered in the province.

SHANDONG'S OPEN DOOR,
A MEANS TO ECONOMIC DEVELOPMENT

The "open door" policy is an invitation to help the province of Shandong dispense with factors that tend to inhibit radical economic reforms. In the process, difficulties are inevitable. To co-ordinate a centrally planned economy with a market economy is altogether difficult. Mistakes are likely to be made and have been made. Nevertheless, in the transfer process, an emphasis on advanced technology, technological expertise and management skill—requirements of the market economy—is slowly gaining force. The past 10 years of reform and opening to the outside world have seen remarkable gains. Although the major quotas of the national economy per capita are still low, the economy of the country in general, and the province in particular, is steadily improving. China has unquestionably improved its overall economic relations with many countries. It is rational that China not only maintain economic contacts with Third World countries but become a balance between them and the developed countries. From the developed countries, China has obtained technical assistance, but to them China has opened a vast market. The most important trade partner of China at present is Japan. It could well be the twin factors of history and geography or the business acumen of the Japanese that has brought this about. Next to Japan are the USA and Western Europe. The contacts between China and the "four little dragons", referred to previously, have also developed rapidly. It is, however, regrettable that the economic ties between China and Canada are not comparable with those of the other countries just mentioned.

With a more or less similar northern location and territorial extent, and almost a similar international economic position, China and Canada differ markedly in demographic weight. China's population is almost 50 times that of Canada. Equally contrasting is their domestic status. The per capita GNP of China is about one-fiftieth that of Canada. But despite the differences, the Chinese people have always cherished friendly feelings for Canada and Canadians. Canada is the homeland of Norman Bethune, the Canadian medical doctor who, as Dale correctly points out in Chapter 1, is highly respected and admired by the Chinese people. In developing foreign trade, China has always placed emphasis on establishing friendship with its partners. In this respect, Canada has an advantage in forging economic co-operation with China. The twinning relationship established between Jinan, capital of Shandong Province, and Regina, capital of the Province of Saskatchewan, could be considered a promoting force in this respect. It is hoped that the business sectors of both countries will exploit this relationship to their mutual benefit. Shandong Province has much to offer in terms of trading, and the people of Shandong can be regarded as trustworthy and entirely dependable trade partners.

CONCLUSION

It is true that the political turmoil which occurred in 1989 has cast a shadow over relations between China and the Western world. However, ideological differences should not be a hindrance to economic relations. The diplomatic relations which China established with Western countries in the 1960s and 1970s should remain intact. It is at present inconceivable that China, with nearly one-fourth of the world's population, should isolate itself from the rest of the world. This would neither be in the interest of China nor of the West. The recent rapid growth of China's national economy illustrates the inestimable trade potential of China, enough to excite far-sighted Western entrepreneurs to rush to China, especially to Shandong Province, where divers opportunities await them.

REFERENCES

Province of Shandong. (1990). *Shandong statistics yearbook*. Beijing: China Statistics Press.

Governor Zhao Zhihao. (1990). *Firmly carry out the policy of opening to the outside world, Jinan*. Unpublished.

ACKNOWLEDGEMENT

As in Chapter 8.

Appendix 1,10   Corporations under the Provincial Foreign Trade Bureau

1. China National Cereals, Oils & Foodstuffs Import and Export Corporation, Shandong Cereals & Oils Branch

2. China National Cereals, Oils & Foodstuffs Import and Export Corporation, Shandong Foodstuffs Branch

3. China National Native Produce and Animal By-Products Import & Export Corporation, Shandong Native Produce Branch

4. China National Native Produce and Animal By-Products Import & Export Corporation, Shandong Animal By-Product Branch

5. China National Textiles Import & Export Corporation, Shandong Branch

6. China National Textiles Import & Export Corporation, Shandong Clothing Branch

7. China National Light Industrial Products Import & Export Corporation, Shandong Branch

8. China National Metals and Minerals Import & Export Corporation, Shandong Branch

9. China National Chemical Import & Export Corporation, Shandong Branch

10. China National Machinery Import & Export Corporation, Shandong Branch

11 China National Handicrafts Import & Export Corporation, Shandong Branch

12. China National Handicrafts Import & Export Corporation, Shandong Drawwork Branch

13. China National Packing Imports & Export Corporation, Shandong Branch

14. Shandong National Medicine and Keep-Fit Necessities Import & Export Corporation, Shandong Branch

15. China National Foreign Trade Transportation Corporation, Shandong Branch

16. China National Machinery Equipment Import & Export Corporation, Shandong Branch

17. China National Tobacco Import & Export Corporation, Shandong Branch

Appendix 1,10 (continued)

---

18. China National Technical Import & Export Corporation, Qingdao Branch

19. China National Silk Import & Export Corporation, Qingdao Branch

20. Qingdao Textiles United Import & Export Corporation

21. Qingdao Drinks Import & Export Corporation

22. Qilu Advertisement Corporation.

11 CAPITAL, TECHNOLOGY AND TRANSFER

J.H. Song and Y.C. Ma

Biology Institute, Academy of Sciences, Jinan, Shandong

INTRODUCTION

Shandong Province covers an area of 153,300 square kilometres and has a population exceeding 80 million people. With industry and agricultural production occupying a prominent position, it has become an area of comprehensive resource development and processing. Shandong's industrial and agricultural output has placed it second among China's other provinces. In addition, it is the largest coastal open economic zone in China, and an ideal place for foreign investment.

In accord with China's open policy towards the outside world, Shandong has been attracting foreign investment increasingly. Over the past 10 years, the province has approved 2,269 contracts, involving a total foreign investment of two billion dollars US, imported more than 1,805 sets of advanced equipment and related technologies, and established more than 41 foreign-funded enterprises and 794 joint ventures (Government of Shandong, 1990).

Shandong is attractive to foreign investors owing to its advantageous geographical position. A coastal province, its neighbours include both Japan and South Korea. Besides, Shandong has made a great effort to improve its investment climate to ensure that the legitimate rights and interests of foreign investors are protected. In Shandong, foreign investors have not only good prospects of gain, but also harmonious relations with their Chinese partners.

Over the past decade, Shandong has spent Y20 billion in improving its investment environment (Government of Shandong, 1990). At present, power and water supplies are available, as well as convenient transport and communications facilities, sufficient factory buildings and warehouses, and skilled labour. In short, conditions for effective business operation are gradually being improved.

In addition, Shandong has made a considerable effort to improve the 'soft' investment environment. Foreign entrepreneurs coming to the province will discover that procedures for establishing wholly foreign-funded enterprises or joint ventures are simple. To set up a foreign-funded enterprise, the foreign entrepreneur needs only to submit an application to the local government or appoint someone else to do it. After gaining approval, he/she then registers with the local Department of Industry and Commerce and obtains a business licence. With this, his/her business is considered established. As for a joint venture, the foreign business person needs first to find a partner, and then report his/her co-operative arrangements to the local Economic Planning Department for examination. Next, he/she submits an application, along with feasibility-study reports, to the local government. Finally, upon approval in Shandong, he/she must register with the local Department of Industry and Commerce.

FOREIGN INVESTMENT AND ASSISTANCE

The interests of foreign businesses in Shandong are absolutely guaranteed. To protect such legitimate rights and interests, the Shandong Government has worked out a series of laws and regulations, and assures their implementation. These laws and regulations are strictly observed, contracts are respected, and the rights and interests of foreign businesses are upheld. Concerned departments conscientiously implement policies regarding the preferential treatment given to foreign-funded enterprises. Charges levied against them are removed when found to be unreasonable This is done with the aim of establishing an effective system of administration and production in compliance with international practice.

The Shandong Insurance Company provides services for foreign-funded enterprises, including ocean-going freight insurance, ship insurance, property insurance, investment guarantee insurance and employer-responsibility insurance. In short, Shandong offers every type of insurance that is available elsewhere in the world. This insurance company has received appreciative comments on its convenient procedures and prompt compensation for losses.

Within the limits allowed by the State, Shandong grants foreign investors the most favourable treatment possible. In the areas of investment and guarantees, Shandong extends whatever benefits it can provide. It ensures that foreign-funded enterprises have autonomous rights in management and, within the limits of their contracts, allows them to work out production and management schedules on their own, raise and use funds, purchase the materials or production and sell their products however they wish. In respect to taxation, foreign-funded and joint-venture enterprises in open economic coastal cities, such as Jinan, Qingdao, Weihai and Yantai, can enjoy preferential treatment in enterprise income tax, and industrial and commercial consolidated duties. Income tax on foreign-funded enterprises established in the development zones of the province is levied at the reduced rate of 15 percent. Those enterprises, projected to operate for a period of 10 years and more may be exempt from income tax for the first two years, and allowed a 50 percent reduction during the third to fifth years. If the enterprises pertain to high technology, they are further allowed to turn over half of their due income tax during the sixth and eighth years (*Beijing Review*, 33(3), 1990: 13).

Foreign entrepreneurs can obtain assistance from the foreign Investment Administration and Service Centre which is directly controlled by the Shandong Government. This centre provides a series of services, such as information and advice, determination and approval of a project, as well as any help that may be needed after the funding of an enterprise. Leaders of local governments in Shandong often make inspection tours of foreign-funded enterprises, and thus can help them to remove difficulties.

At present, the number of foreign entrepreneurs in Shandong is increasing. They are seeking to plan more investment projects or expand present production. With the coming of more foreign investors to Shandong, a foreign 'boom' is anticipated. Most of these investors are from the United States, Japan, Europe, and Hong Kong. At present, investigation has revealed no Sino-Canadian joint venture in Shandong. It is hoped that soon such a joint venture can be established, and that Saskatchewan or Canadian investors will find Shandong a satisfactory place in which to do business.

In China, introduction of advanced technology is guided by State policies. Shandong especially needs such technology and expertise. Over the next five years, emphasis will be placed on the following:

(a) introducing the latest in advanced technology for establishing a group of scientific research centres in the fields of high energy physics, electronics, bio-engineering, space technology, maritime engineering,

(b) importing new and key technology for such basic economic sectors as energy, transportation, post office and telecommunications, and agriculture,

(c) importing new techniques, materials, and facilities that can help to improve the quality of export products.

In importing technology, design and manufacturing technology will be given priority, so as to promote the development of new equipment and new products, and thus improve the quality of products. In addition, more software technology will be imported in the future (*Beijing Review*, 33(23), 1990: 24).

POLICY OF THE SHANDONG GOVERNMENT

Shandong's aim in importing foreign technology is to improve industrial output and to achieve and maintain optimal technical efficiency. Thus attention will be given to the importation of basic parts and components of machinery, electrical equipment, and standardized devices. Accordingly, the provincial government will give priority to agricultural and industrial projects. Agricultural projects will involve cultivation of high-yield crops, seed-breeding, soil improvement, prevention and control of plant disease, elimination of pests, rational application of fertilizer, and water conservation. Attention will also be given to poultry farming and the development of new varieties of aquatic products. Increasingly, prosperity for the farmer will depend on his familiarity with technology, especially in the areas of preservation and storage, transport, and processing. Industrial projects which are to be given priority include the development of new textile materials, silk dyeing and printing. Advancement in mining techniques, the development of computer technology (including software systems and applications, fibre-optic communications, facsimile transmission—'Fax'—and computer-controlled switchboards), precision-lathe techniques, technological advances in truck and tractor manufacturing, energy conservation, industrial pollution, and treatment of industrial waste are all given top priority.

To accelerate the introduction and development of advanced technology in Shandong, technological development zones have been established in the cities of Jinan, Qingdao and Weihai. Weihai is the largest and important base for China's advanced technological industry. This zone is jointly operated by the State Science and Technology Commission, and the Weihai Municipal Government which has announced preferential policies for the development of high technology. These policies are designed to attract foreign capital and technology. Furthermore, these development zones are attempting the organization of research institutes. Schools of higher learning as well as large-and medium-sized enterprises are encouraged to establish companies in the area. China's central and provincial governments will be more willing to transfer funds to commercial and industrial production, in addition to guiding and promoting developmental projects still in the preliminary stages. Compared with such places as Hong Kong, South Korea, and Thailand, Shandong appears to offer better conditions for investment, as well as better opportunities for financial returns.

In relative terms, the province of Saskatchewan is in a better position to provide badly needed technology and expertise to Shandong. Shandong's needs and Saskatchewan's technical superiority indicate a complementarity for exchanges in agriculture, mining, computer technology, and optical fibre communication. In these areas Saskatchewan's development precedes that of Shandong by about 20 years.

Since China adopted its open policy, Shandong has introduced computer-controlled telephone equipment from Belgium and West Germany. This is to improve communication conditions in cities like Jinan, Qingdao, and Yantai. Despite these improvements, communication facilities remain backward. Public telephones are difficult to find anywhere in the province. In the cities, 3 out of 100 persons have the use of a telephone. To obtain a private telephone in Jinan, the capital city of Shandong, one first submits an application form along with Y3,000 ($660 CN). It should be noted that the monthly salary of a person employed in the city is approximately Y200 ($44 CN). And it would take at least six months before the telephone could be installed. Conditions are worse in the countryside.

TECHNOLOGY AND EQUIPMENT

Shandong needs to improve communication facilities, but the province lacks capital, technology and equipment. For example, SaskTel possesses the latest in advanced technology and equipment. The company uses digital technology, fibre-optic transmission, and it has well-trained, dedicated employees, thus well able to meet and overcome the challenge presented by inadequate communications in Shandong. Here the promise of investment is very real.

Most of the computers in Shandong are publicly-owned, and were imported from the United States, Japan, and France. The largest is an IBM 3083 which is used by the Sheng Li Oil Field Company. Shandong has approximately 1,000 micro-computers, most of which use the Intel 8088, 8086 or 80286 microprocessor chip, with smaller numbers of Intel 80386 processors. There are 90 large or medium-sized computers in use. Approximately 3,000 people are involved with computer software in the province. The major areas of involvement are data processing, process control, software development, Computer Aided Design (CAD), and telecommunications. According to the quality of research teams, the level of research projects, and application level of computers, Shandong occupies a middle position among the provinces of China (*Annals of Shandong Science and Technology*, 1990: 2, 4-12).

Conceivably there are many problems associated with the transfer of computer technology to Shandong. The chief are the lack of fully qualified employees and some eighty different brands of computers in use, which makes it difficult to establish a computer network. Also many of the companies with computers keep them for prestige purposes or merely as 'decoration.' Equally, the level of computer research is backward, for the main interest is in quick financial returns from the sale of software rather than in developing the software itself.

The opportunities for Shandong and Saskatchewan to work together to improve conditions and solve problems regarding the transfer of computer technology appear to be very good. Since 1980 the Shandong Academy of Sciences and the Shandong University have established academic and technological co-operative relationships with the University of Regina, Saskatchewan. This relationship should be continued and extended, and special attention given to the training of personnel in the use of computers, and to academic exchange. Furthermore, a joint-venture software company could be established to develop software. Shandong has inexpensive labour, while Saskatchewan has technology and capital. Combined, these factors are likely to ensure success.

CONCLUSION

In sum, Shandong is an ideal place for investment. It has a favourable geographical location. China's open policy grants foreign investors preferential tax concessions. In addition, regulations have been established to ensure that contracts are honoured, and the interests and rights of the investor are protected. Saskatchewan investors are welcome in Shandong, especially to establish suitable projects or joint ventures. The prospect of Shandong sending more people to Saskatchewan for training in computer science and in developing computer software should be energetically explored. There is no doubt that Shandong needs the advanced technology that Saskatchewan can offer. China is a developing country, and its provinces, in particular Shandong, have need of technology and capital transfer. Both sides, Saskatchewan and Shandong, should continue to strengthen their relationship. More contact should create understanding and mutual co-operation.

REFERENCES

Annals of Shandong Science and Technology, Computer Section. Jinan, Shandong, 1990, pp. 2, 4-12.

Beijing Review. Vol. 33, No. 3. Jan. 15-21, 1990, p. 13.

Beijing Review. Vol. 33, No. 23. June 3-10, 1990, p. 24.

Government of Shandong. (1990). *Document of foreign trade*. Jinan, Shandong.

12 CONCLUSION

Edmund H. Dale
University of Regina

The Asian-Pacific region is undergoing momentous change. The so-called "four little dragons"—South Korea, Taiwan, Thailand and Malaysia, together with Singapore and Indonesia, have become economic entities of global significance and are attracting considerable foreign investment. Add Japan and Hong Kong to the group and economically, the region is seen as the fastest growing entity in the world at present. Each has a market economy that is paying spectacular dividends. China, in contrast, grounded in a "gerontological immobility" and steeped in a Marxist-Leninist philosophy and Mao Zedong Thought, had for decades refused to adopt the marketing mechanism of its Pacific neighbours. But in 1978, Deng Xiaoping, then the Chinese leader, renounced China's historic closed-door policy and introduced plans for the modernization of agriculture, industry, national defence, and science and technology. To achieve his ends, he flung open, albeit partly, the doors of China to foreign investors, established five Special Economic Zones (SEZs), as Wong has pointed out in Chapter 7, and invited in foreign investment, foreign capital, foreign-owned enterprises and foreign manufactured goods, including television sets (black-and-white, and coloured), tape recorders video-cassettes, washing machines and refrigerators.

Introduction of the market economy, first in agriculture, soon liberated the peasants from the collective sector and caused the commune system to come tumbling down. The creative energies of the people, long held captive and now stimulated by the market reforms, suddenly burst into activity and resulted in increased production and rapid economic growth. The same spectacular results were achieved in industry, despite a degree of resistance to the new reform measures.

What is altogether remarkable is the speed of the increased productivity and unprecedented growth which resulted from the introduction of the market economy, an essential feature of the capitalist system. Almost overnight it achieved what decades of socialist central planning of the economy failed to accomplish in China, as in other socialist States, including North Korea (in contradistinction to South Korea under the market system), the East European States, Mongolia and the former Soviet Union itself. In all these States, a centrally-planned economy had resulted in low efficiency, low production, strangulation of initiative, and generally, we are told, in a very depressed atmosphere.

It is a well-known fact that the greatness of a nation is its ability to dream dreams and to bring them to fruition, to feel free to plan for the future, to yearn for and realize a degree of grandeur and destiny. Until 1978, this free spirit had been held in check in China. Notable past achievements like the Great Wall, among others, are today sad reminders of the millions of lives that were sacrificed in their construction or execution. In every century and in every age in China, the history is marred by oppression, repression and civil wars. It cannot be denied that the Cultural Revolution of 1966-76 was anything more than wanton destruction, blatant waste of energies that could have been harnessed into advancing China to its rightful place among the leading nations of today. Poised by its early inventions to reach that stage, the country succumbed instead to internal weakness, subjugation and oppression. In short, China has always found itself in a dilemma.

It would seem that history is repeating itself in China, for at present China seems to be at a crossroads, apparently uncertain as to which way to go. Politically, ideologically, theoretically, it declares adherence to a centrally-planned economy but in practice encourages a shift to a market economy. Is this a contradiction of policy, or is it that Beijing is juggling the two systems—distinct and incompatible, as they are—to see if the one can be incorporated into the other? But surely, the failure of socialist central planning in the former Soviet Union and its satellite states to improve the economy and provide the nations with what they now seek from the introduction of the market economy should convince the politically astute that a political marriage of the two systems would lead ultimately and irrevocably to an unpleasant divorce.

Surely, too, the long history of China shows the Chinese to be a market-oriented people, attested recently by the immediate success of the market reforms that were introduced. The readiness of the Chinese to trade and to make a profit is endemic, and most likely will take precedence over ideology in the long run, howsoever repressive or aggressive that ideology may be. Communism, it must be admitted, is born of force and is perpetuated by force, but that force has woefully and persistently failed so far to bring about economic benefits for those it seeks to control.

China's central government has repeatedly stated that it intends to continue the open-door policy. Witness its further opening of 14 coastal cities (all major seaports), the whole island province of Hainan, and a few deltaic and peninsular areas to foreign investment. Note, too, the government's plan for the future, namely, to open areas and regions beyond the SEZs for the same purpose. Indeed, Beijing has gone even further to give a surprising degree of autonomy to its provinces, municipalities and counties. With this measure of freedom to plan and direct their individual economies, the administrative units are beginning to make headway, as Chen Longfei and Yan Aihua have shown in the case of Shandong. This province, like other Chinese provinces, is improving its existing infrastructure, especially the modernization of port facilities, the construction of communication and transport facilities (railways, highways, airlines), the revitalization of existing old industries and the creation of new ones, the shift from labour-intensive to a technology-intensive type of production, de-emphasizing state ownership, and encouraging private-collective ownership and individual ownership. From agriculture to industry, to communications, to commerce, to trade, to real estate, the changes spawning development are wide-ranging. From seeming lethargy, the administrative units are at last attempting their development with a certain dispatch, optimism and confidence. There seems to be no turning back.

What conclusions may the social scientist draw from these changes if Beijing continues to reiterate its cleavage to socialist central planning? Certainly, the contradiction of policies recommends itself to uncertainty or hesitancy on the part of potential foreign investors. However, as the prosperous southern provinces of Guangdong and Fujian exploit more and more the market system, gain experience, earn considerable foreign currency for the nation, and draw closer to their capitalist neighbours of Hong Kong and Taiwan, so perhaps will the central government realize more and more the importance of the market system and exercise more flexibility in the development of the country's economy.

Attempting to follow in the footsteps of Guangdong and Fujian, the province of Shandong (also Jilin) is utilizing its new-found freedom in the most adroit fashion. It is focusing its attention not on strengthening planned state control but on economic efficiency, the development and expansion of the forces of production according to the demands of the market. It is encouraging foreign entrepreneurs to establish joint ventures and co-operative enterprises in the province, and its attempts had been meeting with varying degrees of success up to June 1989.

Shandong has a preferential policy for foreign investors to invest and establish enterprises in all its cities, townships and counties. Chen and Yan have elaborated on this in Chapters 8 to 10, as have Song and Ma in Chapter 11. Export-oriented enterprises using state-of-the-art technology get an exemption of fees for public installation of public utilities. They are also given priority treatment in the supply of water, electric power, steam and gas. Other incentives include the exemption or reduction of taxes, legal advice in such matters as accounting, foreign trade, tourism, project engineering and construction, and ensuring the autonomy of foreign-funded businesses. To expedite matters, the Jinan Foreign Economic Relations and Trade Commission has been established to help foreign investors to co-ordinate and unify arrangements. On the whole, there is a positive attitude and a marked readiness to lure foreign business and to replace the out-dated technology and equipment of old enterprises by importing advanced technology.

Shandong does not regard its attempts to industrialize with the latest technology as the panacea for all its economic problems. Such problems demand an assault on all fronts, and this is exactly what the province is attempting to do. The infrastructure is effete. Most of it was built over a long period and cannot meet the demands of modern industry and increasing population growth. Roads, railways, port facilities, the telephone system, power stations and water supply need to be modernized and new ones built or installed. Without them industries cannot be developed. Equipping with modern technology and providing the trained expertise to maintain them involve a considerable capital investment that is far beyond the means of a developing country like China or any of its provinces. But the supply of capital is the key to the development of Shandong or any of the other provinces. It is for that purpose that the local governments are encouraging co-operative enterprises and joint ventures that will produce export goods to earn foreign exchange to pay for those commodities that must be imported. In addition, the municipalities encourage enterprises that will give the local labour force training and provide them with a good income, and in so doing increasingly raise their standard of living. Of necessity, then, the local governments assess carefully ventures that appear viable and offer maximum contribution to all sectors of the economy.

It is to be expected that the shift to a market economy will be an enormous challenge for Shandong and the rest of China. Acquiring knowledge of the system and how it works will be daunting by virtue of inexperience, as Yam elaborates in Chapter 5. Introduction of the system requires training for the workers, agents and decision-makers alike. It demands massive cuts in State spending, an understanding by workers and managers alike of the importance of competition and speed in meeting production dead-lines, and generally how to run a business and the ethics of business. It must be understood quickly that the free market resists bureaucratic bungling, political ineptitude and mismanagement; that it thrives on long-term, as opposed to short-term, planning and, above all, that freedom to transact, freedom to hire and dismiss, freedom to manage are the prerogatives of the business or enterprise. Neither does it entertain hindrance to market expansion and production. In part, these make up the credo of the market economy of the capitalist system. If any province of China is to adopt this system, it must be fully aware of its demands and free to meet them.

On the other hand, foreign investors have lessons to learn, too, if they want to do business with one-quarter of all humanity. Their customary speed of doing business in the West and their customary impatience will need to be tempered. They must, above all, blend business acumen with patience, perseverance, prudence, courage and vision, as Yam has taken pains to point out. They must realize that whereas they were brought up in the free-market system, the Chinese were not. Unaccustomed to local Chinese conditions, they should be prepared to asses local advice carefully, and be flexible and adaptable.

Perhaps the greatest difficulty to be overcome is investors' confidence. Investors are a cautious breed, and rightly so. They will not invest in a climate of political uncertainty. This was made eminently clear, for example, to President Mikhail Gorbachev of the former Soviet Union at the 17th Summit of the world's seven leading industrial democracies in London in July 1991. Forced by necessity, President Gorbachev requested of the seven Summit leaders financial assistance to prevent the Soviet economy from collapsing. The Summit was sympathetic enough but refused to give the huge sums of cash required. It promised technical assistance, and individual members, Canada, for example, gave small amounts for specific purposes. The reason for the refusal was quite obvious. Centrifugal forces in the Soviet Union were dividing the nation, pitting one faction against the other. The one group was insisting on the retention of socialist central planning, the other was loudly clamouring for the dethronement of the system, and a speedy shift to democracy and market reforms. We have since witnessed the successful return to nationhood of the three former Baltic Republics, the dissolution of the former Soviet Union, and the emergence of a new Commonwealth of Independent States of the remaining former republics except Georgia. But the new Commonwealth is a house divided, vulnerable, and could succumb to political and economic chaos. The G7 leaders were far-seeing in declaring that sweeping changes in Soviet political, economic and military policies should necessarily precede the infusion of the billions of dollars needed. Prime Minister Mulroney of Canada, acting independently of the Summit, told the Soviet leader that once the right climate was created in the Soviet Union, foreign investment would follow. Another of the Summit leaders figuratively put it another way. He stated that putting cash into the Soviet Union at that time would be like putting money into a pocket with holes. In a word, investor confidence in the Soviet Union was low and would remain low until centripetal forces were in the ascendancy and the market economy fully and properly established.

In a similar fashion, investor confidence in China is low at present, unlike what it was before the Tiananmen Square debacle of June 4, 1989. Between 1980 and 1989 vast sums were lent to China by international financial institutions and equally copious amounts were poured into joint ventures, co-operative deals, infrastructure development and tourism by foreign agencies—all because China had opened its doors to the outside world. There was abroad a pro-China sentiment which augured well for the country and, as stated above, brought outstanding change and optimism in the 1980s. After the Tiananmen tragedy, much of this good will suddenly dried up. The outside world appears to be punishing China for what it perceives as China's lack of remorse for sending heavily armed military forces to do battle with unarmed students who were demanding democracy, the removal of corruption, China's alleged harsh treatment of dissidents and intellectuals, and general disregard for human rights, and China's alleged refusal to ease its rigid imposition of ideological uniformity on its people. Since Tiananmen, most foreign corporations have realized the risks of doing business with China and this has triggered a severe foreign-investment frost in the country. Uncertainty, lack of confidence and trust in the central government, exacerbated all the more by the current, dramatic, unprecedented flight of capital from Hong Kong (instigated by fear of what China may do when Hong Kong reverts to Chinese control in 1997)—matters like these, among others, tend to militate against continued co-operation with China by the international business community.

It is not the purpose of this discussion to condemn or denigrate. Rather, the intent is to identify the cause of investors' sudden lack of confidence in doing business in China, and to hope China will find it possible to restore that confidence. The international financial agencies are asking, "Whither goest China?" and it is for China to respond. The whole invites a spirit of generosity and give-and-take. A penchant of the Chinese is to revere friendship, and business that is negotiated in China in friendship is very likely to withstand the vicissitudes of politics and time.

Successful trading, and ultimately economic development, require a good measure of goodwill and harmony, among other requirements. Clearly then, the friendly relations between Saskatchewan and Shandong, resulting from twinning arrangements, are an asset in their endeavour to forge successful trade with each other. Moreover, the two areas are embraced in a splendid complementarity in respect to trade. Saskatchewan's capital city, Regina, is the centre for software and computer services, and Saskatoon, the largest city, dubbed the "Silicon Valley" of the province, as Maguire and Lim have outlined in Chapter 6, is engaged in the production of telecommunication systems and fibre optics cable, data switching systems, the design and manufacture of control systems for manufacture, agricultural technology and expertise—all state-of-the-art technology in very good supply. Carlson in Chapter 3 and Pretty in Chapter 4 have come to the same conclusion in respect to Saskatchewan's potentiality for supplying agricultural products and agricultural technology, and potash deliveries and expertise for a potash agronomy programme. On the other hand, Shandong, as Chen and Yan, and Song and Ma have attested, is an area which needs for its modern economic development the very goods and services that Saskatchewan/Canada can supply. Without question the supply is assured. Without question the demand is real, even acute; and without question there is a striking dearth of trade between these two acknowledged friends, a gap that is easily closed. If of the two areas Saskatchewan is technically more advanced by more than 20 years, according to Song and Ma (Chapter 11), economically more developed, and has a greater spending power, it follows that Saskatchewan is the better able to seek out avenues of trade in Shandong. This means competing aggressively with agents of the business sectors of Hong Kong, Taiwan, Singapore, Japan, Germany, Italy, France, the United States and other countries, who are actively knocking on the administrative doors of the Shandong Government. The repeated charge that the Saskatchewan business sector is somewhat complacent, mildly competitive, and seemingly non-aggressive is not easily refuted when it is realized that Shandong is willing and eager to do business with Saskatchewan/Canada and is indeed attempting to remove whatever obstacles to trade that may have existed as the market mechanism is gradually understood and applied. The next move in the pursuit of trade between the two is surely Saskatchewan's.

Close observation between 1983 and 1990 reveals that throughout China, from north to south, east to west, the Saskatchewan, if not Canadian, entrepreneur has a markedly low profile compared with that of others from other countries. Why is this? Is the business sector of Saskatchewan lacking in enterprise, or afraid or unwilling to accept the challenges offered, or that it refuses to exercise the patience, which Yam expounds in Chapter 5, and to expend the energy and time that trade negotiations with China demand? Whatever the reason, favourable opportunities in Shandong for the Saskatchewan business sector remain regrettably unexplored— a decidedly tragic circumstance because Saskatchewan and Shandong need each other's commodities and expertise to transform their economies and to further the development of the human and material resources of their areas.

Shandong's large labour pool, various resources, old and nascent industries are being mobilized and developed according to planned development. More than an ideological manoeuvre, it is an economic exercise in which Saskatchewan, with its advanced technology in many spheres of economic activity, can make a contribution par excellence, spectacular and profitable to both areas. This, in sum, is what the authors of the many chapters of this book declare. In detail, they have shown the paths to effective trading between two friends, Saskatchewan/Canada and Shandong China.

THE CONTRIBUTORS

ELAINE CARLSON is a Regina-based freelance writer who provides professional communications services to an extensive list of corporate, non-governmental and government clients in Saskatchewan.

In the past two decades, Ms. Carlson's work has appeared in *The Financial Post*, *Trade and Commerce*, *Saskatchewan Business*, *HealthCare Canada*, *Benefits of Canada*, and other regional and national publications. On behalf of provincial government departments and other clients, Ms. Carlson has also researched and written an extensive list of materials for public consumption. Her special interests are agriculture, personal financial planning and money management, consumer information, Native issues, health, education, social services, energy and resources, and business.

Ms. Carlson has prepared Chapter 3 for the Department of Agriculture, Government of Saskatchewan.

CHEN LONGFEI, President, Shandong Teachers' University, Jinan, Shandong, China; Professor of Geography.

Professor Chen has been engaged in the teaching and research of human geography at Shandong Teachers' University since 1956. He is Chairman of the Shandong Geographical Society, and Editor-in-Chief of the journal *China Population, Resource and Environment*.

EDMUND H. DALE, Professor Emeritus, former Head, Department of Geography, University of Regina, Saskatchewan.

Dr. Dale is a geographer. He graduated from the University of London, England, with a BSc (Honours) and an MSc in Geography, from the University of Alberta with a PhD, and from King Alfred's College, Hants., England, with a Teacher's Diploma. He taught at the University of Alberta and the University of Victoria before coming to the University of Regina where he has taught for nearly 20 years. He has also taught in Jamaica, London (England) and in the People's Republic of China.

Dr. Dale's main interests are Urban Geography, Urban Planning, Political Geography, the Caribbean area—areas in which he has published extensively. In recent years he has taken a keen interest in the People's Republic of China.

DEREK LIM, M.Sc. in Computer Science

Mr. Lim obtained his MSc from the University of Regina in 1991. His thesis topic was "Computerized Image Processing and Analysis of Sedimentary Rocks." He is now working in Regina with a computer consulting firm.

R. BRIEN MAGUIRE, Professor of Computer Science and Former Head of Department of Computer Science, University of Regina

Dr. Maguire received a BA (Honours) from the University of Saskatchewan and a PhD from the University of Waterloo. He is an adviser to the Academy of Sciences of Shandong Province and has visited and worked with academic and industrial institutes in China since 1984. His active research interests include software engineering and the use of hypermedia in educational settings, particularly in the support of distance education via television.

KENNETH M. PRETTY, Agronomist/Soil Scientist

Dr. Pretty obtained his BSA at the Ontario Agricultural College (now the University of Guelph) and his MSc and PhD degrees at Michigan State University. Internationally recognized as a soil scientist with special interest in institutional, human, and project development, and the integration of numerous factors which impact on food production and quality, his leadership earned him several national and international awards.

Dr. Pretty is recently deceased.

SONG JIAHUA, Engineer, Vice-Director of the Biology Institute, Academy of Sciences, Jinan, Shandong Province, China

Mr. Song Jiahua graduated from the Biology Department, Shandong University, Jinan, with a BSc degree. He worked for many years in the Foreign Affairs Department of the Academy of Sciences of Shandong Province, the Shandong Provincial Planning Commission, and the Shandong Science Technological Commission before studying Administration at the University of Regina from 1985 to 1988. In addition to his administrative duties, he is involved in developing relationships and joint ventures between the Biology Institute and organizations outside China.

EDY L. WONG, BSc, MSc, PhD Economics, Assistant Professor, Grant MacEwan College, Edmonton Alberta. He also teaches Economics at the University of Alberta, Edmonton.

Dr. Wong's area of specialization is Chinese economic development and Pacific-rim economics.

AL M. YAM, Manager of Product Marketing, Saskatchewan Telecommunications (SaskTel)

Mr. Yam is a professional engineer. After graduating with BSc and MSc degrees in electrical engineering at the University of Alberta, he joined SaskTel in 1975 where he has since held various managerial positions. In 1984 he joined the newly established SaskTel International and, as General Manager of Canadian Communications International, a consortium of the international subsidiaries of SaskTel, B.C. Tel and Edmonton Tel, he was active in the China market. He returned to SaskTel in 1988. Mr. Yam has published in *Physics Letter* and in *Videodisc & Optical Disk*.

YAN AIHUA, MSc in Geography at the Shandong Teachers' University in Jinan

Mr. Aihua is currently assistant researcher at Shandong Agricultural Commission, concentrating on the agricultural development of the Yellow-Huai-hai River area.

MA YONGCHUN is a student of Canadian history who helped Song Jiahua with background research and with the translation of his chapter.